DOCTOR WHO
TWELFTH NIGHT

'Invaluable reading for intellectually-engaged devotees of the programme.'

DOCTOR WHO
TWELFTH NIGHT

ADVENTURES IN TIME AND SPACE WITH PETER CAPALDI

Edited by
Andrew O'Day

I.B. TAURIS
LONDON · NEW YORK

Published in 2019 by
I.B.Tauris & Co. Ltd
London · New York
www.ibtauris.com

Who Watching

ISBN: 978 1 78831 363 6
eISBN: 978 1 78672 471 7
ePDF: 978 1 78673 471 6

A full CIP record for this book is available from the British Library
A full CIP record is available from the Library of Congress

Library of Congress Catalog Card Number: available

Text design and typesetting by Tetragon, London
Printed and bound by CPI Group (UK) Ltd, Croydon, CRO 4YY

CONTENTS

PART ONE
The Doctor and His Companions

PART TWO
Further Politics and Themes

LIST OF FIGURES

CONTRIBUTORS

Paul Booth, PhD, is Associate Professor at DePaul University. He is the author of *Crossing Fandoms: SuperWhoLock and the Contemporary Fan Audience* (London, 2016), *Digital Fandom 2.0: New Media Studies* (New York, 2016), *Playing Fans: Negotiating Fandom and Media in the Digital Age* (Iowa City, 2015), *Game Play: Paratextuality in Contemporary Board Games* (New York, 2015), *Time on TV* (New York, 2012) and *Digital Fandom: New Media Studies* (New York, 2010). He has edited *Seeing Fans: Representations of Fandom in Media and Popular Culture* (New York, 2016, with Lucy Bennett), *Controversies in Digital Ethics* (New York, 2016, with Amber Davisson) and *Fan Phenomena: Doctor Who* (Bristol, 2013).

David Budgen received his PhD in History from the University of Kent, and recently completed his first book, *British Children's Literature and the First World War: Representations since 1914* (London, 2018). He is also a contributing editor for the website International Encyclopedia of the First World War. His work on Great War YA fiction led him to *Doctor Who*, and he has written several chapters on the subject. Most recently he has contributed to an edited volume on Joss Whedon's *Firefly* (*Firefly Revisited: Essays on Joss Whedon's Classic Series* (2015)), in which he examined American Civil War analogies. He teaches at both Kent and Canterbury Christ Church University.

Robin Bunce, PhD, is a historian based at Homerton College, University of Cambridge. His research and teaching focuses on the history of political thought. His most recent publication, *Renegade: The Life and Times of Darcus Howe* (London, 2017), written with Paul Field, deals with the Black Power movement in Britain. He has also published on seventeenth-century European political theory, and on moral philosophy and the Daleks.

Brigid Cherry is a researcher working in the areas of fan culture and cult media. Dr Cherry has recently published work on Clive Barker, *Doctor Who* fandom, the steampunk community, and Southern Gothic television. Her most recent work, *Cult Media, Fandom and Textiles: Handicrafting as Fan Art* (London, 2016), looks at fan crafts. Her chapter in this book was completed as part of a Research Fellowship in Screen Media at St Mary's University, Twickenham.

Andrew Crome, PhD, is Lecturer in Early Modern History at Manchester Metropolitan University. He works on apocalyptic thought in Christian history, as well as writing about contemporary pop culture and fandom. He was co-editor (with James McGrath) of *Religion and Doctor Who: Time and Relative Dimensions in Faith* (London, 2013) and edited a special edition of the journal *Implicit Religion* (2015) on the programme. He is also the author of *The Restoration of the Jews: Early Modern Hermeneutics, Eschatology, and National Identity in the Works of Thomas Brightman* (London, 2014) and editor of *Prophecy and Eschatology in the Transatlantic World 1550–1800* (London, 2016).

Richard Hewett has a PhD in Television Studies, and is Lecturer in Media Theory at the University of Salford. He has contributed articles to *The Journal of British Cinema and Television*, *Adaptation*, *The Historical Journal of Film, Radio and Television* and *Critical Studies in Television*. His book, *The Changing Spaces of Television Acting: From Studio Realism to Location Realism in BBC Television Drama*, was published by Manchester University Press (Manchester, 2017). Research interests include the impact of changing production context upon television performance, and adapting literary texts for television.

Matt Hills, PhD, is Professor of Media and Film at the University of Huddersfield, where he is co-director of the Centre for Participatory Culture. Matt has written six sole-authored monographs, including *Fan*

Cultures (London, 2002), *Triumph of a Time Lord: Regenerating Doctor Who in the Twenty-First Century* (London, 2010) and *Doctor Who: The Unfolding Event* (Basingstoke, 2015), as well as editing *New Dimensions of Doctor Who: Adventures in Space, Time and Television* (London, 2013). He has also published more than a hundred book chapters/journal articles on fandom and cult media. Matt is co-editor on the 'Transmedia' book series for Amsterdam University Press, and regularly contributes reviews to the Doctor Who News website.

Eric Leuschner, PhD, is Associate Professor and Chair of the Department of English at Fort Hays State University, Kansas. His teaching and research interests include the history of the novel, academic fiction, protest and conspiracy literature, and film adaptation. He has published articles on Henry Fielding, William Godwin, Henry James, Ellen Glasgow and Wallace Stevens.

Douglas McNaughton has a PhD in Television Studies and is a Senior Lecturer in Film and Screen Studies at the University of Brighton. He has published articles on the intersection of space, technology and labour in television production in *The Journal of British Cinema and Television* and *Historical Journal of Film, Radio and Television*. His other publications include book chapters on television fandom, television melodrama and camerawork as performance.

Sonia Michaels earned her BA and MA in English from the University of Washington. She has taught English and Communications for more than 25 years, and has also worked extensively in admissions and career services. In her current position at DigiPen, she teaches English (with a focus on speculative fiction) and professional communications. She has been a presenter and panellist at the Game Developers Conference (GDC), PAX Dev (Penny Arcade Expo Developers) and GeekGirlCon.

Dene October is a Senior Lecturer at University of the Arts London. His recent publications include the monograph *Marco Polo* (Edinburgh, 2018) and the co-edited collection *Doctor Who and History: Critical Essays on Imaging the Past* (Jefferson, NC, 2017). His essays on *Doctor Who* include contributions to *Mad Dogs and Englishness: Popular Music and English Identities* (London, 2017), *New Worlds, Terrifying Monsters,*

Impossible Things: Exploring the Contents and Contexts of Doctor Who (published online by PopMatters Media, 2016) and *The Language of Doctor Who: From Shakespeare to Alien Tongues* (New York, 2014). He is also the author of several articles on David Bowie, including in *David Bowie: Critical Perspectives* (London, 2015) and *Enchanting David Bowie: Space/Time/Body/Memory* (London, 2015).

Andrew O'Day received his PhD in Television Studies from Royal Holloway, University of London. His thesis concentrated on meta-fiction in telefantasy with an emphasis on the 'classic' *Doctor Who* series. He is co-author (with Jonathan Bignell) of the book *Terry Nation* (Manchester, 2004), and editor of *Doctor Who: The Eleventh Hour – A Critical Celebration of the Matt Smith and Steven Moffat Era* (London, 2014). He has contributed to a range of edited collections on *Doctor Who*, both old and new, and has also published on Jack the Ripper in media and popular culture and on LGBT (Lesbian, Gay, Bisexual and Transgender) Studies. He also studied Law at the University of Birmingham and at King's College London. He can be found on the Web at www.hrvt.org/andrewoday.

NOTE ON TERMINOLOGY

There are several contentious issues regarding labelling the Steven Moffat/Peter Capaldi era. First, the revival of *Doctor Who* is sometimes referred to as 'NuWho' or the Steven Moffat years as 'new new *Who*'. However, throughout this book, the original series will be referred to as the 'classic series' and the Moffat years, like the Russell T Davies ones, as 'new *Who*'. Second, there is the issue of how to number the seasons. Rather than the new series following on with the numbering of seasons from the classic series, this collection will follow the DVD numbering, which began at 'series one' for the revival of the programme, and refer to the seasons of the Moffat/Capaldi era as 'series eight, nine and ten'. Finally, there is the issue of how to number Capaldi's Doctor, given the presence of John Hurt's War Doctor in 'The Day of the Doctor' (2013) and the Doctor's earlier use of regeneration energy in 'The Stolen Earth'/'Journey's End' (2008). At the end of 'The Time of the Doctor' (2013), the Time Lords give the Doctor a brand-new cycle of regenerations, so Capaldi's Doctor may be the Fourteenth Doctor or the First Doctor of this new cycle. However, this book will follow the official BBC branding of Capaldi as the Twelfth Doctor.

ACKNOWLEDGEMENTS

The idea for this collection came as soon as Peter Capaldi was announced as the Twelfth Doctor, but circumstances meant that the initial deadline had to be extended. I am therefore indebted to Philippa Brewster from I.B.Tauris for having the faith to commission this volume of essays and also for her patience in awaiting the final draft. Thanks also go to everyone else at I.B.Tauris for making the production process as smooth as possible. Furthermore, I acknowledge Professor Jonathan Bignell, Professor Matt Hills and Dr Matthew Kilburn for their assistance, as well as Professor Leonée Ormond (the former head of my MA from King's College London) for her encouragement. All the contributors were a delight to work with; however, a special round of applause must go to Dr Brigid Cherry, who offered editorial advice and who additionally composed the graphs reproduced at the end of the book. Gratitude must also be extended to Robin Prichard and Trisha Wood for the photograph of Carriad Eager-Hobden as Osgood, and thanks go to Matt Parsons and Phil Hogarth for introducing me to Carriad, and to the convention organisers and helpers for enabling such smooth-running photographic sessions.

As always, I am indebted to the great friendship of Tim Harris, which has spanned several decades, as well as that of Adam Emanuel. I also thank the 'Oxford Massive', Paul Dunn and Richard Harris, for many a humorous evening at Oxford's finest restaurants, as well as friends of 'The Massive', Patrica Dempsey, Gill Selwyn and Phil Newman, and also Colin Jones and Rob and Sharon Worthington, whom I renewed my friendship with after many years. Richard Harris deserves further thanks for unreservedly giving me lifts to *Doctor Who* conventions and sparing me a great deal of inconvenience, as does Andrew Stocker. Mention must also be made of the 'Gloucester Duo', consisting of Ian Kubiak and Francis Moloney, with whom I went on a fun tour of *Doctor Who* locations. It is furthermore with great fondness that I remember Nicholas Courtney, since this collection features a chapter on UNIT, and the unveiling of a plaque by 'the Brig' at the Eagle and Child in Oxford in 2000, organised by Garron Martin. From the LGBTQ community, Simon Heritage deserves a special mention for his loyalty, as do those who joined me for many a dinner or a coffee. I also take this opportunity to nod towards all my other Facebook friends and Twitter followers, including those from the *Doctor Who* and LGBTQ communities and from my time as a student in the English Department at McGill University; I shall not single further individuals out because of the risk of omitting people: everyone is important.

While I was completing this book, I was enrolled as a student on the MSc degree on Mental Health, Ethics and Law at King's College London. I thank the staff there and my fellow students for providing an inspiring environment in which to study and in which to complete this book. I also thank the Whitechapel Society for comradeship. But it is with great sadness that I have to say that the Terrence Higgins Trust, Oxford, for which I volunteered for many years, was forced to close in April 2017 during work on this book.

Finally, I offer appreciation to my younger brothers, Daniel and Matthew Englander, for their love and support. But this collection is dedicated to my parents, Professor Rosemary O'Day (Englander) and the late Dr Alan Earl O'Day. My father tragically lost his long, courageous battle with cancer in May 2017 as this volume progressed, and I hope that he would be proud of the results.

INTRODUCTION

Andrew O'Day

Having spanned over 54 years, *Doctor Who* has constantly been regenerated, both in terms of changes of lead actor and variations in the production team. But over that time there have been constant nods to the past, which have been important to appeal to the programme's wide fan base and remind one that the series remains the same one as before. Just as the book *Doctor Who: The Eleventh Hour* was devoted to the Matt Smith era of the series (2010–13), this tome focuses on the Peter Capaldi one (2014–17). However, unlike when David Tennant stepped down and was replaced by Matt Smith (2010), and Russell T Davies left as showrunner, the Matt Smith and Peter Capaldi eras have been overseen by the same executive producer: Steven Moffat. Such a bridge had previously been seen on occasion in the 'classic' series, and also in new *Who* when David Tennant replaced Christopher Eccleston (2005) under the watchful eye of Davies. Moffat, however, had also written for Davies's new *Who*. Therefore, it is unsurprising that, in the Capaldi era, Moffat, who, like Davies, had grown up as a fan of the classic series, includes nods to his own new *Who* as well as to the programme's recent and distant past. This was also evident in Moffat's work for the Matt Smith era, which, for example, featured images of past Doctors ('The Eleventh Hour', 2010), roles for actors who had previously played the Doctor (in the 50th anniversary episode 'The Day of the Doctor', 2013), as well as the standard old characters and monsters. 'The Name of the Doctor' (2013), meanwhile, featured clips from the classic series, even though these were remoulded to include current companion Clara (Jenna Coleman).

The promotion of the Twelfth Doctor era involved nods to the past. In the actual series, the presence of Clara as the continuing companion, the appearance of the Paternoster Gang (Madame Vastra (Neve McIntosh), Jenny Flint (Catrin Stewart) and Strax (Dan Starkey)) and the return of the Clockwork Droids from 'The Girl in the Fireplace' (2006) are not the only bridges marking the change in Doctor. Also, towards the end of 'Deep Breath', Clara receives a call on her mobile phone from Matt Smith's Doctor. Smith's Doctor tells Clara that he is calling from Trenzalore before he changed and that it is all still happening for him, but that she should be there for his new incarnation, who is more scared than anything she could imagine. When the phone call ends, Capaldi's Doctor, who has emerged from the TARDIS, says that the Doctor on the phone asked Clara whether she would help him in his new form and says that he was not listening in but that it was him talking. She sees the new Doctor standing in front of her and embraces him. Moffat's authorial signature is evident here, where he plays with time, just as his trademark is evident in 'Listen', which recalls 'The Girl in the Fireplace', written for Davies's *Who*: in both there is *something* under a child's bed and, in the later episode, there is again a play with time where Clara, hidden beneath the bed, grabs the child Doctor's leg, which caused the TARDIS to take her there in the first place. Clara says that the Doctor would one day return to the barn to reverse Gallifrey's destruction in the Time War, and this is accompanied by a shot of the War Doctor (John Hurt) from the earlier episode 'The Day of the Doctor' by the barn, which would again be seen in 'Hell Bent'.

'The Girl Who Died' provides an explanation for the Doctor's presence, linking this to Peter Capaldi's appearance in a guest role during Davies's tenure. This is not the first time that an actor has played more than one character in new *Who*. In Davies's new *Who*, Eve Myles played Gwyneth in 'The Unquiet Dead' (2005) before taking on the regular role of Gwen Cooper in *Torchwood* and in Davies's *Doctor Who* episodes 'The Stolen Earth' and 'Journey's End' (2008). In the latter of these episodes, the Tenth Doctor (David Tennant) comments on Gwen descending from this old Cardiff family. Freema Agyeman, meanwhile, played Adeola, working for Torchwood at Canary Wharf, in 'Army of Ghosts' (2006) before playing her cousin, companion Martha Jones, from 'Smith and Jones' (2007) onwards (the family relationship being explained in that episode). In 'The Girl Who Died', the Doctor (Peter Capaldi) sees his reflection in a barrel of water and, as he says he knows that he got this face to remind him that he is the Doctor who saves people, there are clips from 'The Fires of Pompeii' (2008) of Donna Noble (Catherine Tate) pleading with the Doctor (David Tennant) to save someone from the volcano, and of the Doctor beckoning Caecilius (also Peter Capaldi) and his family to come with him in the TARDIS. The Doctor therefore realises he can bring Ashildr (Maisie Williams) back to life, placing her within a line of such figures.

During the Capaldi era, there are also dialogue and sets which recall previous narratives, including ones from Davies's tenure and from the classic series. For example, the series ten episode 'Thin Ice' recalls the previous showrunner's 'The Shakespeare Code' (2007), since Bill Potts (Pearl Mackie) ponders what will happen to history if she kills a butterfly. And the series ten finale 'The Doctor Falls' sees the Twelfth Doctor recall the famous line of Tom Baker's Fourth Doctor: 'Would you like a jelly baby?' The TARDIS in which the Doctor and Clara travel in 'Hell Bent', meanwhile, with its white walls with roundels, echoes the design of that in the classic series.

As one would expect, there are reappearances of monsters – Daleks, Cybermen, Ice Warriors and Zygons – from the classic series; from, in the case of Daleks and Cybermen, Davies's new *Who*; and, in all cases, from the Moffat/Smith era. There are also references to old creatures. There are visual echoes: 'Into the Dalek', which sees a lone Dalek attached to tubing, and 'Hell Bent', where a Dalek appears in chains, recall Davies's new *Who* episode 'Dalek' (2005), while Cybermen walking down the steps of St Paul's Cathedral at the end of 'Dark Water' echo a similar scene from 'The Invasion' (1968). There are other ways in which the past is conjured up. 'The Magician's Apprentice', for example, is placed in a lineage of classic *Doctor Who* serials: there are audio clips of encounters between the Doctor and Davros from a range of classic stories, and a visual clip from 'Genesis of the Daleks' (1975), in which the Fourth Doctor (Tom Baker) ponders his right to destroy the Dalek mutations in the incubation room. And, in 'World Enough and Time', the Master (John Simm) announces that what is being witnessed is a 'genesis of the Cybermen', giving them a different origin narrative from that of the parallel-Earth Cybermen in Davies's new *Who* and placing this episode in the lineage of the Tom Baker Dalek serial.[1] The Ice Warriors, meanwhile, had first been seen in a serial of that title (1967) and in 'The Seeds of Death' (1969), from the Patrick Troughton era, and had made reappearances in the Jon Pertwee era and in the Matt Smith episode 'Cold War' (2013), penned by Mark Gatiss. In 'Empress of Mars', also written by Gatiss, an army of the creatures is awoken, and not only is Gatiss's 'Sleep No More' referenced, but the episode also recalls the Troughton serial 'The Tomb of the Cybermen' (1967), a connection made by Matthew Kilburn, among many.[2] In the series ten premiere 'The Pilot', meanwhile, the Movellans, first seen in the Fourth Doctor serial 'Destiny of the Daleks' (1979), make a cameo appearance with the Daleks, while in 'Empress of Mars' there is a brief appearance by Alpha Centauri, who featured more extensively in the Jon Pertwee serials 'The Curse of Peladon' (1972) and 'The Monster of Peladon' (1974), along with the Ice Warriors, and who is again voiced by Ysanne Churchman. Such appearances can be nostalgic: in a 'star letter' for *Doctor Who Magazine*, lifelong fan Tim Harris reveals that this 'golden moment' occupied a 'special warm place in [his] heart' while noting that 'casual viewers would have taken' the moment 'with a pinch of instantly forgotten salt'.[3]

Moffat reintroduces UNIT in the Capaldi era, and the fact that Osgood (Ingrid Oliver) is an expert on the Doctor reminds us of his previous ties with the organisation during the programme's history. Osgood is the ultimate cosplayer, who recalls the recent and distant past. In addition to referencing Matt Smith's Doctor, Osgood has done her research, since in 'The Zygon Invasion'/'The Zygon Inversion' there are question marks on her shirt collar, of the type seen on the Doctor's costume throughout the 1980s. Furthermore, in the video of the two Osgoods, one of them wears a multicoloured scarf of the type of Tom Baker's Fourth Doctor. Fans also cosplay Osgood

Figure 1. Cosplaying as Osgood

cosplaying the past (see Figure 1). Another figure who bridges the recent past and present in the era of the Twelfth Doctor is River (Alex Kingston), who is given a 'swansong'.

Moffat also reintroduces the Master in the Capaldi era. The Master, as played by Roger Delgado, first appeared in the Jon Pertwee serial 'Terror of the Autons' (1971), and was a semi-regular up until 'Frontier in Space' (1973). Following this, the character was seen in decayed, yet obviously male form, as played by Peter Pratt in 'The Deadly Assassin' (1976) and Geoffrey Beevers in 'The Keeper of Traken' (1981) – both Tom Baker stories. Throughout the 1980s, when Tom Baker, Peter Davison, Colin Baker and Sylvester McCoy were playing the Doctor, the Master was portrayed by Anthony Ainley, and in the TV Movie of 1996, starring Paul McGann, Eric Roberts took on the role. In Davies's new *Who*, the villainous Time Lord was played first – briefly – by Derek Jacobi and then – more extensively – by John Simm. Moffat presents the Master, however, in female form as 'Missy', played by Michelle Gomez. Moffat also plays on the older idea of multi-Doctor serials by having a multi-Master serial at the end of series ten, in which John Simm joins Gomez, prior to the multi-Doctor Christmas special 'Twice upon a Time'.

So far, we have seen how nods to the past in the Moffat/Capaldi era mark the fact that this is the same programme as before. Following on from the 50th anniversary special, in Capaldi's first series the presence of Coal Hill School is felt. This harks back much further, to the very first episode of *Doctor Who*, 'An Unearthly Child' (1963), which was also referenced in 'Remembrance of the Daleks', screened in the programme's twenty-fifth year (1988). There are also connections to *Doctor Who* in the spin-off *Class* (BBC, 2016), designed to get viewers of the parent programme to tune in and watch, just as David Tennant and Matt Smith's appearances in *The Sarah Jane Adventures* (BBC, 2007–11) as the Tenth and Eleventh Doctors respectively (2009, 2010) would have brought in viewers of *Doctor Who* to that series.[4] *Class* was set in Coal Hill Academy, on the same site as the old school, which is built on a rift through which aliens appear. The first episode, 'For Tonight We Might Die', features Peter Capaldi as the Twelfth Doctor telling the young main characters to keep up the good work fighting enemies.

Additionally, it is important to note that the production techniques of the Moffat/Capaldi era bear similarities with the new *Who* that preceded it. For example, similar visual effects are employed, such as that of water oozing from Heather's (Stephanie Hyam) body in the series ten premiere 'The Pilot', which recalls the extremely effective use of such imagery in Davies's new *Who* episode 'The Waters of Mars' (2009).[5]

About this collection

Turning to this collection, the first section concerns the Doctor and his companions. Richard Hewett and Douglas McNaughton examine key characteristics of the Twelfth Doctor. Hewett argues that Capaldi's age is key to considering pace in the new series as well as thinking about themes such as the effects of ageing on the memory, the fact that long life is more a curse than a blessing, and the point that old does not necessarily mean decrepit. McNaughton's chapter, meanwhile, departs from those making traditional readings of Englishness in the programme and investigates the space for Scotland and Scottishness that is opened up in the series. McNaughton looks at a 'set of place-myths' in the representation of Scotland in television drama, including in *Doctor Who*, and goes on to probe Capaldi's Scottishness in relation to authorship, political and broadcasting contexts. Sonia Michaels, meanwhile, turns her attention to the Doctor's companions Clara and, to an extent, Courtney Woods. Michaels probes the controversial episode 'Kill the Moon' and argues that the episode is more complex than simply delivering an anti-abortion message, since it deals with Clara's autonomy and lack of independence. Just as Dee Amy-Chinn argued in the book *The Eleventh Hour* that there is the possibility of a double reading of gender, in which one can see women as empowered or not, so too does Michaels.[6]

The second part carries on an investigation of politics in the Capaldi era as well as dealing with other themes. It develops Raymond Williams's argument that culture is the expression of social forces and expands on Bernadette Casey et al., who argue that science fiction 'allows a framework for difficult philosophical and political debate'.[7] Robin Bunce begins the part by examining the presence of war in the new series in the context, for instance, of the twenty-first-century War on Terror, and notes the impossibility of telling friend from enemy. Eric Leuschner's chapter acts as a companion piece to Bunce's, investigating UNIT from the classic series to the Capaldi era. The chapter looks in depth at the original militaristic direction of UNIT and also at the recent scientific, yet still martial, path of the organisation. Turning to look at broader themes, Andrew Crome investigates the controversies surrounding the afterlife in the Moffat/ Capaldi era, arguing, for instance, that the series's denial of an after-life is likely to be controversial, as is the suggestion that one might feel the effects of cremation after death. Crome points out that, as a public-service broadcaster, the BBC was quick to warn viewers about such distressing content. He concludes his chapter by looking at the programme's standard position on death and immortality. David Budgen then completes the section, arguing that the uncanny recurs in the Christmas specials.

The third and fourth parts of this collection take us beyond the actual episodes. Matt Hills sets the tone for the penultimate section, looking in a cutting-edge fashion at promotional discourses in, or which affect, the United Kingdom, which is followed by an equally groundbreaking chapter by Paul Booth, probing promotional dis-courses for series eight in the United States. The final section of the collection examines fandom. Brigid Cherry's chapter concerns fan imaginings of the Twelfth Doctor after it was announced that Peter Capaldi would be playing the role but before the broadcast of any of his episodes. Dene October, meanwhile, rounds off the volume with an investigation of the varied responses to casting a female actress as the Master – Moffat is known for creating strong female characters, but in this case the character was one hitherto played by men. Elsewhere, Hills has written about how this change heterosexualised the relation-ship between the Doctor and the Master; this may remind one of the relationships between Avon and Servalan and Tarrant and Servalan in *Blake's 7* (BBC, 1978–81), but October's investigation highlights that in the case of the Master there is much discontent with changing a pivotal character's gender.[8]

It is important to note, then, that the chapters in this collection also include examination of how the Capaldi era makes nods to the programme's history while, in some cases, deviating from the past. However, these discussions are placed in different contexts than that in the first section of this introduction. This is the case with the chapter by October on Missy and with Leuschner's work on UNIT. Crome's chapter, meanwhile, deals with the programme's past differently. Crome points out the importance of the production team's maintaining canonical consistency around the issue of immortality, and refers to previous narratives that reflect a standard position on the topic of which the production team and fans would be aware. Budgen's chapter, furthermore, connects the Capaldi Christmas specials with Davies's new *Who* (River Song's fate written by Moffat as well as other narratives) and with the classic series (the multi-Doctor episode) in detail. I also noted at the beginning of this introduction that promotion of the Capaldi era had involved nods to the past, and these can be seen in Hills's chapter as well as Hewett's first chapter, which additionally contains other references to the past, helping us to understand the Doctor as played by the relatively mature Capaldi.

Finally, although a book on the Moffat/Capaldi era evidently raises a set of concerns, as Booth persuasively argues elsewhere, there is a danger of oversimplification in periodising the programme into eras.[9] For example, Booth points to the way in which, in the classic series, the Barry Letts/Terrance Dicks/Jon Pertwee era has been classed as 'Earthbound', and the Sylvester McCoy era has been labelled as fitting into the 'Cartmel masterplan', named after the script editor of the time (Andrew Cartmel), of portraying a darker, more manipulating Doctor, when, in fact, only some serials from those eras fit into these patterns. Booth also observes that there are Gothic narratives outside what is commonly classed as the 'Gothic era' of Philip Hinchcliffe and Robert Holmes in the early years of Tom Baker's Doctor. Likewise, we shall see later in this book, for instance, both that the Capaldi Christmas specials follow a pattern seen in earlier such specials and that there are different types of Christmas special within the Capaldi era. Conversely, in Chapter 8, Hills argues that, while Booth noted that periodisation is important for fans, who point to their own favoured era and also are connected with one another by organisational principles (for example, labelling early Tom Baker seasons as 'the Gothic era'), brand-focused paratexts are important in smoothing over transitions between eras of different Doctors. So, while this book does introduce a set of concerns, and while periodisation into eras can take place, the lesson is that one must be on one's guard and tread carefully in arguing that the Capaldi era is always distinctive and consistent.

Notes

1   There was an origin narrative for the Mondasian Cybermen in 'Spare Parts' (2002), an audio drama by Marc Platt for Big Finish Productions, and for the parallel-Earth Cybermen in the Davies episodes 'Rise of the Cybermen' and 'The Age of Steel' (2006). Indeed, the name of the character of Yvonne from the audio was used in 'Army of Ghosts'/'Doomsday' (2006).

2   Matthew Kilburn, 'Empress of Mars', Doctor Who Reviews [website] (10 June 2017). Available at http://reviews.doctorwhonews.net/index. php?search=Doctor%20Who%20(series%2010) (accessed 7 January 2018).

3   From *Doctor Who Magazine* 514 (2017), p. 12.

4   For more on this see Ross P. Garner, 'Friends reunited? Authorship discourses and brand management for *The Sarah Jane Adventures* "Death of the Doctor"', in Andrew O'Day (ed.), *Doctor Who: The Eleventh Hour – A Critical Celebration of the Matt Smith and Steven Moffat Era* (London, 2014), pp. 246–64.

5   I thank Tim Harris for making this observation.

6   See Dee Amy-Chinn, 'Amy's boys, River's man: generation, gender and sexuality in the Moffat Whoniverse', in Andrew O'Day (ed.), *Doctor Who: The Eleventh Hour – A Critical Celebration of the Matt Smith and Steven Moffat Era* (London, 2014), pp. 70–86.

7   See Raymond Williams, *Culture* (London, 1981) and Bernadette Casey et al., *Television Studies: The Key Concepts* (London, 2002), p. 209.

8   Matt Hills's article is 'Time stands still for Doctor Who, despite the Master's sex change', The Conversation [website] (8 November 2014). Available at https://theconversation.com/time-stands-still-for-doctor-who-despite-the-masters-sex-change-33963 (accessed 27 July 2017).

9   Paul Booth, 'Periodising *Doctor Who*', *Science Fiction Film and Television* vii/2 (2014), pp. 195–215.

PART ONE

THE DOCTOR AND HIS COMPANIONS

1

A YOUNG–OLD FACE

Out with the New and in with the Old in *Doctor Who*

Richard Hewett

Introduction

'I approve of your new face, Doctor – so much more like mine.' This line, spoken by the now ancient, enervated and seemingly dying Davros in 'The Magician's Apprentice', is just one of many age-related barbs directed at the Twelfth Doctor during Peter Capaldi's reign, serving as a constant reminder that the Time Lord is no longer (if, indeed, his on-screen self ever was) a young man.[1] Throughout his tenure, friends and foes alike highlighted the latest incarnation's wrinkled, somewhat cadaverous visage, grey hair and scrawny body, the Doctor being variously described as a 'desiccated man crone' ('Robot of Sherwood'), a 'grey-haired stick insect' ('Listen') and a 'skeleton man' ('Last Christmas'). Although she ultimately comes to regard him affectionately as a 'daft old man' ('The Woman Who Lived'), in 'Deep Breath' Clara (Jenna Coleman) struggles to comprehend how the Doctor's face can have so many wrinkles when it is brand new (much to the similarly long-lived Madame Vastra's [Neve McIntosh] disapproval). Stalwart ally Kate Lethbridge-Stewart (Jemma Redgrave) and former spouse River Song (Alex Kingston) both suggest it might be advisable for the Time Lord to touch up his roots ('Death in Heaven'; 'The Husbands of River Song'), and even a mildly embarrassed Bill (Pearl Mackie) feels the need to pass the Doctor off as her grandfather in front of contemporaries ('Knock Knock').[2]

Announced in 2013, Peter Capaldi's appointment as the Doctor added a new dimension to the frenzy of media coverage already surrounding *Doctor Who*'s 50th anniversary. Much of this centred around the fact that, at 55, Capaldi was the same age original Doctor William Hartnell had been when he took on the role, and showrunner Steven Moffat swiftly claimed this as his USP (unique selling point), stating that 'to emphasise the senior consultant over the medical student for once reminds people that he's actually a terrifying old beast'.[3]

Establishing the Doctor's exact age is problematic. As given on screen, it veered between 450 and 953 in the original series, but by 'The End of Time' (2010) had been retconned to a reassuringly precise 906.[4] However, the Eleventh Doctor's (Matt Smith) extensive off-screen adventures made it increasingly difficult to pin down accurately – something the Time Lord himself admits in 'The Day of the Doctor' (2013). His lengthy sojourn on Trenzalore only added to the confusion, though by 'The Zygon Inversion' the Twelfth Doctor is able to state with confidence that he is 'over two thousand years old.' This approximation still stands in the later 'Smile' and 'Thin Ice', despite the Doctor having previously been trapped in his Confession Dial for four and a half billion years ('Heaven Sent').

Perhaps appropriately, the apparent age of the Doctor's physical body has also varied wildly. While it was possible that the first 'regeneration', in 'The Tenth Planet', was indeed a 'renewal' – as the Doctor himself described it – in the sense of his body becoming younger, this has not always been the case since; the Doctor can also grow visibly older, as occurred with Jon Pertwee and Colin Baker's incarnations.[5] However, it is the casting of a younger actor that is usually deemed most newsworthy, Peter Davison and Matt Smith having received particular coverage on these grounds. Since its own 'renewal' in 2005 the series has placed the emphasis more firmly on youth, with the then 40-year-old Christopher Eccleston the most senior of the lead actors prior to Capaldi's casting.

This was a trend that showrunner Steven Moffat initially intended to reverse upon taking the helm in 2009, but his plan to cast an older Doctor was sidelined when the 26-year-old Matt Smith impressed him during auditions. However, the introduction in the 2013 anniversary special 'The Day of the Doctor' of John Hurt as the grizzled War Doctor could be seen as paving the way for a more mature actor to take the lead – a move compounded by Capaldi's own (brief) appearance in the episode, the return of a visibly older Tom Baker as the 'Curator' (a possible future incarnation of the Doctor) at the narrative's close, and the subsequent ageing of Smith's incarnation while on Trenzalore ('The Time of the Doctor', 2013).

Although in the original era the pace of the show was often constrained by its multi-camera studio format, which made scenes of physical combat challenging to stage convincingly, the single-camera model of the Davies and Moffat series has often seen the Doctor functioning more as high-octane action hero than cerebral sage, complete with elaborate post-production special effects that could only have been dreamed of by the original series production team. Capaldi's arrival, therefore, raised several questions with regard to age and ageing in *Doctor Who*, in terms of both characterisation and narrative form. With the Doctor played by younger men for so much of his recent tenure, Moffat's re-establishment of the Doctor as a middle-aged hero was a daring move in a televisual era that featured few such role models, even the quinquagenarian Inspector Morse having been replaced by his twenty-something counterpart in *Endeavour* (ITV, 2013–). This chapter will therefore investigate the narrative and performative strategies employed to accommodate this approach, and the impact Capaldi's arrival had upon the pace and style of *Doctor Who*.

In need of assistants?

In a direct mirroring of the 1963 series, Capaldi's era saw the Doctor initially accompanied by a teacher from London's Coal Hill School, Clara Oswald ostensibly representing a counterpart to original series companion and history tutor Barbara Wright (Jacqueline Hill). While Clara was a hangover from the Matt Smith years, her role at Coal Hill had only been established in Smith's penultimate adventure, 'The Day of the Doctor', and at first seemed little more than a nostalgic nod to the classic series in its anniversary special. When it was announced that she would be joined in Capaldi's first year by soldier turned maths teacher Danny Pink (Samuel Anderson), it could have been surmised that Danny's inclusion in the regular cast was intended to replicate the role originally played by science master Ian Chesterton (William Russell), who had been included in the TARDIS crew to take care of any physical business that may have proved too demanding for Hartnell/the First Doctor.[6] Following Ian's departure, the Doctor was similarly 'assisted', first by astronaut Steven Taylor (Peter Purves), and latterly by sailor Ben Jackson (Michael Craze). Although in 1966 Hartnell was replaced by the younger Patrick Troughton, the new lead's cerebral approach meant that action sequences were for the most part undertaken by brawny Scot Jamie McCrimmon (Frazer Hines), the Second Doctor rarely embarking upon any form of physical engagement. This formula was attempted again in 1974, the character of naval surgeon Harry Sullivan (Ian Marter) having been conceived before the Fourth Doctor was cast. In the event, Tom Baker's incarnation proved perfectly adept at handling combat scenes, and Harry's stay proved brief indeed. John Tulloch and Manuel Alvarado have previously highlighted the issue of the 'running and punching' role of the male companion, but in the event this satellite archetype was one that Danny Pink would largely deviate from.[7]

Ultimately, Clara and Danny were less the mature guides envisaged by the 1963 production team than a youthful counterpoint to the casting of Capaldi, their ill-fated romance providing an emotional spine to the new Doctor's first year and reminding the audience (and Clara) that the Doctor was, in his own words, not her boyfriend ('Deep Breath'). The programme's move to a later time slot meant that the need for youthful points of identification had become increasingly moot, and any similarities between Clara and Danny and the original Coal Hill duo proved superficial at best. Indeed, Danny Pink could only be said to play a 'traditional' companion role (i.e. assisting the Doctor in his endeavours) in two stories: 'The Caretaker' and 'In the Forest of the Night'. In the former, Danny's efforts serve only to frustrate the Doctor's plan to neutralise the Skovox Blitzer, sparking a mutually antagonistic relationship atypical of that enjoyed by the Time Lord with the majority of his previous male companions, while in the latter the spirit is more one of competition than collaboration.[8]

Much of the Twelfth Doctor's resentment of Danny seems to stem from the latter's former career as a soldier, and from this perspective it is interesting to compare the Twelfth Doctor with the Third, played by Jon Pertwee. It is series script editor Terrance Dicks's oft-employed description of Pertwee's 'young–old' face in his Target novelisations of the broadcast stories that provides this chapter's title, and – like Capaldi – Pertwee was a 'senior' performer (aged 50 at the beginning of his term) who had little need of the 'action men' frequently surrounding him in the form of Brigadier Lethbridge-Stewart (Nicholas Courtney) and his UNIT troops. Indeed, Pertwee's was arguably the most physical Doctor of all: his description of himself as 'quite spry' for his age ('The Green Death', 1973) and the numerous action sequences in which Pertwee (or occasionally his stunt double, Terry Walsh) took part suggest that age need not be a barrier with regard to the Doctor performing as action hero. The number of visual and narrative signifiers in Capaldi's era that recall Pertwee's characterisation are difficult to ignore. In the photo shoot revealing the new Doctor's costume in January 2014, Capaldi struck a pose strongly reminiscent of Pertwee in his own early publicity shots, pointing directly into the lens of the camera, and the similarities between their respective outfits in terms of colour scheme (white shirt, black jacket, red lining) were swiftly picked up on by press and fans alike. The Twelfth Doctor subsequently donned a necktie almost identical to that worn by the Third (at least in his early adventures) for 'Mummy on the Orient Express', and his later favouring of a velvet frock coat would doubtless have met with his predecessor's approval. In addition, Capaldi's hair – initially cropped unflatteringly – grew increasingly bouffant with each passing year, much as Pertwee's had. In 'Robot of Sherwood' and 'World Enough and Time' the Doctor employs the long-neglected art of Venusian aikido pioneered by his third incarnation (Capaldi even mimicking Pertwee's 'Hai!') to disarm, respectively, Robin Hood (Tom Riley) and Jorj (Oliver Lansley), and 'The Girl Who Died' sees him 'reversing the polarity of the neutron flow' on a Mire helmet – recycling the line originally adopted and memorised by Pertwee to deal with overly complicated technological jargon.[9]

However, the Third Doctor and the Brigadier's relationship, while occasionally frosty, seldom became as fractious as that between the Twelfth and Danny Pink. It is implied throughout Capaldi's first year that the Doctor both reviles the role of the military man and yet is aware of himself as a soldier of sorts, possibly as a result of his experiences as the War Doctor, but also in a broader sense as one who frequently involves others in his battles against evil, often at the cost of their lives – as proves to be the case with series ten companion Bill Potts.[10] Tellingly, it is Danny who hails the Twelfth Doctor as a 'blood-soaked old general', and this militaristic antipathy is taken to extremes in 'Death in Heaven', when the Doctor is disturbingly (at least for fans with long memories) disdainful of the Brigadier's hitherto unstated desire – as revealed by his daughter, Kate – that the Time Lord salute him, just once: 'He should have said'. This lack is, however (perhaps predictably), rectified by the episode's close.

While the Twelfth Doctor is, like the Third, Fourth and Fifth, shown to be adept with a sword, offering to train a Viking village in self-defence in 'The Girl Who Died', he is also happy to subvert swashbuckling norms by facing off against Robin Hood armed only with a spoon.[11] In fact, Capaldi's performance often undercuts the notion of the Doctor as action hero, arguably for the first time since the series was relaunched in 2005. Whereas Christopher Eccleston, David Tennant and Matt Smith played running and fighting scenes 'straight', Capaldi introduces a comedic, stiff-jointed run when the Doctor takes flight. Described by Bill as resembling 'a penguin with its arse on fire', this less than heroic gait provides a frequent visual reminder of the Doctor's great age. What could be regarded as his first 'action' sequence – mounting a horse and galloping to meet the dinosaur he has accidentally transported to Victorian London during his regeneration trauma – is played primarily for laughs; the Doctor is dressed only in a nightshirt, and visibly struggles to control his steed. By the time of 'The Woman Who Lived', the Doctor has become a more capable horseman – though viewers may doubt that Capaldi is performing his own stunt.[12] In this respect, while action still forms a significant part of Capaldi's narratives, he is neither the near superhuman figure cut by Pertwee or Tom Baker (and at times by Peter Davison, Colin Baker and their post-2005 successors), nor the more physically passive type of Hartnell, Troughton or Sylvester McCoy, who typically relied on intellect over physicality. While the pace of his episodes is as frenetic as that of any other post-2005 Doctor, the Twelfth did not fulfil the more recent tradition of the action hero role to quite the same extent.

Changing the pace?

As mentioned earlier, modern *Doctor Who* is made in a very different production context from the original series, whose primarily multi-camera studio process was already becoming outmoded when the programme was cancelled in 1989. Television drama today is largely the domain of single-camera location, though an effects-heavy programme such as *Doctor Who* makes greater use than most of studio sound stages. These are usually of the type more commonly associated with feature-film production, more suitable both for 'green screen' CGI (computer-generated imagery) and sizeable 'standing' sets such as the TARDIS interior, which would have been difficult to accommodate in the era of Television Centre and Lime Grove Studio D (the first production site of *Doctor Who*).

The impact of this change in production process is evident in the increased number of action sequences featured in the series post-2005, the more dialogue-heavy sequences of the original having given way to 'set pieces' of a type that would have been impossible to stage in the 'classic' era. This is not to say that scenes of emotional intensity, with the focus on verbal sparring or conflict between the Doctor and his antagonist of the week, no longer have any part to play. Rather, they provide periods of calm between the storms of expansive action sequences, frequently driven by orchestral scores from Murray Gold and the BBC National Orchestra of Wales. The climax of the series's 2005 premiere featured the explosive demise of the Nestene Host, while the following week saw the similarly incendiary end of the world in special effects sequences that would have been near-impossible to realise on the original series's comparatively meagre budget.

This same aesthetic is apparent throughout Russell T Davies's new *Who* and that of his successor Steven Moffat, and is also visible in the Capaldi years. While there is, perhaps, a slightly greater reliance on longer conversational sequences, these continue to be sandwiched between spectacular scenes of destruction and/or flight. 'Death in Heaven' and 'The Witch's Familiar' are both cases in point. Each forms the second instalment in a two-part adventure, and features lengthy segments which the Doctor spends in conversation with an old adversary (Missy and Davros, repectively), while companion Clara takes on much of the physical 'business' of confronting the monster of the week (the Cybermen and the Daleks, repectively). In this respect, each episode in a sense replicates the pace of the more studio-bound original series serials, in which the Doctor's confrontations with foes such as the Master or Davros were primarily verbal. When physical combat was attempted, it was compromised by the multi-camera set-up and the need to accommodate the action taking place in real time, as with Jon Pertwee and Roger Delgado's sword fight in 'The Sea Devils' (1972). Both of the aforementioned new series episodes culminate, however, in action sequences in which the Doctor plays a prime role (escaping in his Presidential ship, and then facing off against the Cyber-army/confronting a Dalek army, before escaping in the TARDIS), and are not lacking in spectacle when compared with similar escapades of the Ninth, Tenth and Eleventh Doctors. 'Under the Lake' is equally high-octane, and illustrates how far the modern series has travelled from its multi-camera origins. While centring around the 'base under siege' premise that formed a template for many of the stories in Patrick Troughton's era as the Doctor (such as 'The Moonbase', 1967, 'The Ice Warriors', 1967, or 'The Seeds of Death', 1969), 'Under the Lake' is more ambitious and expansive in terms of both the sets employed and the use made of them. Lengthy underground corridors and the pressurised doors that seal them off form a major part of the plot, as both Clara and various base personnel decoy the 'ghost' members of the crew subsequently revealed to have been created by the Fisher King. Such sequences would have been difficult to accommodate in the limited studio space of Lime Grove or Riverside, which also provided a production home for the original series.[13] However, it is notable that, for these tantalising 'action' sequences, the Doctor plays a relatively static role, coordinating events via communicator from a control chamber where he surveys events on a monitor, rather than joining in the running and hiding, as Tennant or Smith's incarnations might have done. The same logic applies to 'Sleep No More', where lengthy, dialogue-based scenes are interspersed with more action-oriented sequences, in which the rescue crew do battle with the Sandmen. In the 'Monks trilogy' from series ten ('Extremis', 'The Pyramid at the End of the World' and 'The Lie of the Land'), the Doctor's ability to perform as action hero is impeded by his temporary blindness, which leads to increased physical hesitancy and a greater reliance than usual on companions Bill and Nardole (Matt Lucas), the latter often narrating what is happening before them for the Time

Lord's benefit. However, these mid-series episodes also feature some of the year's more epic and adrenalin-fuelled set pieces (not least the Doctor and Erica's [Rachel Denning] attempt to avert biochemical disaster). Such stories demonstrate that, while Capaldi's Doctor at times plays a more sedentary role, the overall pace of the stories is in no way slowed; by way of exception, his 'action' scenes in 'The Doctor Falls', in which he vigorously dispatches a number of Cybermen on the field of battle before being struck down, are as physical as those of any previous Doctors.

Showing his age?

The fact of the Twelfth Doctor's more visibly aged appearance (disallowing Tom Baker's cameo in 'The Day of the Doctor', the Twelfth is the first grey-haired 'regular' Doctor since Pertwee) is highlighted in his earliest episodes, only to be gradually downplayed as Capaldi establishes himself. The costume chosen by the new Doctor for his first two stories (and trailed heavily in the aforementioned publicity shots) is stark and severe, as is the haircut Capaldi sports for most of his first series, which has the effect of further emphasising the actor's age. Even when the Doctor begins wearing the ultimate emblem of 2010s teen culture (the hoodie) it serves only to emphasise the scrawniness of the actor's neck. In Capaldi's second year the Doctor temporarily exchanges that long-serving *deus ex machina*, the sonic screwdriver, for sonic shades, and returns to them the following year in order to mask his blindness. However, the adoption of sunglasses – and a new penchant for contemplatively strumming an electric guitar (the modern equivalent of Troughton's recorder) – while positing the Time Lord in the iconic pose of the anti-authoritarian, still cast him more as old rocker than youthful hipster. His musical repertoire, ranging from the 1960s pop of Roy Orbison's 'Pretty Woman' to the more traditional 'Amazing Grace' and Beethoven's Fifth, also reflects this, as does his 'retro' choice of pseudonym when leaving a voicemail on Clara's mobile, 'Doctor Disco' ('The Zygon Invasion'). The positioning of the Doctor in diametric opposition to 'youth' culture is further highlighted in 'Thin Ice' via his anachronistic linguistic attempts to demonstrate that he is 'down with the kids' ('You guys hang tight. Laters!').

When publicising Capaldi's appointment, Steven Moffat claimed that, just as predecessor Matt Smith 'had something of the demeanour of a much older man [...] [Capaldi] is terribly boyish and young at times'.[14] Like several of his predecessors, Capaldi's Time Lord has a penchant for yo-yos, and sarcastically offers his Dalek captors a game of dodgems after appropriating Davros's wheelchair in 'The Witch's Familiar'.[15] However, there is no escaping the physical fact of the Twelfth Doctor's advanced years, and in truth his great age – and his implied 'immortality' – increasingly come to the fore as a theme in Capaldi's second year. The Doctor's relationship with Ashildr/Me (Maisie Williams) is on one level a retread of the Captain Jack (John Barrowman) storyline (a fact acknowledged in the script of 'The Woman Who Lived', the Doctor assuring Me that Jack will 'get round to her' eventually), though with the distinction that this time it is the Doctor himself, tired of 'losing people', who has bestowed the dubious gift of eternal life, rather than his companion Rose Tyler (Billie Piper).

The effects of ageing on the memory are certainly more evident in Capaldi's Doctor than in previous incarnations – natural enough given that, at double their age, he has twice as much to remember. In 'Deep Breath', he has a nagging feeling that he should recognise his clockwork antagonists (a reference to the Tennant story 'The Girl in the Fireplace'), but ultimately fails to place them. He also vaguely recalls having seen his new face somewhere before ('Who frowned me this face?'). These initial lapses of memory could, however, simply be symptoms of regeneration trauma.[16] Although Clara Oswald is ultimately wiped from the Doctor's memory ('Hell Bent'), his tenure at St Luke's University sees him commemorating two other significant females in his life – granddaughter Susan (Carole Ann Ford) and the departed River Song – via the surprisingly traditional means of framed photographs on his office desk ('The Pilot'). It is difficult to imagine this sentimental touch on Steven Moffat's part being applied to earlier incarnations of the Doctor, the character until this point usually having been one who looks firmly ahead rather than back. Other memories the Doctor has little difficulty recalling include his childhood nightmares and lapsed telepathic abilities ('Heaven Sent'), the fact that the Tereleptils began the Great Fire of London ('The Woman Who Lived'), his previous encounters with Earth survival ships ('Smile') and the many previous occasions on which he has vanquished the Cybermen ('The Doctor Falls'). In addition, in 'The Zygon Inversion' he can clearly recollect both the events of 'The Day of the Doctor' and his low opinion of former companion Harry 'the imbecile' Sullivan's intellect.[17] Memory is a particular theme of the latter serial, the Time Lord revealing at the denouement that the face-off between Kate Lethbridge-Stewart and Bonnie the renegade Zygon is nothing new, and the former has already been through the Osgood Box scenario '15 times' prior to having her memory wiped. It thus becomes clear that the Doctor – along with Osgood (Ingrid Oliver) – has taken on the role of perpetual watchdog: aware, perhaps, that he will always be needed.[18]

The fact that long life is more a curse than a blessing is not a new path for the series to tread, but Capaldi's status as an 'old' Doctor lent it a pathos that would arguably have been less effective if played by one of his younger predecessors.[19] Just as the Tenth Doctor was at first uncomfortable in the company of the immortal Jack Harkness, so the Twelfth is unwilling to take Ashildr/Me with him on his travels ('The Woman Who Lived'), despite being personally responsible for her situation. Like him, she has lived so long that she no longer uses her original name, which she claims to have forgotten. When she assures the Doctor that she will, in the future, be looking out for his 'leftovers', as their patron saint, his response is not entirely that of a man reassured. While aware that he at times needs a watchful eye, the fact that there is someone else in the cosmos with the potential to match him for longevity does not sit easily. Tellingly, in 'The Girl Who Died' he is keen that Ashildr have the option of choosing a similarly immortal companion, reflecting the ultimate loneliness of the reluctant Lord of Time. This is, after all, a Doctor who has clearly spent much of his later life alone – to the extent that he sometimes finds it difficult to focus on any conversation not directly relevant to his own train of thought, even when a gun is literally being held to his head ('The Woman Who Lived').[20] Unlike Ashildr, however, the Doctor has not lived long enough to forget the value of human life entirely. His developing relationship with Clara is also indicative of his increased sensitivity with regard to the passage of time.[21] Just as the Tenth Doctor warned Rose that, though she could spend the rest of her life with him, he could never have the same experience with her ('The Satan Pit'), so the Twelfth by turns pushes Clara away (in series eight, towards Danny) before pulling her back (even learning, eventually, to hug); their final stories in particular reveal a growing insecurity at the thought of losing her. Perhaps by way of compensation for Clara's later absence, the Doctor opts to spend a single night of 24 years with River Song on the planet Darillium ('The Husbands of River Song'). Although aware that she is fated to die after this meeting – an event his tenth self has already witnessed ('Forest of the Dead', 2008) – he is determined to prolong their encounter for as long as possible. By series ten the Doctor is seemingly resigned to watching over Missy in the Vault for the thousand years it will take to rehabilitate her: a possible acknowledgement that hers is one of the few lifespans to match his own, and perhaps a desire for company in his later years. As Missy later reproves him in 'World Enough and Time', only Time Lords can be friends with each other; anything else is cradle-snatching. As ever, though, the Doctor is uncomfortable growing old (or older) in any one place or time, and it is Bill (against whom Missy's admonishment is directed) that proves the catalyst for the Doctor renewing his wanderings in time and space (and, ironically, indirectly causing Missy to be released from the Vault).

Another subtext to Capaldi's later episodes is the fact that 'old' need not necessarily mean decrepit – particularly when even an aged Time Lord still has regeneration energy available to draw upon at will. In 'The Witch's Familiar' it is this ability that 'renews' both the ailing Davros – just as the Kaled scientist intended – and the decaying, near-liquefied remains of the 'old' Kaled mutants that populate the sewers of Skaro. These 'regenerated' Daleks then turn, in time-honoured fashion, on their own descendants, their attack on the present-day Daleks facilitating the Doctor and Clara's escape. In 'Empress of Mars' it is the veteran Ice Warrior Friday (Richard Ashton) that provides the impetus both to revive his leader, Iraxxa (Adele Lynch), and to launch a new, golden age of Ice Warrior–human relations. Capaldi's Doctor is often derided and dismissed on first appearance as an 'old man', much as Hartnell's and even Pertwee's sometimes were; in 'The Girl Who Died' he is not among the strongest and best selected by the Mire for culling from the Viking settlement (though he admittedly works hard to avoid detection), and in 'Knock Knock' the Caretaker (David Suchet) states that, as he is of advanced years, the Doctor will possess less energy than the house's younger victims (though he will be harvested just the same). However, the Twelfth Doctor usually proves to possess both the intellect and energy required to resolve the situation, and a recurring theme of his first year in particular is the ceding to him of leadership by initially dismissive authority figures ('Into the Dalek'; 'Time Heist'; 'Kill the Moon'; 'Mummy on the Orient Express'; 'In the Forest of the Night'). In 'Dark Water' he is even made 'President of the World' – a role for which he is seen to have developed a certain relish in 'The Zygon Invasion', and that he has taken entirely for granted (much to Bill's surprise) by 'The Pyramid at the End of the World'.

Conclusion: the new (older) statesman

The introduction of Peter Capaldi as the Doctor could be read both as a return to the elder-statesman style of lead actor that predominated for the first 18 years of the original series, and a continuation of the more action-oriented hero of the relaunch. While much was made of Capaldi's advanced years in terms of scripting and characterisation, the Twelfth Doctor proved more than adept at keeping pace with his more youthful predecessors. The programme's single-camera production model, and the increased volume of post-production special effects, allowed for a far greater emphasis on visual spectacle than was possible in the era of the multi-camera studio, and the fact that the Doctor's body was slightly older than contemporary audiences may have been used to in no way militated against this faster-paced narrative style. If, upon its 2005 relaunch, *Doctor Who* could have been seen as a case of 'out with the old and in with the new', the Moffat/Capaldi era refined this to draw upon the best of both classic and modern *Who*, demonstrating that an older and wiser head need not necessarily preclude the high-octane style of storytelling that now predominates in so much twenty-first-century television drama. This chapter has therefore demonstrated the impor-tance of thinking through ideas of ageing in the Peter Capaldi era; however, in their later chapters for this collection, Matt Hills and Paul Booth look at the way in which Capaldi's age was, in some cases, highlighted paratextually, but also at the way in which this was sometimes sidestepped.

Notes

1   Missy's comments to Clara in the same episode suggest that the Doctor was female for at least part of his early life.

2   Interestingly, the Doctor himself seems oblivious to the increased age of his physical appearance, twice assuming that Bill Potts thinks he looks younger than his years ('The Pilot'; 'Knock Knock').

3   Steven Moffat, 'Day of the Doctors', *Radio Times* (17–23 May 2014), p. 13.

4   The Second Doctor estimated that he was 450 years old in Earth terms in 'The Tomb of the Cybermen' (1967), while the Third stated that he had been a scientist for several thousand years in 'The Mind of Evil' (1971). The Fourth gave his age as 749 in 'The Brain of Morbius' (1976), and as 750 in 'The Robots of Death' (1977), but according to Romana had aged to 759 by 'The Ribos Operation' (1978). He then turned 760 in 'The Power of Kroll' (1978). The Sixth Doctor gave his age as 900 ('Revelation of the Daleks', 1985), and the Seventh as 953 in 'Time and the Rani' (1987). The War Doctor would subsequently state that he was 400 years younger than the 'twelve hundred or something' Eleventh Doctor in 'The Day of the Doctor', making him around 800 years old. The Ninth Doctor claimed to be around 900 years old in 'Aliens of London' (2005).

5   The process was not specifically referred to as 'regneration' until eight years after 'The Tenth Planet', in 'Planet of the Spiders' (1974). The Sixth Doctor also liked to think of the process in terms of 'renewal' ('The Twin Dilemma', 1984), though in his case his body has clearly aged in comparison to his fifth incarnation.

6   On the one occasion Hartnell's Doctor does engage in physical combat, tussling with a would-be assassin in 'All Roads Lead to Rome' (1965), the actor is left palpably short of breath.

7   John Tulloch and Manuel Alvarado, *Doctor Who: The Unfolding Text* (London, 1983), p. 229.

8   While the Fifth Doctor's relationship with female travelling companion Tegan was, like the Sixth's with Peri, sometimes antagonistic, this was not the result of the battle over another's affections, as is implied for the Twelfth Doctor and Danny with Clara.

9   While the Third Doctor 'reversed polarities' on several occasions, Pertwee only delivered the line in full in 'The Sea Devils' (1972) and 'The Five Doctors' (1983). It should be noted, however, that Capaldi's borrowings are not limited to the Third Doctor alone, the Second's favoured line 'When I say run, run!' featuring in 'Sleep No More'.

10   Although her physical body dies when she is converted into a Cyberman, Bill Potts's personality survives – and she is later resurrected thanks to the Pilot.

11   The Third Doctor takes up arms against the Master in 'The Sea Devils' and the Fifth in 'The King's Demons' (1983), while the Fourth tackles

both Count Federico's troops in 'The Masque of Mandragora' (1976) and master swordsman Count Grendel in 'The Androids of Tara' (1978).

12 In the Blu-ray commentary for the episode, producer Derek Ritchie confirms that a stunt double was used, with Capaldi seated on a mechanical horse for his close-ups.

13 In the Blu-ray commentary for the episode, actress Sophie Stone reveals that only two corridor sets were in fact used at the Roath Lock studios in Cardiff, though these are clearly substantial enough to 'double' for a complex network of walkways – something that would have been difficult to replicate in the earlier, multi-camera studios.

14 Steven Moffat, 'Day of the Doctors', *Radio Times* (17–23 May 2014), p. 13.

15 Both the Fourth and Twelfth Doctors use the yo-yo to perform a gravity test ('The Ark in Space', 1975, and 'Kill the Moon'), and a gold model is one of the possessions stolen from the Seventh Doctor by Chang Lee, and subsequently returned to the Eighth, in the 1996 TV Movie.

16 The Fourth Doctor initially struggles to recall the names of Sarah and the Brigadier in 'Robot' (1974–5); the Fifth requires the healing powers of the Zero Room before he can recognise Tegan and Nyssa in 'Castrovalva' (1982), and the Sixth continues to misname Peri for some time after his first adventure ('Attack of the Cybermen', 1985).

17 The Fourth Doctor originally came to this conclusion in 'Revenge of the Cybermen' (1975) after Harry had inadvertently caused him to be buried under a rockfall.

18 In this regard, it is tempting to speculate as to whether the Twelfth Doctor continues to execute the long-term duties of care undertaken by previous Doctors, such as the Tenth's annual visit to Daughter of Mine as revealed at the close of 'The Family of Blood' (2007).

19 Even when swathed in layers of prosthetics, as Tennant and Smith were in 'Last of the Time Lords' (2007) and 'The Time of the Doctor' (2013) respectively, these actors fail to convey the full poignancy of the Doctor's long life to the same extent as Capaldi. Indeed, Matt Smith is arguably more convincing as an 'old' man when playing against his own, naturally boyish visage. The notion that long life is more a curse than a blessing is first demonstrated in 20th-anniversary story 'The Five Doctors' (1983).

20 That the Doctor has spent much of his later life alone is witnessed by his monologues to camera in the prologues to 'Listen' and 'Before the Flood'.

21 However, he later dismisses this as 'an illusion' in one of his university lectures ('The Pilot').

2

'I'M SCOTTISH … I CAN REALLY COMPLAIN ABOUT THINGS NOW'

Discourses of Scotland and Scottishness in *Doctor Who*

Douglas McNaughton

Since 1963, the BBC television drama *Doctor Who* has featured a range of actors as its central character, the Doctor. Despite the quintessential 'Englishness' often claimed for the programme, the Doctor has now been played by three Scottish actors – Sylvester McCoy (1987–9), David Tennant (2005–10) and Peter Capaldi (2013–17).[1] This chapter examines how Scotland and Scottishness have been represented in *Doctor Who*. It considers both 'classic *Who*' (1963–89) and new *Who* (2005–17), in which Scottishness derives from wider cultural discourses which have inevitably affected both showrunner Steven Moffat and Twelfth Doctor actor Peter Capaldi. The programme's representation of Scottishness draws upon cultural discourses spanning both the classic and the new series, and the chapter will discuss how both series draw on, and develop, those discourses.

This chapter first sketches some of the arguments around representations of Scotland and discusses the set of place-myths involved in the 'Scottish Discursive Unconscious', the store of images and tropes associated with Scotland in the popular imaginary. It then summarises the way in which Scotland and the Scots have been represented in classic *Doctor Who* and how those representations relate to the chapter's earlier discussions around place and identity. The second half considers the period under showrunner Steven Moffat, and in particular Peter Capaldi's portrayal of the Doctor. The chapter focuses on discourses surrounding Capaldi's casting as the Doctor, specifically through analysis of primary material such as interviews with Moffat, followed by textual analysis of episodes. It concludes by linking these discourses to Scottish devolution and the emergence of plural, playful and complex post-industrial twenty-first-century Scottish identities.[2]

Colonialism, tartanry and kailyard

In order to construct a framework for understanding *Doctor Who*'s representation of Scots, Scotland and Scottishness, some understanding of Scotland's position within the UK is necessary. Cairns Craig's 1996 *Out of History* argued that Scotland has long seen itself as inferior to England due to its colonial history, but not due to any intrinsic lack of cultural value – rather, this is due to colonialist paradigms for quality imposed by dominant English culture. English culture, against which Scottish culture is measured, thus passes for universal while in fact being local or regional. This is a situation clearly untenable in a post-modern age of cultural relativism. *Out of History* discusses the way in which Scotland is seen as being out(side) of official British history and, as will be explored later in this chapter, representations of Scotland in *Doctor Who* have represented it as 'Other' and outside history. Such representations frequently fall back on the tropes of 'tartanry' and 'kailyard'.[3]

Many critics, such as Colin McArthur, divide twentieth-century Scottish culture – much of it produced outside Scotland – into 'tartanry' and 'kailyard' (cabbage patch). Tartanry is represented by the works of Sir Walter Scott and romantic tales of pageantry and medieval valour, as well as the adventure yarns of Robert Louis Stevenson. Kailyard is represented by the works of J. M. Barrie, comprising the parochial, the Calvinist and a temperamental tendency towards the dour and grim. Cairns Craig, writing in Colin McArthur's *Scotch Reels*, thus contrasts Scott's 'realm of imaginative grandeur' with Barrie's 'world of grotesquely impoverished human potential'.[4] For Craig, Scott's and Barrie's worlds 'became the foundation of myths of national identity in a country whose individual identity has been swamped by its incorporation into the United Kingdom'.[5] Cultural representations of Scotland, therefore, are filtered through a form of Orientalism, whereby Europe (and, in this case, specifically England) defines its own identity by balancing itself against the identities of peoples on its periphery and encountered through colonial domination, who are perceived as (and in part shaped into) binary opposition to what the dominant core considers itself to be.[6]

Out of these eighteenth- and nineteenth-century traditions emerges a construction of Scotland as a pre-modern wilderness, using the vast, majestic but often bleak landscapes of the Highlands and Islands to stand in for the whole of Scotland.[7] Both of these modes involve an ambiguous form of nostalgia. In the tartanry paradigm this untamed wilderness, infested by wild and hairy Highland clans rebelling against the union between England and Scotland, was a site of both romantic nostalgia and horrified fascination. Rumours of cannibals abounded through the legend of Sawney Bean and his savage Ayrshire family waylaying travellers and eating them. Within the kailyard tradition, Scotland is a land of tight-knit and insular communities, with canny pre-industrial natives using their peripheral status to confound the modernising forces of urban bureaucracy: 'Here Scotland's isolated position on the edge of "civilized" Europe is evoked to suggest a magical land seemingly untouched by, and indeed – due to its wily Kailyard folk-wisdom – *resistant* to, modernity.'[8]

It should be noted that McArthur's *Scotch Reels* was part of a *Screen*-related Marxist project to look for politically progressive screen texts. In the later *From Limelight to Satellite*, John Caughie identified and developed Scotland's third dominant myth, that of Clydesideism, which explored the crisis of working-class masculinity after the decline of the shipbuilding and manufacturing industries in the latter half of the twentieth century.[9] The industrial 'hardman' is linked to *No Mean City* (1937), Alexander McArthur and Herbert Kingsley Long's influential novel about Glasgow's Gorbals slums.[10] *No Mean City* investigated urban communities, poverty and gangland

'Razor Kings' – incorporating tropes of damaged masculinity, industrial labour and trade unionism (the Red Clydeside 'myth'). For Caughie, the three models of tartanry, kailyard and Clydesideism were useful in that they provided Scottish culture with concepts and identities with which to work through major social change. Latterly, Duncan Petrie has opened up that debate through his discussion of New Scottish Cinema to look at the wider range of identities represented in post-industrial twenty-first-century Scottish screen texts, involving a cultural renaissance – from the Marxian moment to a 'Nietzschian moment marked by the construction of new myths about Scottish identity and history'.[11]

Discussing the notion of Scottish television, John Cook comes up with the term 'three ring circus': drama about, by and for Scotland.[12] These different production models inflect the culture, recycling, recirculating and reshaping these myths which in turn feed back into culture.[13] How have the paradigms sketched above contributed to representations of Scotland and Scottishness in screen media?

Early British cinema and television: Scott, Stevenson, Barrie

Early British cinema drew on the work of Scottish authors Sir Walter Scott, Robert Louis Stevenson and J. M. Barrie within what Richard Butt calls 'a generic regime of adventure narratives' featuring 'romantically minded heroes, drawn into daring adventures in carefully crafted Scottish landscape'.[14] Another strand is a humorously sentimental cycle of Ealing-style comedies, including *Whisky Galore!* (1949), in which canny Scots run rings around humourless English opponents. Meanwhile, an alternative industrial version of Scotland was on offer in 'Clydeside' films such as *The Shipbuilders* (1943) and *The Gorbals Story* (1950). As Butt points out, despite their apparent realism, critics see Clydeside films as providing 'just as mythologised a view of Scotland as the "Scotland/Highland" comedies in their nostalgic representation of a once great industrial city'.[15]

The nascent medium of television drew from both literature and cinema in its adaptation of Scottish narratives: Butt comments that 'the literary canon again lent its authority to a screen medium trying to establish its cultural legitimacy and, in the adaptation of Scottish literature, the Scott–Stevenson–Barrie triumvirate again dominated the early years of this process'.[16] Such historical adventure stories contribute to a process of canonisation in which the same literary texts are adapted again and again, because they have been canonised through earlier acts of adaptation. Butt remarks: 'Such privileging, then, foregrounds a vision of Scotland for later film and television that is conditioned by a vision of "Scotland" shaped by the earlier oligopoly.'[17] Visions such as these feed back into culture and shape understandings of Scottishness on a wider level.

Place-myths

Rob Shields develops Henri Lefebvre's work on the production of space to examine the process of social spatialisation, 'the ongoing conjunction of the spatial at the level of the social imaginary (collective mythologies, presuppositions) as well as interventions in the landscape (for example, the built environment)'.[18] Place, then, is constituted through both physical landscape and place-myth, which in turn comprise place-images. Place-myths are cyclically reinforced materially and ideologically, through both the circulation of images and the restructuring of physical space. The ideological significance of this approach is expressed methodologically in Shields's analysis not of physical sites, but of their intertextual representations: advertising materials, fictional depictions, media images and so on. For example, the 'Highland myth' obscured social upheaval in nineteenth-century Scotland,[19] and these always already constructed 'discursive positions' are perpetuated in media representations of Scotland.[20]

Queen Victoria's fondness for Scotland is key to popularising myths about the country, with the rise of 'Balmorality' and the construction of a mythical geography closely connected with the paintings of Edwin Landseer.[21] This iconography was reproduced and circulated in the rush for American dollars after World War II, laying the foundations of the modern tourist industry.[22] The wildly artificial Hollywood musical *Brigadoon* (1954) also plays a key role in reinforcing these myths. For McArthur, *Brigadoon* is the prime locus of films sentimentalising Scotland through intertwined signifiers of both tartanry and kailyard.

Such films contribute to the Scottish Discursive Unconscious – the core of which is an ensemble of images and stories about Scotland as a highland landscape of lochs, mists and castles inhabited by fey maidens and kilted men who may be both warlike and sensitive – which serves internationally to signify 'Scottishness'.[23]

These hegemonic discourses mean that 'other possible narratives about Scotland, for example as a centre of philosophical inquiry in the eighteenth century or as a source of industrial innovation in the nineteenth century, have largely been evacuated from popular memory'.[24] Examination of classic *Doctor Who* serials confirms the significance of the Scottish Discursive Unconscious in the series's engagement with Scotland and Scottishness.

Representations of Scotland in classic *Doctor Who*

A significant representation of Scottishness comes in the form of the character Jamie McCrimmon (Frazer Hines). Jamie is introduced in 'The Highlanders' (1966–7), and his travels in the TARDIS span virtually the entire Second Doctor era, with the character appearing in all narratives apart from the first serial. Set in the aftermath of the Battle of Culloden, 'The Highlanders' sees the Doctor (Patrick Troughton) and his companions Ben (Michael Craze) and Polly (Anneke Wills) encountering fleeing Scots rebels, including the Laird Colin McLaren (Donald Bisset), his resourceful daughter Kirsty (Hannah Gordon) and his piper Jamie McCrimmon. The unscrupulous Solicitor Grey has devised a plan to transport Highlanders to the colonies on a slave ship. Using a ruse in which Jamie is supposed to be Bonnie Prince Charlie, the Doctor escapes from Grey (David Garth) and returns to Culloden to find the TARDIS. Jamie joins the Doctor and his companions on their travels.

'The Highlanders' owes a great deal to Sir Walter Scott's novel *Waverley* (1814), and in addition draws much of its inspiration from the BBC's classic serials of the time, which safely adapted 'classic' works of literature, thereby again offering the cultural legitimacy of an earlier literary form. Matthew Kilburn notes the serial's debt to Robert Louis Stevenson's *Kidnapped* (1886), and points out that the launch of the first series of *Doctor Who* in November 1963 shared its press launch with a Sunday afternoon dramatisation of that novel. Kilburn thus positions 'The Highlanders' within the BBC's public-service remit, as both drawing on the familiar tropes of a respectable literary source and demonstrating the improving qualities of an educational programme. It thus fulfils 'the BBC's duty as a national broadcaster by interpreting the collective past to the viewer. Almost every historical story saw the Doctor and his companions encountering a society which had an influence on the nature of British identity.'[25] Comparing the serial to Peter Watkins's controversial BBC film *Culloden* (1964), Kilburn shows that while *Culloden* was intended to 'challenge viewers' understanding of the nation', 'The Highlanders' offered a 'cosy, unthreatening worldview'.[26] As evidence, he points out that while *Culloden* shows that there were more Scotsmen fighting Bonnie Prince Charlie than were in his own army, the *Doctor Who* serial 'enthusiastically depicts the Jacobite army – whose cause is never properly explained – as the Scots, and their opponents as the English'.[27]

Since the serial no longer exists, it is difficult to offer close textual analysis. However, working from the remaining fragments – soundtrack, tiny clips, off-screen telesnaps and production photographs – it assembles various signifiers of tartanry such as the Battle of Culloden, sparsely populated bleak moorland, tartan, kilts, tam-o'-shanters, redcoats, Bonnie Prince Charlie, Highland lairds, loyal pipers, bonnie yet feisty lassies, epic but noble failure – in a classical representation of the Scottish Discursive Unconscious. The serial thus confirms McArthur's 'highland landscapes' of 'fey maidens' and 'kilted [...] warlike and sensitive' men.[28] Jamie conforms to a number of tropes in terms of stereotypical representations of Scotland – he is a bagpiper, uneducated but loyal, protective of women; he speaks Gaelic (although his knowledge of the language is basically reducible to his battle cry '*Creag an tuire*'), and he always wears a kilt. To depict his return to his own time in 'The War Games' (1969), signifiers of tartanry are deployed again as Jamie is seen chasing an English redcoat across bleak moorland, crying '*Creag an tuire*' as bagpipes play on the soundtrack. The name Jamie suggests a debt to Stevenson's *The Master of Ballantrae* (1889), which was also a film in 1953 starring Errol Flynn. And the character influenced Diana Gabaldon's *Outlander* series (Starz, 2014–present), showing the way in which media representations feed back into culture in an ontological circle.

A few Scottish characters appear in further Second Doctor serials. In 'The Ice Warriors' (1967), Europe in the far future is gripped by an ice age, and the sparsely populated glaciers covering the UK are now inhabited by wolves and bears. Staff at Britannicus Base – a preserved Georgian mansion under a protective dome – struggle to turn back the ice using their Ioniser machine. The hunter Storr encounters the Doctor when Martians from a crashed spaceship are defrosted from the glacier. On the page, Storr seems to be a typical hairy Highlander – cunning, resourceful and gruff as he negotiates an inhospitable snowy landscape in furs and a beard – but as played by diminutive Glasgow actor Angus Lennie, he comes across as petulant, ineffective and, frankly, camp. Writing and performance therefore throw up some interesting frictions, offering a potentially subversive interpretation of the tartanry stereotype.

'The Krotons' (1968–9) features a distinctly Scottish subtext, with its isolated city surrounded by bleak mountains and colonised natives in thrall to the imperious alien Krotons. The Kroton spaceship landed on the unnamed planet of the Gond people generations ago, killing a large proportion of the population and rendering much of the landscape into a bleak, uninhabitable 'wasteland', a situation with echoes of the Highland Clearances. The dormant Krotons have been culling the brightest of the population to refuel their ship, while suppressing the education of the remainder in order to discipline the subaltern population. While the visual-effects model for the city exterior features strange triangular houses ('Inca, perhaps?' suggests the Doctor's companion Zoe [Wendy Padbury]), the tartanry-inflected interior sets (using BBC stock elements shared across a number of productions) feature vaguely baronial stone walls, pillars and wall decorations of shields or targes. The presence of the Glaswegian-sounding Selris (Helensburgh-born James Copeland) and the less strongly accented Beta (Fife actor James Cairncross) adds to the general effect of Scottishness.

Another depiction of Scottishness comes in 'Death to the Daleks' (1974) and space marine Galloway (his name and accent working together to accentuate his Scottishness). Played by Scotland-raised Duncan Lamont, this grizzled old pragmatist comes across as a taciturn Red Clydesider unwillingly propelled into the future, challenging authority like a space union leader and prone to gruff pronouncements such as: 'He's scared of the wee salt-shakers.'

The next sustained depiction of Scotland comes in 'Terror of the Zygons' (1975), which draws together well-worn signifiers of Scottishness, just as 'The Green Death' had done with its Welsh coal miners, slag heaps, Blodwens and comedy-accented milkmen in 1973. Written by Scottish writer Robert Banks Stewart, 'Terror of the Zygons' opens with the destruction of an oil rig off the Scottish coast. Summoned by his sometime employer Brigadier Lethbridge-Stewart (Nicholas Courtney), the Doctor (Tom Baker) discovers that the rig has been destroyed by the Loch Ness monster, which is really a huge aquatic cyborg under the control of the alien Zygons, whose spaceship has been hidden for centuries under the loch. The Zygon homeworld has been destroyed and the shape-shifting creatures masquerade as locals, including the Duke of Forgill (John Woodnutt), as part of a larger plan to terraform the Earth and populate it with other Zygon survivors from around the galaxy.

The myth of the Loch Ness monster often begins with St Columba's encounter with the monster in the sixth century, and highlights the confrontation between paganism and Christianity, as well as, implicitly, the tension between tradition and progress:

> St Columba reputedly banished the monster back to the depths with powerful words, presumably (we must infer) as he did any existing pre-Christian beliefs. This particular recounting of St Columba's encounter with the monster illustrates precisely Nessie's typical use as prehistoric Other against which the 'civilised' defines itself. In the nineteenth century Nessie was transformed from mythological beastie to dinosaur.[29]

David Martin-Jones acknowledges that Nessie's transformation during the nineteenth century was due to prevailing scientific thinking, and also notes the way in which Nessie's celebrity status emerged in the 1930s alongside new media technologies that encouraged newspaper, photographic and cinematic coverage of the monster. Modern technology was brought to bear in the metaphorical context of a backwards and remote landscape, positioning Scotland as *not* civilised: 'Thus, the idea of an anachronistic dinosaur in a loch came to define Scotland as a nation, meshing with the already existing British myth of Scotland as wilderness (the myth of tartanry), that emerged after the Highland clearances.'[30] Journeys to geographical peripheries are often figured as journeys to social and even historical peripheries. Discussing uncanny landscapes on screen, Peter Hutchings argues that British screen narratives often involve journeys to geographical peripheries which involve a return to primitivism and the 'savage-rural'.[31] It is therefore appropriate that *Doctor Who*'s first present-day trip to Scotland should involve a science-fictional rationalisation of a myth involving what appears to be a prehistoric monster, reinforcing 'othering' views of Scotland as a geographically and historically peripheral wilderness 'out of time'.

The serial deploys many of the tropes of tartanry and kailyard in order to tell its story. The very English Brigadier Lethbridge-Stewart ('the clan Stewart!') is mocked for wearing Highland dress, while the Doctor dons a tartan scarf and tam-o'-shanter hat. The oil company and the forces of the blimpish Brigadier represent encroaching modernity and the bureaucratic centre, in tension with the isolated and close-knit villagers and their laird, the Duke of Forgill. The local landlord Angus (Angus Lennie again) is an Ealing Comedy canny Scot, playing bagpipes to irritate the English soldiers and the American oil executive, and claiming to have the second sight. Location filming in West Sussex used heathery moors and pine forests to stand in for the countryside around Loch Ness. Forgill Castle is represented by a still of Dunvegan Castle on Skye, and by an interior studio set composed mostly of Gothic castle elements from the BBC's scenic stock rather than any convincing attempt at matching Dunvegan's actual interior or approximating Scottish baronial architecture. But this narrative site is one redolent of myths of Scotland. As McArthur points out, '"baronialism" offers a site, the dark Scottish castle, within which certain kinds of specifically "Scottish" stories – principally hinging on treachery and the betrayal of hospitality – can be played out.'[32] Forgill Castle figures as a 'baronial' site of betrayal when the Doctor's companion Sarah (Elisabeth Sladen) visits to use the library there and the unhospitable duke, whose disdain for the oil workers and English troops is clear, is revealed to be a shape-shifting Zygon. Creating an on-screen diegesis combining West Sussex, Skye and studio sets at Television Centre, the serial constructs a peripheral Scotland as seen from the metropolitan centre, which conforms to a range of prevailing place-myths but has little relationship to modern Scotland.

As Hutchings says, modernity can invade the rural, but the rural can strike back in unexpected ways.[33] Loch Ness becomes a threatening and uncanny marginal site, an atavistic landscape threatening identity in the present as the shape-shifting Zygons threaten the cohesion of the national body through their takeover and copying of the protagonists' physical bodies. In utilising the myth of the Loch Ness monster, then, the London 'centre' visits the Scottish 'periphery', but the serial's climax takes place in London – the Highlands of Scotland offer a remote and isolated wilderness in which giant uncanny creatures can roam unseen, but in order to generate any real jeopardy the narrative must return to the industrial and political centre to have any impact. In the final episode, the Zygons send their creature to attack an energy conference in London, bringing the hostile (implicitly prehistoric) periphery into the modern urban centre. Post-colonial fears of invasion from the periphery feature, as the 'return of the repressed' from the colonised margins intrudes into the heart of the British establishment. 'Timelash' (1985) visits a studio-bound Scottish cottage in 1885 for another dip into the Loch Ness myth, contradicting 'Terror of the Zygons' by claiming that the monster is the Borad, a humanoid/reptile hybrid, deposited in the Loch by a time corridor.

'The Highlanders' and 'Terror of the Zygons' draw on traditional myths of Scotland, making use of well-worn signifiers of place and character already thoroughly established in literary and screen cultures and in the popular imagination. The serials utilise the Scottish Discursive Unconscious to assemble signifiers of Scotland, a discourse of place consonant with previous media representations in what Charles Jencks calls the *musée imaginaire* of history, drawn from a variety of sources.[34] Scotland is positioned as geographically and culturally 'Other' – somewhere to be visited by the benignly paternalistic gentleman explorer Doctor. However, in 1987–9, the Doctor was himself played by a Scottish actor, Sylvester McCoy.

Sylvester McCoy's accent

In his analysis of the Doctors and their relationships to their historical contexts, Nicholas Cull notes that Peter Davison 'was the most obviously nationally marked of the set as he appeared in an [*sic*] Victorian cricket outfit and cultivated the air of a gentleman explorer'. His successors are called 'variations on the same theme', and it is noted that

> McCoy carried one further particularly British prop: an umbrella, with a handle in the shape of a question mark. Thus elements of a national self-image were preserved and projected into space, where this reassuringly British character encountered a succession of British cultural and historical obsessions.[35]

This analysis ignores McCoy's Scottishness, in failing to mention his accent and in not pointing out the undermining of identity implied by the question marks incorporated into the prop and McCoy's costume. If the umbrella is 'particularly British', what does it mean that a question mark is incorporated into its structure?

Murray Smith notes the gap between 'official' language and vernacular: most colonised countries require their inhabitants to speak two languages – minority, post-colonial subjects occupy (at least) two linguistic worlds.[36] While McCoy's Scottish accent is not laboured within the series beyond some pointed pronunciations of 'loch', its significance lies perhaps in its presence. In his chapter in McArthur's *Scotch Reels*, Cairns Craig points out that popular culture did offer a means of expression for the working classes of Scotland and a site to find identity and experience mirrored. In her profile of McCoy's Doctor, Lynne M. Thomas does not mention his Scottishness, focusing instead on the programme's troubled relationship with the internal politics of the BBC and its increasingly political content, but noting that

> *Doctor Who*'s casting during the McCoy era featured a more diverse pool of actors […] than had been seen in the series for quite some time. This conscious choice to reflect a more diverse society of viewers in casting carries through to the reboot.[37]

McCoy's accent may be seen as another articulation of this greater diversity in an increasingly multicultural Britain.

Since the end of the 'classic' series in 1989, Scotland's position within the UK has seen substantial change. The 1998 Scotland Act created an elected Scottish Parliament with greater control over domestic policy, and in May 1999 the Scottish Parliament held session for the first time since its dissolution in 1707. In 2014, Scotland held an independence referendum in which 44.75 per cent of those who voted favoured Scotland's independence from the UK.

'Lots of planets have a north': nations and regions in new *Who*

When Christopher Eccleston took on the part of the Doctor in 2005, his Salford accent was explained with the line 'Lots of planets have a north!' ('Rose', 2005). The casting of Paisley actor David Tennant, therefore, raised the potential for a Scottish-accented Doctor. According to the *Scotsman* newspaper:

> When Tennant joined the hit show as the tenth Doctor in 2005, he said: 'I'd love to be the first Time Lord to wear a kilt.' But writer Russell T Davies said he did not want the Doctor's voice 'touring the regions'.[38]

The one episode in which Tennant briefly uses his own accent – 'Tooth and Claw' (2006) – offers a new *Who* example of an episode set entirely in Scotland with which it is productive to compare previous representational strategies. 'Tooth and Claw' also offers a provocative reading of representations of Scotland within *Doctor Who*, one that raises important questions around the theme of colonialism touched on by, for example, Craig, as discussed above.

In 'Tooth and Claw', the Doctor and his companion Rose (Billie Piper) arrive in Scotland in 1879. In an apparently deserted glen, they encounter Queen Victoria (Pauline Collins) on her way to Balmoral. The queen spends the night at the Torchwood Estate, a typical baronial castle, not realising that the house has been taken over by sinister monks. The monks are assisting a lycanthropic alien being which has possessed the bodies of locals over many generations, periodically transforming into a werewolf-like creature. The Doctor discovers that the late Prince Albert planned to use the Koh-i-Noor diamond in an advanced form of telescope housed at Torchwood to repel the creature's essence. He completes the Prince's plan, but the episode ends with the suggestion that Victoria, infected with the alien essence, may now carry lycanthropy back to London.

The presence of a werewolf in what is only *Doctor Who*'s third sustained narrative set in Scotland may not be a coincidence. In his discussion of Scottish horror films, David Martin-Jones traces a line from Robert Louis Stevenson's Burke and Hare story 'The Body Snatcher' (1884) to contemporary rural horror, positioning Scotland as, again, an atavistic periphery – a hostile, marginal wilderness at the edge of the UK (as a geographical space) and also at the edge of civilisation (as a social space). But he also draws on Stevenson's *Strange Case of Dr Jekyll and Mr Hyde* (1886), with its respectable, educated doctor transforming into an uncouth, hairy beast at night – significantly, under the influence of drink – and this idea of the Freudian 'return of the repressed' is key to the Scottish psyche.[39] Scottish Presbyterianism controls and suppresses a recently wild, uncivilised, notably masculine past. It also informs our understandings of Scottish history and identity as a colonised country, 'out of history' with much that is policed, stifled and driven underground.

The combination of Scotland, werewolves, Queen Victoria and the Koh-i-Noor points to the serial's post-colonial subtext. Danielle Kinsey notes the way in which the Koh-i-Noor diamond functioned on a number of different and contradictory levels in British imperial culture. On the one hand, it was used within colonial discourses to cast British rule in India in a progressive light; on the other, it was a highly negative symbol of plunder imperialism.[40] The Queen was inextricably associated with the Koh-i-Noor, and Kinsey argues that consequently much Victorian media discourse around the diamond feminises it. The diamond contrasted with another form of carbon, coal, which produces real light and heat where the diamond only borrows it – positioning coal as masculine, useful and industrial, and diamond as decorative and feminine. Its origins in India meant that it was also seen as suspiciously 'Oriental', and Kinsey argues that Prince Albert's recutting of the diamond into a new symmetrical shape using the latest British science and technology was 'an attempt to reposition the artifact in British material culture as a symbol of the British Empire's civilising mission in India'.[41] Superior British technology is thus brought to bear in an attempt to Westernise and 'civilise' a problematic Oriental object.

The 'classic' serials discussed earlier fall back on well-worn myths of Scotland – the Jacobite uprisings as retold through the adventure tales of Robert Louis Stevenson in 'The Highlanders', and the Loch Ness monster in 'Terror of the Zygons'. 'Tooth and Claw' similarly utilises key tropes of the Scottish Discursive Unconscious – paradigmatic tartanry signifiers of deserted glens, hairy savages, stone castles, the Scottish baronial trope of betrayal of hospitality, and Queen Victoria's 'Balmorality'. Scotland is here still positioned as a colonial periphery, as exotic and dangerous in its own way as unruly nineteenth-century India. Within this context, the Koh-i-Noor diamond thus functions as a symbol both of eighteenth-century imperial plunder and of nineteenth-century scientific modernity; both, however, are colonial discourses. It is therefore appropriate in 'Tooth and Claw' that a diamond which represents these discourses – simultaneously an 'artifact of British conquest' and a contentious symbol of the British Empire's 'civilising mission'[42] – is used to contain and repel the 'return of the repressed' in a Scottish-set wilderness narrative in which the queen of England is menaced by a Scottish werewolf. The episode therefore points to the colonising role of the British Empire and, in its suggestion that Victoria becomes lycanthropic, Scotland's own potential to resist and reverse that colonisation.

This chapter now turns to the Steven Moffat era of *Doctor Who* (2010–17) in order to consider Moffat's contribution to discourses of Scottishness within the series, and how these discourses fit within contemporary changes in the programme's social, political and broadcasting contexts.

Scottishness in the Steven Moffat-produced Matt Smith era

In the twenty-first century, Scotland has undergone drastic social change in terms of attitudes to national identity and self-determination. As Nowlan and Finch note, with the re-establishment of the Scottish parliament in 1999 and the devolution of significant self-governing authority and national autonomy to a Scottish government elected by the Scottish people, Scots are increasingly identifying primarily as Scottish rather than British.[43] Scottishness features strongly in showrunner Steven Moffat's era of *Doctor Who*, initially in the character of Amy Pond (Karen Gillan), the Eleventh Doctor's first companion. Born in Scotland but living in the English village of Leadworth, Amy (Amelia, played by Caitlin Blackwood) is seven when the Eleventh Doctor (Matt Smith) arrives in her garden. Although he promises to take her adventuring in space and time, he accidentally leaves her behind for twelve years. The image of Amy sitting in the garden on her suitcase, gazing longingly at the stars, is a key one in her first episode.

Christopher Harvie makes the distinction between 'Red' Scots (mobile, outward-looking, high-achieving) and 'Black' Scots (stable, insular, conservative).[44] The 'Red' Scot is a peripatetic figure driven by aspiration as well as alienation. As Harvie explains, the 'Wandering Scot' is a high-achieving figure who goes back at least to the fourteenth century, and who has a strong association with universities.[45] Amy's 'Otherness' as a Scot in England is paralleled with the Doctor's status as an exile and the last of his kind when, in 'The Eleventh Hour' (2010), he remarks: 'You're the Scottish girl in the English village and I know how that feels.' Furthermore, her accent is no mere signifier of Scottishness, but indexical of her strong sense of self and desire to travel, seemingly situating Amy as a questing 'Red Scot'. Again in 'The Eleventh Hour', the Doctor states: 'All these years living here, most of your life, and you've still got that accent, yeah, you're coming.'

While Amy's retention of her accent seems to point to a strongly assertive Scottish identity within England, the notion of Scottish independence is referenced in Amy's next episode, 'The Beast Below' (2010), when she visits *Starship UK*, a space-going vessel escaping solar flares on Earth. *Starship UK*'s culture is composed out of nostalgic signifiers of a 'selectively reconstructed mid-twentieth century of red telephone boxes and school uniforms [...] a stylised representation of the New Elizabethanism of the 1950s'.[46] Scotland, though, is explicitly absent from this metonymic United Kingdom:

GIRL: You sound Scottish.
AMY: I am Scottish, what's wrong with that? Scotland's got to be here somewhere.
GIRL: No. They wanted their own ship.
AMY: Ha. Good for them. Nothing changes.

Amy's slightly defensive reaction (the unnecessary 'what's wrong with that?') invokes the shadow of the subaltern, but is reversed when she finds out Scotland has struck out on its own ('Good for them'). This throwaway line has a deeper import, however, suggesting that there is not perhaps much left of the UK, despite the 'British' iconography of the episode. A large Union flag decorates the starship's exterior, and more flags festoon the interior sets and serve as screen graphics, but its tower blocks are all named after English counties, and the interiors draw on the iconography of the London Underground. There is thus a tension between the name of *Starship UK* and its semiotic construction, suggesting that the ship is a function of the convention that the south-east of England regularly stands metonymically for the UK.

The episode engages with democratic politics in a very direct way, as the inhabitants of *Starship UK* regularly vote to wipe their minds of the knowledge that the ship is powered by an enslaved space whale:

THE DOCTOR: Once every five years, everyone chooses to forget
    what they've learned. Democracy in action.
GIRL: How do you not know about this? Are you Scottish too?
THE DOCTOR: Oh, I'm way worse than Scottish. I can't even see
    the movie, won't play for me.

Scottishness in *Starship UK* functions as exclusion from democratic participation, a process from which the Doctor is specifically excluded ('worse than Scottish') on the grounds of his non-human Otherness. In reducing the UK to south-east England in this way, the vessel might better be called *Starship UKIP*.

In the next episode, 'Victory of the Daleks' (2010), the iconography of World War II is engaged through signifiers of national identity – principally the Union flag again – but Scottishness features interestingly here too. Churchill (Ian McNeice) is using Daleks to fight the Nazis, believing them to be a new weapon invented by Professor Bracewell, played by Scottish actor Bill Paterson. Again, Scottishness is seen as worthy of comment:

CHURCHILL: Fellow's a genius!
AMY: A Scottish genius too. Maybe you should listen to him.

Bracewell says: 'Ideas just seem to teem from my head,' and Amy comments approvingly on his origins: 'Not bad for a Paisley boy!' Acknowledging the presence of another 'Red' Scot, Bracewell comments: 'Yes, I thought I detected a familiar cadence, my dear.' Accent is a key signifier of Otherness here, articulated through Paterson's performance – he pronounces Dalek as 'Dallek', although nobody else does. No matter how positively Amy's approving 'Scottish genius' frames Bracewell, drawing attention to nationality inevitably Others it. It transpires that the ideas that 'teem' from Bracewell's head are a result of his origins as a Dalek android. Amy directly appeals to their shared Scottishness to help them fight the Daleks, several times calling him 'Paisley': 'In your own time, Paisley boy, because right now we need your help.' And in the episode's conclusion, it is Amy who defuses the bomb within the android Bracewell by appealing to his implanted memories of an early love, Dorabella. Churchill comments: 'She's good, Doctor. As sharp as a pin.'

Engagement with Scottishness throughout the remainder of the season is less pointed. The Bishop Octavian (Iain Glen) has a Scottish accent, but the point is not laboured ('The Time of Angels'/'Flesh and Stone', 2010). In 'Vampires of Venice' (2010) Amy slips into Scottish idiom, asking Rory (Arthur Darvill): 'Why did you make the sign of the cross, ya numpty?' In 'The Hungry Earth'/'Cold Blood' (2010) the Scottish accents of the reptile Silurians Alaya and Restac (Neve McIntosh) are not commented on. McIntosh returns as another Scottish-accented Silurian, Madame Vastra, in later episodes. In 'Vincent and the Doctor' (2010), Van Gogh's (Tony Curran) accent is commented on by comparison with Amy's; the suggestion is that the TARDIS translates his Dutch-accented French into a regional British-accented English. Similarly, both characters comment on their ginger hair.

The following season similarly features a scattering of Scottish accents among the supporting cast, for example Jimmy (Mark Bonnar) in 'The Rebel Flesh/The Almost People' (2011). In 'A Good Man Goes To War' (2011), Amy tells Rory: 'No offence to the others [their allies], but you let them all die first', to which he replies, 'You're so Scottish.' When the Doctor is dying in 'Let's Kill Hitler' (2011), the TARDIS uses a voice interface in the image of seven-year-old Amelia Pond; when it dogmatically repeats, 'I am not Amelia Pond. I am a voice interface,' the Doctor comments, 'You are so Scottish!' The interface's unsympathetic repetition of 'You will be dead in 32 minutes' similarly elicits the Doctor's response, 'Scottish. That's all I'm saying.'

Scottishness then is paradigmatic here of an unsentimental instrumentalism, suggesting a utilitarian and hard-hearted 'kailyardism' not given to empathy. However, during Amy's tenure the show seems to lose interest in Scottishness as a trope, suggesting that as the audience gets accustomed to Amy's character, her Scottishness becomes largely unremarkable. Scottishness is to take on renewed importance in the Twelfth Doctor era, as this chapter now discusses.

'Doomed dialogue doesn't half sound great in Scottish': authorship and the Twelfth Doctor

The discussion above shows how the programme draws attention to Amy Pond's Scottishness in the Eleventh Doctor era. Scottishness is also key to Moffat's public statements about the casting of Peter Capaldi as the Twelfth Doctor, and these utterances play a significant part in the discursive positioning of audience understandings of the character and the programme. While Matt Hills is right to say that '*Doctor Who* has been interpreted within fandom as multi-authored, rather than being articulated within any one creative "vision" or authority figure,'[47] it is still the case that as 'quality television', *Doctor Who* is positioned among both fan and industrial discourses as predominantly authored by its showrunner. While creative agency is shared among various production staff in official discourses, this is in part an institutional promotional strategy designed to shape audience understandings of the programme and its production: 'Multi-authorship discourses derived from fandom are thus woven into the new media strategies of new *Who*. The monotheistic "author-God" of "literary" and "television-as-Culture" discourses is decentred, even whilst authorship discourses continue to be mobilised.'[48] As Hills argues, such discourses act as Foucault's 'author-function', legitimising the text as 'authored' television, thereby giving the imprimatur of 'authorship' as a way of positioning *Doctor Who* within the hierarchical structure of television. Inevitably, however, such discourses contain their own hierarchies of value, which continue to privilege the showrunner as primary author of the programme. Steven Moffat therefore enjoys a privileged position as author-function, discursively shaping the positioning of audience understandings of the programme.

Covering Capaldi's casting as the Twelfth Doctor, *The Scotsman* newspaper reported:

> Asked what viewers could expect from the new Doctor, Moffat, originally from Paisley, Renfrewshire, said: 'Scottishness. I think that's the main thing. I mean watching him, and I just watched episode two actually, you don't go around thinking this is an older bloke as the Doctor, particularly. You just think my God, he's Scottish. And doomed dialogue doesn't half sound great in Scottish. You say the world's about to end in a Scottish accent, and you really believe it.' [...] The BBC has said the decision for Capaldi to have a Scottish accent was a 'creative decision'.[49]

Significant is the word 'doomed', linking Scottishness with the tartanry/kailyard discourse of heroic failure and recalling the catchphrase of the pessimistic Private Frazer (John Laurie) in *Dad's Army* (BBC, 1968–77). Also significantly, the article makes a point of mentioning Moffat's own west Scottish roots.

In his 'Ask Steven Moffat' column for *Doctor Who Magazine*, Moffat makes frequent reference to Scottishness. Discussing the episode where Dalek creator Davros, in childhood, meets the Doctor ('The Magician's Apprentice') and later in life starts to wonder if it was the Doctor who saved him, he comments: 'Davros has always known that some grumpy old Scotsman saved him on a battlefield [...] And when he looks out that strange device the Scotsman gave him (probably in his mum's attic), he realises it was true.'[50] It is not only Capaldi's Scottishness of which Moffat is aware. He also discusses his own, and that of other actors connected to the programme. Moffat parallels his journey from Scottish childhood to showrunner of *Doctor Who* with David Tennant's journey from Scottish childhood to star of *Doctor Who*:

> Dan Jacobs asks: Have there been any *Doctor Who* fantasies from your childhood that have made it into the show now you're the man in charge?

> I think being the man in charge was the fantasy, and I'm still slightly surprised that one worked out. Particularly as I was having that fantasy in the same town that little David Tennant was fantasising about being the Doctor. That town, by the way, was Paisley, near Glasgow, if you want to pop along and make a wish.[51]

Scotland is positioned here as being peripheral to the London-centric world of *Doctor Who*, and Scottishness as being an obstacle to reaching that world. As already discussed, the 'Red Scot' is seen as a mobile and aspirational figure, eager to leave Scotland and fulfil their potential. In addition, as Angus Calder points out, the ambitiously diasporic 'Red Scot' is instrumental in reproducing canonical, if mythical, representations of Scotland.[52] Both Moffat and Tennant can be read as 'Red Scots' with their aspirational urge to travel and pursue their own brands of self-actualisation by entering into the professional and diegetic worlds of *Doctor Who*.

Peter Capaldi, another diasporic 'Red Scot', also demonstrates an awareness of *Doctor Who* as being a long way from the cultural and political 'core' of London and the BBC. Before becoming the Twelfth Doctor, after meeting David Bradley playing William Hartnell playing the First Doctor in Mark Gatiss's *An Adventure in Space and Time* (2013), Capaldi wrote to Gatiss 'summing up his love affair with the series and what it's always meant to him. He said, "You made the dreams of a little boy from smokey Glasgow come true. He got to meet Doctor Who."'[53]

Conversely, in an interview conducted once he was playing the Doctor, Capaldi was asked about his relationship with the programme:

> What was it that first attracted Peter to *Doctor Who*? Growing up in 1960s Glasgow, BBC Television Centre must have seemed a world away ...
>
> 'Well, yes, regional accents were few and far between on television ... That's how shows were. That's how drama and entertainment was presented. But it absolutely didn't feel a world away. It's odd now when you think about it, as most drama then was London-centric, but we didn't think about that then.'[54]

While the interview stresses the gulf between the both ideological and geographical 'centre' of BBC Television Centre and the colonial 'regional' (actually national) periphery of 1960s Glasgow, Capaldi disavows any sense of the subaltern by stressing 'it absolutely didn't feel a world away'.

Following the casting of Glasgow actress Michelle Gomez as the Doctor's arch-enemy Missy, Moffat again parallels himself with the Scottish actors working on the programme in his 'Ask Steven Moffat' column:

> Clive Lewis asks: Is the Gallifreyan regeneration energy field going through a Scottish cycle of influence at the moment? We've got a Scottish Doctor (Peter Capaldi), a Scottish Missy (Michelle Gomez) and, on audio, a Scottish Rani (Siobhan Redmond).
>
> How about showrunner? Coughs, points at self. Nothing. Oh, never mind. Yes!! Yes, this is our plan for Scottish independence (you ask [director] Douglas Mackinnon – he NEVER TALKS ABOUT ANYTHING ELSE EVER). First, we will secure all positions of cultural and political significance in England. Then we will initiate full separation having created (this is the clever part) TWO SCOTLANDS.
>
> You see? This is why separation is necessary. Two Scotlands would never get on. There would be a mighty war within 12 seconds, destroying most of the landmass, Wales would be left, bobbing alone in the water, wondering why there was nothing at the end of the bridge.
>
> I'll be fine. I've got a house in Cardiff. Me and Peter will start a new Scotland right here. And then split it between North and South.[55]

From 'gay agenda' to 'Scottish agenda'

While acknowledging the multivalent nature of television authorship and the slippery nature of authored 'eras', Matt Hills has discussed the presence of queer identities in *Doctor Who* episodes produced under Russell T Davies and analysed assumptions by both media and fans that Davies had a 'gay agenda': 'Davies' career has been interpreted by critics and fans alike as following specific agendas – or [...] as repeatedly making statements with a distinct cultural politics.'[56] Press and fans noted, not always approvingly, the presence of LGBTQ characters in many episodes in Davies's *Who*. Hills goes on to suggest that 'The reactionary fan label "gay agenda" appears to be rooted discursively in conservative and right-wing furore, as well as in a restrictive view that sexuality should not be written about at all in *Doctor Who*'.[57] In interviews, Davies himself rejects the 'gay agenda', leading Hills to argue that this 'positions Davies as an *auteur* of "non-agenda agenda" television drama in which queer identity resists being a central "issue"'.[58] That said, Moffat wrote the first episode to feature the omnisexual Captain Jack Harkness character (John Barrowman), and his work has included gay characters such as Madame Vastra (Neve McIntosh), Jenny Flint (Catrin Stewart) and the first openly gay companion, Bill Potts (Pearl Mackie).

This chapter has explored how Steven Moffat positions the Twelfth Doctor as Scottish in a range of paratextual discourses which contribute to audiences' understandings of the character. As well as positioning both actor and character of the Twelfth Doctor as Scottish in such paratexts, Moffat includes intradiegetic reference to the character's Scottishness. Even in script directions, Moffat mentions Capaldi's Scottishness. In the script for 'Hell Bent', predicting Capaldi's reaction to being on a pastiche version of the original 1960s TARDIS set: 'The Doctor is flying around the classic console, like a distinguished Scottish actor who's slightly too excited for his own good.'[59]

Before examining the episodes themselves, it is worth mentioning an interview which gives some insight into Moffat's conception of Scottish identity. Discussing Peter Capaldi's reaction to being told he will be carrying an entire episode ('Heaven Sent') alone, Moffat comments:

> You know, Peter's the kind of guy who responds with the same dour Scottish nod to whatever news he's given [...] He has great emotional range as an actor, but, you know, he's Scottish; it's a sign of weakness to have a reaction.[60]

This notion of Scottishness falls back on kailyard/Clydesideism discourses of the Calvinistic, emotionally repressed Scot. The construction of the Scottish Doctor which emerges in Capaldi's episodes connects Scottishness with lack of emotional intelligence, a trait of some of the previous Doctors, such as Christopher Eccleston's Doctor not doing 'domestic' ('Rose', 2005; 'Aliens of London', 2005) but developed to perhaps its fullest extent with the explicitly Scottish Twelfth Doctor.

'I've gone Scottish': discourses of Scotland and Scottishness in Capaldi-era *Who*

In 'Deep Breath', his first full episode, in the throes of post-regeneration confusion, the Twelfth Doctor sees his new reflection for the first time:

THE DOCTOR: Look at the eyebrows, these are attack eyebrows! You could take bottle tops off with these … they're cross! They're crosser than the rest of my face. They're independently cross! They probably want to cede from the rest of my face and set up their own independent state of eyebrows! That's, Scot, I'm Scottish, am I? I've gone Scottish?

TRAMP: You are definitely Scots sir, I hear it in your voice.

THE DOCTOR: Oh no, that's good! Ohh! Ohhh! That's good I'm Scottish, I'm Scottish, I am Scottish. I can complain about things. I can really complain about things now.

Later, reading about spontaneous combustion in the newspaper, he mutters 'blame the English'.

The Scottish Independence referendum was held on 18 September 2014, less than a month after this episode was broadcast, and this dialogue is a clear reference to the forthcoming vote. The moment the Doctor says 'independent' seems to be the moment he realises he is Scottish and notices his own accent, despite this recognition coming more than 20 minutes into the episode. It also suggests anger ('they're cross') and the fact that they are 'crosser than the rest of my face' ties them metonymically to Scotland's desire to declare its independence from the rest of the UK (more specifically, from England), as well as the trope of the grumpy or angry Scottish male ('I can complain about things').

Anger seems key to the Capaldi persona. Reviewer Graham Kibble-White notes of the Twelfth Doctor:

> Where the former was almost puppyish, this one's a fighting dog [...] From the off, a sense of rage precedes the Twelfth. Indeed, the story quivers, slightly, as if waiting for him to lose it ('Don't look in that mirror, it's absolutely furious!')[61]

The review goes on to emphasise the frightening qualities of the new persona, calling him 'this fearsome, lonesome man with a long reputation and a rather disdainful take on the human race'.[62]

Anger and the capacity to induce fear are evoked by the new Doctor and his Scottishness. When Dr Chang (Andrew Leung) reads a fake government inspector ID from the Doctor's psychic paper, he asks, 'Why's there all this swearing?' The Doctor replies, 'Oh, I've got a lot of internalised anger.' Tropes of the rampaging Scottish football fan are mobilised as the Doctor tries to evacuate the area around St Paul's as the Cybermen march out: Missy calls out, 'Sorry everyone, another ranting Scotsman in the street, I'd no idea there was a match on' ('Dark Water'). Having saved a schoolgirl from wild animals, the Doctor is told 'from being almost savaged by a tiger, abducted by a Scotsman, she's allowed any nervous ticks she likes' ('In the Forest of the Night').

The Tennant or Smith Doctors would not be described as an Englishman quite so specifically in an equivalent context. There is clearly something Othering about these references, and about the implication that being abducted *by a Scotsman* is comparable to being savaged by a tiger and sufficiently alarming to bring on nervous ticks. Similarly, the playfully demented Missy (Glasgow actress Michelle Gomez) is explicitly identified by having a 'Scottish accent' ('Death in Heaven'); none of the previous actors who played the same character (originally the Master) was ever described as having an 'English accent'.

The Doctor's sound and appearance are related to his national identity. In a play on poor Scottish diets, Robin Hood (Tom Riley) tells the Doctor 'you have a sickly aspect to you. You're pale as milk. It's the way with Scots, they're strangers to vegetables' ('Robot of Sherwood'). Beyond the occasional 'och' or the Glaswegian 'big man' ('Time Heist'), the Doctor uses very little in the way of actual Scots idiom, but even the sound of the Doctor's Scottishness seems to possess its own menacing qualities: having travelled to the end of the universe, the Doctor is talking about ghosts when the lights in the timeship darken in a sinister fashion. Clara (Jenna Coleman) says, 'Do you have your own mood lighting now, because frankly the accent is enough' ('Listen'). Scottishness functions as a form of implied threat (of anger): 'We can't phone the Doctor and bleat, he'll go Scottish!' ('The Magician's Apprentice'). In 'Hell Bent', the Time Lord homeworld of Gallifrey is described as 'sort of Glasgow, space Glasgow', and the Doctor's companion Clara interprets the founder of Time Lord society, Rassilon (Donald Sumpter) through the *No Mean City* lens: 'And there was this gang boss and he wanted to kill you?' And in 'Smile', in Capaldi's final series, Bill Potts raises the issue of Scottishness again:

BILL: Why are you Scottish?
THE DOCTOR: I'm not Scottish, I'm just cross.
BILL: Is there a Scotland in space?
THE DOCTOR: They're all over the place, demanding independence
on every planet they land on!

Thus, both intradiegetically and extradiegetically, discourses of Scottishness are reinforced through tropes of anger and lack of emotional intelligence. Through his paratextual discourses in *Doctor Who Magazine* and other journalistic sources, Moffat positions both Peter Capaldi and the Twelfth Doctor as emotionally distant, socially restrained, dour, cross, even frightening. And within the episodes, the narrative goes to great lengths to reinforce this understanding with repeated reference to the character's lack of empathy, discomfort at discussing emotions, intimidating presence, and need for human companions to act as emotional translators bridging the emotional gap between the Doctor and other human characters (and the programme's audience).

With Moffat, Capaldi and the Doctor himself all functioning as 'Red Scots' within this period of the programme's history, it is tempting to see parallels between showrunner, star and title character. Fans on the online forum Gallifrey Base discussing the Twelfth Doctor's accent identified a specifically 'Scottish agenda' and explicitly paralleled the Doctor with Moffat himself. Using the term 'Moffia' they discussed the showrunner's Scottish influence on the show, and in a thread entitled 'Has Moff cast a Doctor in his own image?' suggested that aggressive, acerbic elements of the Twelfth Doctor reflected aspects of Moffat's own personality.[63]

While this speculative connection between showrunner and Doctor might seem to be tenuous, Moffat did offer an instructive reply to a question in *Doctor Who Magazine*:

> Jason Gott asks: If you had to cast one more Doctor, who would your dream pick be?
> Steven Moffat: Me.[64]

Conclusion: out of history

A Capaldi episode set entirely in Scotland again mobilises well-worn tropes of the Scottish Discursive Unconscious. In 'The Eaters of Light', the Doctor, Bill and Nardole (Matt Lucas) arrive in second-century Aberdeen and encounter interdimensional creatures. Welsh hillsides offer an approximation of visual conventions for depicting the Scottish Highlands, with glowering grey skies above bleak misty glens dotted with polystyrene standing stones. 'It's Scotland. It's supposed to be damp,' observes the Doctor.

As with the time corridor in 'Timelash', Scotland is depicted as a place where other worlds are close to the surface. The Doctor comments: 'Picts, early Celts, loved stone cairns. They built them under the ground but close to the sky. They think they're doors between worlds.' The episode ends with scenes set in the present day in which a contemporary girl hears other-worldly faux-Celtic music. Karen Ralls-MacLeod notes how the 'enchanting music of the Celtic Otherworld is portrayed as being heard from a dimension not of this world'.[65] The episode thus positions Scotland as a site of liminal overlap between the worlds of magic and reality through the 'spiritual or supernatural dimension of music'.[66] Furthermore, using the same bleak location for present-day Aberdeen implies that Scotland, or vast tracts of it, has not changed at all between the second century and the twenty-first, reinforcing discourses of a land 'out of history'.

Hills notes that having passed the 'burden of representation' of Wales over to *Torchwood* (BBC, 2006, 2008, 2009, 2011), the new *Doctor Who* has continued in its metropolitan, London-centric narratives with London companions Rose, Martha and Donna, and distinctive

London landmarks such as Westminster Bridge, the London Eye and Buckingham Palace:

> If the programme can be viewed as a centralised London commission allocated to BBC Wales for both contingent, deal-brokering and devolutionary BBC policy reasons, then in diegetic terms, BBC Wales's *Doctor Who* nevertheless treats London as its narrative centre [...] the Doctor's implicit home, 2005–9, is surely England's capital city [...] As such, the show's networked success resonates with Steve Blandford's observation that 'the BBC's faith in the need for a broader, more flexible idea of Britishness does not yet extend to its commissioning of programmes that they hope will have genuinely broad appeal'.[67]

Russell T Davies's *Doctor Who* is thus critiqued for its continuing London-centric qualities as failing to adequately represent the broader 'nations and regions' of the BBC's modern broadcasting remit. However, Scottish companions and Scottish Doctors in the subsequent Moffat era offer examples of a 'broader, more flexible idea of Britishness'. This is not to reduce Scottish identity to tartanry, kailyard and Clydesideism; but there is a tension between the Scottish stereotypes mobilised and reflexively satirised within the programme and the presence of a Scottish actor as the central hero of what is still a highly successful UK-networked and transnationally sold telefantasy action-adventure.

As David Martin-Jones has argued, popular culture which employs these tropes may offer more progressive potential than previously considered.[68] In providing an alternative to 'official' histories of a unified, colonial Britain, popular culture can represent both a traditional Anglocentric desire to use old myths in repressive ways (the *Scotch Reels* position), and simultaneously offer the image of Scottish history and identities (the *Out of History* position). These binaries are themselves complicated by views which seek to open out existing positions. The tropes of tartanry, kailyard and Clydesideism, with which this article opened, have been increasingly critiqued since the publication of *Scotch Reels* in 1982. Colin McArthur himself has talked of the need for Scottish identity to be reconceived, at a historical point at which '(national) identity needed to be theorised as open, complex and hybrid'.[69] And a variety of scholars have responded to the increasingly complex range of identities at work in Scottish society and popular culture: 'Over the course of the last three decades [...] this (*Scotch Reels*) line of criticism has receded in popularity, with most scholars today interpreting common mythic representations of Scotland and Scottishness in more positive (or at least ambiguous) terms.'[70] Recent critics have preferred to see representations of Scotland as playful, celebratory and exploratory, or as contradictory and open to positive reappropriation.[71] Capaldi's Scottish Doctor is both a reappropriation and a pastiche of established tropes about Scottishness, and also a post-industrial, hybrid and progressive performance of Scottishness as a grumpy, unsentimental but nonetheless heroic polymath.

This chapter therefore highlights that while representations of Scottishness in *Doctor Who* do have some roots in the *Scotch Reels* identities, recent eras of the programme offer new formulations of these identities which are indeed 'open, complex and hybrid'. In turn, the representations of Scottishness in *Doctor Who* do themselves help to shape contemporary Scottish identity. The programme therefore mirrors the increasingly fissiparous tendencies of the UK as regional and national identities assert themselves in a progressively pluralistic society. There is still something of a view from the centre at work here, in the programme's use of London as a central dramatic site (e.g. 'Dark Water'/'Death in Heaven'), but the number of Scottish actors in the programme playing parts *as* Scottish reflects both the increasing recognition of the diversity of British identity and a less London-centric approach to TV drama production as well as, perhaps, a degree of authorial commentary on Moffat's part.

If Nicholas Cull's classic Doctors '[project] something from a better past into an uncertain future',[72] then perhaps the recent Doctors extend across a geographical, national/regional axis rather than a temporal/historical one, in line with the BBC's commitment to serving the 'nations and regions' in terms of representation of the diverse identities within the UK. To return to Craig's *Out of History*, the title has four potential interpretations. Firstly, it suggests a country which has *run out* of history – which is now reduced to a touristic set of signifiers in thrall to its colonial masters. Secondly, it suggests a country *outside* history, one which is so peripheral that literally nothing of any national import happens there. Thirdly, it suggests a country which has been *written out* of history, a set of identities suppressed within and exscribed from the official histories of the UK. But in the fourth reading, it suggests a country emerging *out of* history – one emerging from the obscurity and suppression of its historically colonised status and ready to come into focus and explore a progressive and self-determining post-colonial future.[73]

Capaldi's Doctor then exists within a complex set of tensions around national and regional identities. Duncan Petrie has argued for the progressive nature of the new Scottish identities emerging in film, and as David Martin-Jones suggests, fantasy may offer a 'return of the repressed' inserting Scotland back into history and offering a way forward for twenty-first-century Scottish identity.[74] Therefore, Capaldi's use of his own accent, the plethora of Scottish actors playing Scottish and the programme's self-reflexive engagement with Scottishness suggest a negotiation with Scottish devolution and independence, the increasing plurality of the UK's regional identities, and confidence with Scots being Scots. Reading the Twelfth Doctor not across Cull's diachronic historical/nostalgic axis but across a synchronic geographical/regional axis therefore suggests a nation emerging *Out of History*.

Notes

1   For quintessential 'Englishness', see Matthew Kilburn, 'Genealogies across time: history and storytelling in Steven Moffat's *Doctor Who*', in Andrew O'Day (ed.), *Doctor Who: The Eleventh Hour – A Critical Celebration of the Matt Smith and Steven Moffat Era* (London, 2014), pp. 52–69.

2   For reasons of space, this chapter will focus only on televised episodes.

3   Cairns Craig, *Out of History: Narrative Paradigms in Scottish and British Culture* (Edinburgh, 1996).

4   Idem, 'Myths against history', in Colin McArthur (ed.), *Scotch Reels: Scotland in Cinema and Television* (London, 1982), p. 8.

5   Ibid., p. 9.

6   Colin McArthur, 'Scotland and cinema: the iniquity of the fathers', in Colin McArthur (ed.), *Scotch Reels: Scotland in Cinema and Television* (London, 1982), p. 41.

7   David Martin-Jones, *Scotland: Global Cinema: Genres, Modes and Identities* (Edinburgh, 2009).

8   Ibid., p. 25.

9   John Caughie, 'Representing Scotland: new questions for Scottish cinema', in Eddie Dick (ed.), *From Limelight to Satellite: A Scottish Film Book* (London, 1990).

10 Alexander McArthur and Herbert Kingsley Long, *No Mean City* (London, 1978).

11 Duncan Petrie, *Screening Scotland* (London, 2000), p. 7.

12 John R. Cook, 'Three ring circus: television drama about, by, and for Scotland', in Neil Blain and David Hutchison (eds), *The Media in Scotland* (Edinburgh, 2008), pp. 107–22.

13 Richard Butt, 'Literature and the screen media since 1908', in Ian Brown (ed.), *The Edinburgh History of Scottish Literature*, vol. 3: *Modern Transformations: New Identities (from 1918)* (Edinburgh, 2007), pp. 53–63.

14 Ibid., p. 56.

15 Ibid., p. 58.

16 Ibid., p. 59.

17 Ibid., p. 60.

18 Rob Shields, *Places on the Margin: Alternative Geographies of Modernity* (London, 1991), p. 31.

19 See, for example, Malcolm Chapman, *The Gaelic Vision in Scottish Culture* (London, 1978); Trevor Robert Pringle, 'The privation of history: Landseer, Victoria and the Highland myth', in Denis Cosgrove and Stephen Daniels (eds), *The Iconography of Landscape: Essays on the Symbolic Representation, Design and Use of Past Environments* (Cambridge, 1988), pp. 142–61; Hugh Trevor-Roper, 'The invention of tradition: the Highland tradition of Scotland', in Eric Hobsbawm and Terence Ranger (eds), *The Invention of Tradition* (Cambridge, 1983), pp. 15–42.

20 See McArthur (ed.), *Scotch Reels*; idem, *Brigadoon, Braveheart and the Scots: Distortions of Scotland in Hollywood Film* (London, 2003); Martin-Jones, *Scotland: Global Cinema*.

21 Pringle, 'The privation of history'.

22 McArthur, *Brigadoon, Braveheart and the Scots*.

23 Ibid., p. 6.

24 Ibid., p. 19.

25 Matthew Kilburn, 'Bargains of necessity? *Doctor Who*, Culloden and fictionalising history at the BBC in the 1960s', in David Butler (ed.), *Time and Relative Dissertations in Space: Critical Perspectives on Doctor Who* (Manchester, 2007), pp. 69–70.

26 Ibid., p. 70.

27 Ibid., p. 81.

28 McArthur, *Brigadoon, Braveheart and the Scots*, p. 6.

29 Martin-Jones, *Scotland: Global Cinema*, pp. 89–90.

30 Ibid., p. 90.

31 Peter Hutchings, 'Uncanny landscapes in British film and television', *Visual Culture in Britain* v/2 (2004), pp. 27–40.

32 McArthur, 'Scotland and cinema', p. 42.

33 Hutchings, 'Uncanny landscapes'.

34 Cited in David Harvey, *The Condition of Postmodernity* (Oxford, 1990), p. 87.

35 Nicholas Cull, '"Bigger on the inside …" *Doctor Who* as British cultural history', in Graham Roberts and Philip M. Taylor (eds), *The Historian, Television and Television History* (Luton, 2001), pp. 100–1.

36 Murray Smith, *Trainspotting* (London, 2002), p. 21.

37 Lynne M. Thomas, 'Sylvester McCoy', *Science Fiction Film and Television* vii/2 (2014), p. 236.

38 'Peter Capaldi's Glasgow accent "perfect" for Dr Who', *Scotsman*, 21 March 2014. Available at https://www.scotsman.com/lifestyle/peter-capaldi-s-glasgow-accent-perfect-for-dr-who-1-3348971 (accessed 28 August 2016).

39 Martin-Jones, *Scotland: Global Cinema*.

40 Danielle C. Kinsey, 'Koh-i-Noor: empire, diamonds, and the performance of British material culture', *Journal of British Studies* xlviii/2 (2009), p. 392.

41 Ibid., p. 412.

42 Ibid., p. 419.

43 'Introduction by the editors', in Bob Nowlan and Zach Finch (eds), *Directory of World Cinema: Scotland* (Bristol, 2015), p. 6.

44 Discussed in Jonathan Murray, *The New Scottish Cinema* (London, 2015), p. 160.

45 Chris Harvie, *Scotland and Nationalism: Scottish Society and Politics, 1707 to the Present* (4th edn, London, 2004), pp. 44–5.

46 Kilburn, 'Genealogies across time', p. 53.

47 Matt Hills, *Triumph of a Time Lord: Regenerating Doctor Who in the Twenty-First Century* (London, 2010), p. 26.

48 Ibid., p. 29.

49 'Peter Capaldi's Glasgow accent "perfect" for Dr Who'.

50 Steven Moffat, 'Ask Steven Moffat', *Doctor Who Magazine* 492 (2015), p. 6.

51 Steven Moffat, 'Ask Steven Moffat', *Doctor Who Magazine* 484 (2015), p. 6.

52 Angus Calder, 'By the water of Leith I sat down and wept: reflections on Scottish identity', in Harry Ritchie (ed.), *Acid Plaid: New Scottish Writing* (London, 1997), pp. 218–38.

53 Benjamin Cook, 'Robot of Sherwood', *Doctor Who Magazine* 477 (2014), p. 24.

54 Peter Capaldi, cited in Benjamin Cook, 'The DWM interview: Peter Capaldi', *Doctor Who Magazine* 477 (2014), pp. 28–35.

55 Steven Moffat, 'Ask Steven Moffat', *Doctor Who Magazine* 490 (2015), p. 4.

56 Hills, *Triumph of a Time Lord*, p. 34.

57 Ibid., p. 35.

58 Ibid., p. 36.

59 Benjamin Cook, 'The Doctor and me', *Doctor Who Magazine* 494 (2016), p. 20.

60 Moffat, cited in Benjamin Cook, 'Heaven Sent and Hell Bent', *Doctor Who Magazine* 493 (2015), p. 29.

61 Graham Kibble-White, 'The *DWM* review: Deep Breath', *Doctor Who Magazine* 478 (2014), p. 68.

62 Ibid.

63 Kassandra, 'Has Moff cast a Doctor in his image?' (2013), Gallifrey Base. Available at http://gallifreybase.com/forum/showthread.php?t=176481 (accessed 21 August 2016).

64 Steven Moffat, 'Ask Steven Moffat', *Doctor Who Magazine* 503 (2016), p. 4.

65 Karen Ralls-MacLeod, *Music and the Celtic Otherworld: From Ireland to Iona* (Edinburgh, 2000), p. 1.

66 Ibid., p. 3.

67 Hills, *Triumph of a Time Lord*, p. 48.

68 Martin-Jones, *Scotland: Global Cinema*.

69 McArthur, *Brigadoon, Braveheart and the Scots*, p. 113.

70 Bob Nowlan, 'Mythic visions: critique and counter-critique', in Bob Nowlan and Zach Finch (eds), *Directory of World Cinema: Scotland* (Bristol, 2015), p. 92.

71 Ibid.

72 Cull, '"Bigger on the inside ..."', p. 100.

73 Craig, *Out of History*.

74 Petrie's argument can be found in his *Screening Scotland*; Martin-Jones, *Scotland: Global Cinema*.

3

CLARA'S CHOICE

The Political Lunarscape of 'Kill the Moon'

Sonia Michaels

I n 'Kill the Moon', three women must make a life-or-death choice: 'an innocent life versus the future of all mankind'. With few exceptions, reviewers either loved it[1] or eviscerated it, one writer calling it out as 'illogical, unscientific, silly soap opera'.[2] The most negative reviewers and bloggers fell into two clearly delineated camps: those who complained because the episode's science was inaccurate (a strange accusation, considering the customary hand-waving 'wibbly-wobbly' dismissal of hard science throughout the series), and those who reacted viscerally against what they perceived as an anti-choice message. While upon first viewing 'Kill the Moon' could easily be dismissed as a straight-up anti-abortion message dressed in fantasy, upon further examination the episode is significantly more complex than either of these superficial analyses suggests. While the episode does contain certain tropes frequently used by the 'pro-life' movement, it actually asks its audience to examine the issues surrounding women's autonomy and agency – including, but certainly not limited to reproductive choice – at a deeper and more complex level than most viewers and reviewers recognise or acknowledge.

Hatching a plot: gender and pro-life

The pre-credit sequence begins *in medias res* and sets up the dilemma at the core of the episode, in which a distraught Clara Oswald (Jenna Coleman) reaches out to the people of Earth, explaining that 'we have a terrible decision' to make, and that 'the man who normally helps, he's gone'. Following the title sequence, the episode's action reverts to Coal Hill School, where an angry Clara scolds the Doctor for having told her student, Courtney Woods (Ellis George), that she is 'not special'. While this statement aligns with Capaldi's Twelfth Doctor's somewhat abrasive persona, it stands out in stark contrast to Matt Smith's Eleventh Doctor's claim that in 900 years of time and space, he has never met anybody who wasn't important ('A Christmas Carol', 2010). In an attempt to appease Clara, the Twelfth Doctor suggests a school field trip of sorts. His question for Courtney, 'How would you like to be the first woman on the Moon?', serves to highlight the distinction between 'person' and 'woman' – rather than just going back in time and taking Courtney to the Moon before 1969, the Doctor emphasises that her identity *as a woman* is the factor that will make her somehow 'special'. This gendered language is prevalent throughout the episode.

The action that follows includes giant, murderous spiders (actually single-celled germ-like organisms that just happen to be extremely spider-like), a small, hapless and short-lived team of has-been astronauts led by a cynical, world-weary woman (Captain Lundvik, played by Hermione Norris), and the revelation that the Moon is actually a giant egg that is getting ready to hatch. The giant spider-creatures seem to exist as little more than convenient devices to dispatch minor characters, and to chase arachnophobic viewers behind the sofa. The episode's central dilemma is whether to allow the egg to hatch and simply hope that the resulting loss of the Moon (not to mention the mood of whatever hatches from it) will not result in massive loss of life on Earth, or to push the button and destroy the creature inside the egg with a huge cache of nuclear weapons before it can ever 'feel the sun on its back'. Upon arriving on the Moon, the Doctor notes that it has 'put on weight', rather than simply saying that its mass has increased. The Moon itself is presented as a 'gravid' object; within it, the Doctor explains, is 'something that's living [...] something growing [...] just getting ready to be born'. Most of the episode's action on the Moon takes place at the Mare Fecunditatis – the 'Sea of Fertility'. The Doctor's demeanour shifts from exhilaration (upon learning that the Moon is an egg) to anger when Lundvik suggests killing the Moon; he describes it as a 'vulnerable creature' and (potentially) a 'little dead baby'. When Lundvik asks how to kill it, Courtney responds by calling it 'a little baby', and the Doctor explains that they can use the nuclear bombs (more specifically, 'the best *man-made* nuclear weapons' [my italics]). When Lundvik reminds Clara that the creature about to be born is killing people, she responds, 'You cannot blame a baby for kicking.'

The Doctor's impatience extends to Clara, whom he dismissively tells that 'It's time to take the stabilisers off your bike', after which he leaves the three women – 'a teenager, an astronaut and a school-teacher' – to make the life-or-death decision without him, claiming that 'It's your Moon, womankind. It's your choice ... Some decisions are too important not to make on your own.' His departure brings us close to the moment that opened the episode, with Clara frantically deciding to reach out to the people of Earth (notably *all* the people, not just the women) for assistance with the choice that the three women on the Moon must ultimately make.

The population of Earth (at least the part of Earth that is visible to the women on the Moon) turn their lights off, indicating that they wish to kill the Moon; at the last second, Clara defies this decision by disarming the nuclear weapons. The detonator's countdown screen now reads 'ABORTED', but in fact the creature gestating within the Moon is about to be born. In the end, the choice – which turns out to be the 'correct' choice, according to the Doctor's climactic mono-logue – is made by one woman, rather than by consensus.

The three women at the heart of this episode represent three distinct phases of women's lives, which tie into this decision. The women correspond to the classical (and later neopagan) mythology of the threefold goddess: the Maiden, the Mother and the Crone.[3] They also present some of the many faces of intersectional feminism – all women, but each woman separated from the others by age, race, edu-cation and social status. Courtney (the Maiden) is an 'at-risk' black teenager, whose 'acting-out' behaviour (using the Doctor's psychic paper as fake ID to acquire alcohol) is at the heart of Clara's concern early in the episode. Clara (displaying characteristics of motherhood) is a young white professional woman who takes her 'duty of care' for

Courtney extremely seriously and wants to have children of her own. Lundvik (the Crone), the commander of the Moon expedition, is a middle-aged white professional woman with a no-nonsense demeanour, who makes it clear that she chose career over children and who is in charge of a small team of feckless male subordinates. Outspoken, cynical and assertive, she tells the others that they cannot risk the future of humanity 'just to be nice'.

The rhetoric of the abortion debate in 'Kill the Moon'

'Kill the Moon', then, echoes the rhetoric of the abortion discourse, although the episode is about much more. To get to the 'much more' part of this discussion, we must first examine the episode in the context of the abortion issue. Under the Abortion Act of 1967, women in Britain who seek abortions must – even now – acquire the approval of two registered physicians (except in cases of immediate danger to the life of the mother, when a single opinion will suffice).[4] In 2003, Ellie Lee highlighted a significant disparity between the letter of the law and its actual practice:

> A key assumption of the 1967 Act is that women are not best placed to make the decision to have an abortion, and this has drawn considerable feminist criticism. By denying women the freedom to decide whether to continue or end a pregnancy, the 1967 Act denies women their autonomy.[5]

Lee concludes that 'Britain needs to have a law that provides for abortion on request,' thus bringing a woman's decision to have an abortion into legal alignment with the decision to obtain other established medical procedures. While the current law is not stringently enforced, the simple fact of its existence puts women who seek abortions in a precarious position – they are, essentially, relying on the goodwill and cooperation of multiple physicians to obtain an outcome that – for any other elective medical procedure – they would be able to choose for themselves.

In light of this background information regarding the process by which abortion decisions are made in real life, it becomes clear that the choice faced by the women in 'Kill the Moon' bears almost no resemblance to an average real-life situation a woman seeking abortion might face. An egg is not a pregnancy. Whatever laid the egg that humanity perceives as the Moon is long gone – whether the egg hatches or is destroyed, there is no violation of maternal bodily autonomy. The choice to let the egg hatch or to kill the creature inside becomes Clara's (along with Courtney and Lundvik).

The dilemma here is not whether to restrict or violate someone's bodily autonomy, but rather, as Alyssa Franke writes on her 'Whovian Feminism' website,

> it's a Trolley Problem; the question is primarily about numbers and uncertainty. Clara isn't sure it is right to kill the space-dragon, even if its hatching may kill millions more, and is especially uncertain because they simply do not know how many people it could kill.[6]

In truth, the painful decision faced by the women on the Moon has very little to do with the morality of abortion, and everything to do with the (in this case) *male* Doctor's unwillingness to support them as equal partners in this critical decision, all while giving lip service to 'respecting' them. In providing the women with partial information and then leaving them alone in crisis, the Doctor places them in what literary theorist Elaine Scarry defines as a 'concussive situation':

> When one suddenly finds oneself in the midst of a complicated political situation, it is hard not only to assess the 'rightness' and 'wrongness' of what is taking place but even to perform the much more elementary task of identifying, descriptively, what it is that is taking place.[7]

Clara's appeal to the people of Earth is tentative and inarticulate: she asks them to make a decision about the future of the planet without being able to provide them with a comprehensive explanation of the circumstances, stakes and possible consequences. In the end, she ignores their vote; the Doctor later congratulates her for making the 'best' and 'right' choice, but viewers are offered no insight into why she made the choice she did (and there appear to be no negative consequences at all to her subversive action). We are simply asked to trust that Clara's gut instinct is more valid than whatever consensus she is seeking when she reaches out to the people of Earth – a symbolic gesture at best, considering that much of the world is asleep, or at least almost certainly not tuned in to mass media, when she broadcasts her plea. Taken together, all of these complexities and confusions confirm that this episode is not about abortion per se – it is also about the complicated power dynamics that restrict and shape women's choices in the world, and that undermine their confidence in making and executing critical decisions even when they are in a position to effect change. The here *male* Doctor may well believe that he is helping Clara by forcing her into this decision; he forgets – or is perhaps incapable of understanding – that true autonomy is impossible if it depends on another, more powerful person granting it.

After the hatching: what happens next

This is not the first time that the Moon has turned out to be an egg in science fiction; Jack Williamson's 1934 short story 'Born of the Sun' describes a somewhat similar hatching in lurid detail:

> Colossal, triangular, a beak came first, green and shining. Behind it were two ovoid, enormous patches, like eyes, glowing with lambent purple. Between and above them was an enigmatic organ, arched, crested; it was an unearthly spray of crimson flame. Incredible wings – reaching out – stretching –[8]

In this story, the creature that hatches from the Moon serves (quite literally) as a 'wing man' for Foster, the protagonist, as a beautiful woman shudders with fear and promptly falls into his arms. The similarities between the basic premise of this story and 'Kill the Moon' have not gone unnoticed by the Tumblrsphere – one user has even interspersed screenshots of the episode alongside the partial text of the Williamson story.[9]

In 'Kill the Moon', though, the hatching of the Moon into a dragon-like alien creature is barely visible through a cloud of eggshell particles, and this presumably spectacular event ends up playing second fiddle to the here *male* Doctor, who – as he tends to do at Very Important

Moments – launches into a monologue, first pausing for a few seconds, then throwing back his head as the music swells and he starts to explain what will happen next:

> The mid-twenty-first century, humankind starts creeping off into the stars. Spreads its way through the galaxy to the very edges of the universe, and it – endures, till the end of time. And it does all that because one day in the year 2049 when it had stopped thinking about going to the stars, something occurred that made it look up, not down. It looked out there into the blackness and it saw something beautiful, something wonderful, that for once it didn't want to destroy. And in that one moment the whole course of history was changed. Not bad for a girl from Coal Hill School, and her teacher.

The Doctor's explanation of the new-found hope and fertile expansiveness of humanity is compelling in the moment; however, it is also wildly inaccurate, or at best incomplete. As viewers know from having watched the lights go out on Earth through Clara's binoculars, humanity – or at least that portion of humanity that was in charge of the electrical utilities of the Western world – had very clearly voted to destroy whatever might be in that giant egg. One woman – Clara – made the choice, saved the egg, and in fact ensured that humankind would reach out into space and endure. If we are to accept that the people of Earth had a change of heart when they first beheld the creature itself – and when they noted that it did not in fact destroy the Earth but very politely left a replacement egg/Moon before it flew away – we must also acknowledge that the natural human urge for self-preservation very nearly led to a much darker outcome.

The Doctor's monologue appears to claim that humanity's successful expansion to the stars was a result of it *not* wanting to kill something beautiful, thanks in large part to his choice, as a man, to take off and leave the women (and by extension humanity) to make the decision, while his discussion with Clara implies that his actions were specifically linked to some lesson that she – specifically – needed to learn about her own self-determination and her ability to make such a decision even when instructed to do otherwise. His claim that he was empowering and respecting her rings hollow, in part because his statement that he was 'allowing' her to make the decision establishes that the Doctor as *male* is still firmly in control. The Doctor's grandstanding monologue also rings hollow in the wake of the pointless trauma to which he has subjected the three women, and the women – even Courtney – are unimpressed. Even as he patronisingly concludes, 'Not bad for a girl from Coal Hill School and her teacher', Courtney's attention has already shifted to the new egg that the creature has laid in its place. And when the Doctor continues, 'I think somebody deserves a thank you!', Lundvik turns to Clara and thanks her directly, rather than feeding the Doctor's ego. Clara, frowning, her lips pursed in disappointment, remains silent – for now.

Silence will fall: the male doctor as silencer/ regulator of women's voices

There are numerous instances in this episode where the *male* Doctor interrupts and silences all three women. He rudely interrupts Courtney numerous times. Courtney's practically incoherent speech early in the episode ('One small thing for a thing, one enormous thing for a thingy-thing') is certainly irritating, but the Doctor responds with disproportionate harshness; later in the episode, though, especially once the Doctor has left the scene, she gains both clarity and brevity of expression.

The Doctor also tells Lundvik to watch her mouth, immediately after the nuclear explosion has been averted and he returns to take the women back to Earth – she exclaims, 'Bloody irresponsible idiots!' and he responds, 'Would you mind your language please, there are children present.' After her initial angry response, which the Doctor dismisses mockingly, she shifts to a more conciliatory tone: 'Could you please let us see what's happening' – suddenly, she is no longer a mission commander, but rather, here, a woman deferring to a more powerful *man*.

In the episode's final scene, Clara suppresses angry tears as she tells the Doctor, 'I almost got it wrong. That was you, my friend, making me scared, making me feel like a bloody idiot!' Again, instead of responding to the content of Clara's accusation with either a respectful explanation or an apology, the Doctor points his finger at her and says

'Language!' In silencing Clara here, the Doctor dismisses her concerns and absolves himself of responsibility for the agony that being forced into this choice has created for her. The Doctor is used to being in control, and used to having the last word, as Charlie Coile notes in his study of female representation in *Doctor Who* which preceded the announcement about the casting of the Thirteenth Doctor:

> The Doctor himself might be seen as a one-man, or one-alien, symbol of oppression. To paraphrase bell hooks, his being is inherently perceived as superior through the show's myth of Doctor-as-savior (the masculine) allowing him to dominate anything perceived as weak (the feminine) demonstrated through companions, humans, and aliens of all sexes (hooks). Even though he is a force overwhelmingly for 'good', the system is inherently degrading and devalues feminine social constructs; it features only one fully empowered character, the masculine Doctor.[10]

Most viewers are probably used to perceiving the Doctor as a male hero – one who may talk tough sometimes, but who invariably has humanity's best interests at heart. His behaviour in this episode, though, crosses the line into bullying (at one point, he tells Courtney, 'Don't be so stupid!'), and is demeaning ('Take the stabilisers off your bike!') and even gaslighting (diverting the discussion to suggest that Clara is irrational and thus in the wrong), when he dismisses Clara's concerns by policing her language instead of acknowledging that there has been a deep breach of trust between them and attempting to help her understand his motivations and actions. The Doctor refuses to acknowledge any responsibility for the trauma that Clara has undergone, in effect creating still more pain and uncertainty for her.

Becoming the hero of her own life

After Clara angrily sends the Doctor away, she and Danny (her romantic partner, played by Samuel Anderson) meet in her classroom, in front of a whiteboard that contains her teaching notes on Charles Dickens's *David Copperfield* – the story of a young man who tells us in the opening moments of his story that he is unsure whether he will be the hero of his own life, and who, throughout his development, faces countless obstacles and a significant loss of agency created by others who enjoy more privilege and wield greater influence. The novel's opening lines cover most of the board. Below the quotation is a question: 'How auto-biographical is this?' Clara, like countless literature teachers before her, is asking her students to locate and examine the boundaries between fiction and reality; the creators of this episode are, in effect, asking viewers to do the same. David Copperfield is, of course, an invention of Charles Dickens, which means that he will only be the hero of his own life if Dickens allows him to become that. The intertextuality created by the inclusion of the whiteboard in the penultimate scene of the episode informs our understanding of Clara as a woman who is simultaneously trying to maintain agency within her own life and yet exists primarily as a (female) tool who has literally been brought into being for the salvation and support of another (male) life, a dynamic that will change with the Thirteenth Doctor. Clara does not reach out and take her freedom of choice in this episode – she is 'allowed' it. This loss of agency, and the accompanying frustration and pain that Clara experiences, is at the core of the episode, and goes much deeper than the 'red herring' of the abortion discourse that frames much of the action.

Conclusion: 'Run, you clever *girl*!'

This episode creates a concussive situation not just for the women involved in the climactic choice, but also for viewers. It challenges our understanding of how society views and responds to women's choices and opinions, and calls into question not only the commonly held trope that the (up until now male) Doctor always has humanity's best interests at heart, but also that he invariably understands what those best interests are. At its heart, this episode of *Doctor Who* reflects society's apparent deep-rooted apprehension and misunderstanding of what might be occurring in the minds of womankind.

Clara's immediate frustration in the face of her disempowerment dissipates rapidly on the surface, and yet it determines her character arc for the remainder of the series. At the beginning of the following episode, 'Mummy on the Orient Express', the Doctor and Clara have settled into an awkward truce; Clara confides to another character that they are 'not even friends, not any more'. Towards the end of the episode, they are reconciled. Clara chooses to continue travelling with the Doctor, but their relationship dynamic is transformed as she becomes still more determined to gain some agency. In the following episodes, Clara even falsely identifies herself to supporting characters as the Doctor on several occasions. In 'Flatline', the Doctor is disempowered and diminished – quite literally trapped inside a shrunken TARDIS – and Clara becomes his proxy, introducing herself as 'the Doctor', acting with Capaldi's customary brash confidence and even mirroring his vocal patterns. At the episode's climax, she is again faced with a critical choice. Addressing the Doctor in monologue, she asks, 'What would you do now?' and then amends the thought: 'No. What will I do now?' Later, in the series finale, Clara saves herself from 'Cyberdeletion' by once again claiming to be the Doctor in his absence. By the end of the series, an emotional equilibrium has developed between the two characters, each of whom ends their final meeting of the series with a carefully chosen lie designed to protect the other. Clara is making a deliberate choice – at least for the immediate future – to build a life with herself at the centre, moving forward through her pain and grief with neither Danny nor the Doctor at her side. She has not yet reached the end of her journey towards becoming the hero of her own life; she has, however, taken the first tentative steps towards regaining her agency, becoming something more than 'companion' while still something less than 'protagonist'.

This arc culminates toward the end of the following season, when just as in 'The Name of the Doctor' (2013) Clara allowed herself to be splintered in time so as to continually save the Doctor, her heroic efforts result in her death, followed by a resurrection of sorts that essentially allows her to *become* a Time Lord, escaping in a TARDIS with her own willing companion. The Doctor's final attempt to control Clara's destiny, well-meaning though it may be, quite literally backfires on him as he loses his own memories of her. In the season's closing minutes, Clara walks away from the Doctor, stepping into a TARDIS in which Ashildr/'Me' (Maisie Williams) is waiting. Clara is not immortal, but rather has become super-mortal, existing indefinitely in the space between her last two heartbeats, finally in complete control of her own choices. Clara decides to return to Gallifrey and rejoin her destiny 'the long way around'. The journey towards true agency and autonomy that became apparent in 'Kill the Moon' ends not with anger and alienation, but rather with a loving acknowledgement of the relationship between Clara and the Doctor. When the Doctor re-enters his own TARDIS, he finds the chalked message 'Run, you clever boy, and be a Doctor'; as he prepares to do so, Clara is following her own advice, thus truly becoming the hero of her own life at last.

Notes

1   Patrick Mulkern, '*Doctor Who* Kill the Moon review: audacious, hardcore sci-fi that defies the laws of physics', *Radio Times* [website] (4 October 2014). Available at http://www.radiotimes.com/news/2014-10-04/doctor-who-kill-the-moon-review-audacious-hardcore-sci-fi-that-defies-the-laws-of-physics/ (accessed 4 October 2014).
2   Brid-Aine Parnell, '*Doctor Who* becomes an illogical, unscientific, silly soap opera in Kill the Moon', The Register [website] (4 October 2014). Available at https://www.theregister.co.uk/2014/10/04/doctor_who_kill_the_moon_episode_7_review/ (accessed 4 October 2014).
3   Lynn Meskell, 'Feminism, paganism, pluralism', in Amy Gazin-Schwartz and Cornelius Holtorf (eds), *Archaeology and Folklore* (London, 1999), p. 84.
4   Abortion Act 1967, Statute Law Database. Available at https://www.legislation.gov.uk/ukpga/1967/87/contents (accessed 5 November 2016).
5   Ellie Lee, 'Tensions in the regulation of abortion in Britain', *Journal of Law and Society* xxx/4 (2003), pp. 532–53.
6   Alyssa Franke, 'Abortion and "Kill the Moon"', Whovian Feminism [website] (9 October 2014). Available at http://whovianfeminism.tumblr.com/post/99609478072/abortion-and-kill-the-moon (accessed 9 October 2014).
7   Elaine Scarry, *The Body in Pain: The Making and Unmaking of the World* (New York, 1985), pp. 278–9.
8   Jack Williamson, 'Born of the sun', *Astounding Stories* (March 1934). Available at http://hyperwave.tumblr.com/post/99428409130/jack-williamson-born-of-the-sun-astounding (accessed 1 February 2017).
9   'Kill the Moon', Hyperwave [website]. Available at http://hyperwave.tumblr.com/tagged/kill-the-moon (accessed 1 February 2017).
10 Charlie Coile, 'More than a companion: "The Doctor's Wife" and representations of women in *Doctor Who*', *Studies in Popular Culture* xxxvi/1 (2013), pp. 83–104.

PART TWO

FURTHER POLITICS AND THEMES

4

A GOOD MAN GOES TO WAR?

The Twelfth Doctor and the Politics of Conflict

Robin Bunce

'War is the continuation of politics by other means.'
Carl von Clausewitz, *On War*[1]

Peter Capaldi's transformation from Malcolm Tucker, the foul-mouthed political enforcer who can see no further than the end of the current spin cycle, into the Doctor, a Time Lord who walks in eternity, was every bit as profound as the Doctor's latest regeneration. However, swapping television's finest political satire for television's finest science fiction did not entail ditching politics. Series eight and nine have been shot through with references to contemporary conflicts, often ones which are intensely political. Consequently, the Peter Capaldi era has dealt with the complexities of creating peace in the teeth of highly politicised conflicts, and the existential threats created by the peculiarities of modern warfare.

Non-linear wars and culture wars

Many of the Doctor's battles bear an uncanny resemblance to wars that have been fought since 1914. In the era of classic *Who* this was true from the very start.[2] The Twelfth Doctor, meanwhile, faces battles similar to the 'Global War on Terror'. In many ways, the War on Terror is a new kind of conflict. Firstly, there is the question of the enemy: the strategic ambiguity of who constituted the 'Axis of Evil' was helpful to the Bush Administration and Blair government in the early years of the 'War on Terror' as it allowed policy makers to conflate Iraq and Afghanistan and in so doing create a pretext for invading Iraq. This ambiguity over the target of Western action has deepened as the 'War on Terror' has shifted focus. The nature of the West's objectives in Syria is hard to pin down. In 2013 David Cameron made a case for fighting the government of Bashar al-Assad. However, in 2015 Cameron committed British forces to fight ISIL, also known as ISIS, also known as Islamic State, also known as Daish and Daesh, and in so doing fighting in a kind of de facto alliance with forces loyal to al-Assad. The complexities of who the enemy is are heightened by the multi-sided nature of the conflict. The war in Syria involves Hezbollah, forces from Russia, and Iran, Ba'athist and Kurdish militias, ISIS, and Al-Qaeda – almost every enemy the US has faced since 1945, with the exception of the Viet Cong. A second feature of the 'War on Terror' is that it is essentially endless. An American-led coalition has been fighting in the Middle East since 2003, and the danger facing Western states, in the rhetoric of Western politicians at least, is ever present.

The nature of the 'War on Terror' is contested. However, one of the most widely discussed interpretations suggests that it is a culture war, or, put another way, a civilisational conflict. This interpretation is rooted in the work of Samuel P. Huntington. The extent to which the War on Terror is a 'clash of civilisations' (in Huntington's terms) is contested. What is more, there has been widespread criticism of the very foundations of the 'clash of civilisations' thesis, as Huntington conflates numerous Christian and Islamic traditions into two monolithic 'civilisations'. Consequently, he fails to see both the pluralism within the two religions and the large amount of common ground that Christian and Islamic teachings share. Moreover, he ignores the extent to which political actors have weaponised specific aspects of Christianity and Islam to win factional battles within their own polities – George W. Bush, for example, used the notion that America was under attack as a political weapon against Democrats and moderate Republicans.[3] Nonetheless, as Huntington's thesis has proved influential, it is worth considering its essential features. For Huntington, the West's victory in the Cold War was followed by a deeper conflict: 'The great divisions among humankind and the dominating source of conflict will be cultural [...] The fault lines between civilizations will be the battle lines of the future.'[4] Huntington contrasts the superficial 'ideological' differences between East and West during the Cold War with the fundamental 'civilisational' differences between the West and Islam which, he argues, will shape the post-Cold War world. During the Cold War, he argues, citizens could pick sides, or even change sides. However, for Huntington, civilisational conflicts are about essential and immutable identity.[5]

Significantly, for Huntington the clash of civilisations is fought within nations, as well as between them. From this perspective, Huntington argues that 'multiculturalism' is profoundly dangerous, as it allows non-Western – even anti-Western – cultures to flourish within Western nations.[6] In so doing, what Huntington describes as tolerant Western culture allows potentially corrosive opposition groups to undermine Western civilisation from within.

Conflicts in the Crimea and Ukraine have also caused alarm in the West, not so much due to their essential nature, but because of novel tactics. The largely unprecedented nature of Russia's invasion of the Crimea has given rise to the terms 'non-linear' and 'hybrid warfare'. The former term emerged in the short story, 'Without Sky' (believed to be by Vladislav Surkov, former deputy prime minister of the Russian Federation and political advisor to Vladimir Putin), published a few days before Russia's annexation of the Crimea. It describes a future, after a fictional World War V, in the following terms:

> It was the first non-linear war. In the primitive wars of the 19th and 20th centuries it was common for just two sides to fight [...] Now four coalitions collided. Not two against two, or three against one. All against all.[7]

In Surkov's fictional non-linear war, the conflict is in a perpetual state of flux:

> A few provinces would join one side, a few others a different one. One town or generation or gender would join yet another. Then

they could switch sides, sometimes mid-battle. Their aims were quite different [...] Most understood the war to be part of a process. Not necessarily its most important part.[8]

Crucially, non-linear warfare is a form of asymmetric conflict in which a weaker military and economic power, in this case Russia, neutralises a stronger military and economic power, in this case NATO, by obscuring the true nature and purpose of the conflict, as well as the identity of the aggressor. Journalist Peter Pomerantsev, who played an important role in bringing the concept of 'non-linear warfare' into mainstream debate, summarised this non-linear approach to war and politics in the following terms: 'It's a strategy of power that keeps any opposition there may be constantly confused, a ceaseless shape-shifting that is unstoppable because it's indefinable.'[9]

Invasions and inversions

The Doctor's involvement with the Zygons in 'The Zygon Invasion'/'The Zygon Inversion' takes him into the realms of non-linear warfare in which literal shape-shifting ensures that it is all but impossible to tell friend from enemy. Various elements in the design and the script push the audience in the direction of the conflicts of our time. The Zygon rebels appear in a viral video, about to execute Osgood (Ingrid Oliver). The style and purpose of the video are reminiscent of the 2004 video in which Jama'at al-Tawhid wal-Jihad executed Nick Berg, an American engineer who had worked and travelled in Iraq from 2003 to 2004. Indeed, their black and white flag, with its central circle, is clearly modelled on the Black Standard, or *al- rāya*, a flag with numerous variants used by many Islamist groups. What is more, the first time the Zygon rebels attack they use gas, recalling the Ghouta chemical attack of 2013, one of the most publicised moments of the Syrian Civil War.

The Zygon invasion is a kind of clash of civilisations. The rebels' central demand concerns civilisational solidarity and identity: 'We have been betrayed. We were sold. Our rights were violated. We demand the right to be ourselves [...] All traitors will die. Truth or consequences.' This brief manifesto casts the Zygon rebels as insurgents, at war with humanity and with established Zygon leaders. In this sense, the Zygon rebels are similar to various Islamist groups who are at war with both internal traitors and external enemies. Al-Qaeda, for example, have consistently argued that the Saudi Royal Family are 'traitors to Islam' for allowing the US to base troops in their country.

The Zygon invasion is also a clash of civilisations in the sense that it reflects concerns about external and internal threats to peace. The Zygons are presented as migrants. The Zygon family in Clara's (Jenna Coleman) block of flats have taken on the form of people of Asian descent, a group popularly associated in the UK's mainstream media with Islam. The term 'dispersed', which is used several times during the episode to describe the Zygon population, recalls the policy of 'dispersal', implemented by Conservative governments in the 1950s and 1960s as a way to force migrant populations to assimilate (although the process was described in the rhetoric of 'integration') 'British values' – whatever they might be.[10] Finally, the 'NO DOGS/NO BRITISH' sign that Kate Stewart (Jemma Redgrave) sees in Truth or Consequences is surely a reference to the infamous signs 'No dogs, no Irish, no Coloureds' which appeared in the windows of London's B & Bs and bedsits during the 1950s.[11] By presenting the Zygons as a migrant population the episodes again play with the tropes of the 'clash of civilisations' narrative. However, at the same time, the confusion between Zygons and British in the minds of the Americans pushes British viewers to consider the experience of migrants and question the hysteria that surrounds the contemporary immigration debate.

Turning from style and rhetoric to tactics, similarities between the Zygon rebels and Islamist insurgents fall away. Instead, the Zygon rebels fight much more like 'little green men' – a phrase that shows that just as science fiction borrows from politics, so politics borrows from science fiction – the 'unaffiliated soldiers' who appeared as if from nowhere and played a decisive role in the Ukraine crisis of 2014. Indeed, the Zygon rebels seem to fight using the 'non-linear instruments' outlined in the 'Gerasimov doctrine'.

While Surkov set out the general concept of the non-linear war, Russian Chief of the General Staff Valery Gerasimov has described the specific tactics used by Russia in order to destabilise and then dominate Ukraine. Known as 'non-linear instruments' or 'hybrid' forms of war, three main techniques are used by the Russian army under Gerasimov to destabilise states and advance Russian interests. First, there is military might. Crucially, Gerasimov favours the use of small groups of highly trained and highly mobile troops, operating in a context where war has not been declared and where their allegiance is hidden. Gerasimov's 'little green men' are trained to use minimal force, and to engage their enemies in places and situations that put their enemies at a considerable disadvantage. Moreover, Gerasimov favours using force during periods of ceasefire or peace talks to create narrative confusion and hide the true nature of what is taking place.[12]

Gerasimov's second 'non-linear instrument' is intelligence. Significantly, for Gerasimov this includes spreading disinformation and encouraging defections. Finally, Gerasimov's forces are backed by a media war which undermines the enemy's narrative; indeed, it undermines any coherent narrative about the causes and nature of the war, as well as the progress of the campaign. Gerasimov's 'battle for the narrative' also focuses on spreading conspiracy theories.

The scene in Turmezistan, a fictional country which sounds like it might have once been part of the Soviet Union, contains many of these elements. Zygons appear, but it is impossible to tell that they are Zygons. They talk peace. They circulate conspiracy theories claiming, 'It's not us who are the imposters, don't let them trick you. It's your commanders, your chief, they're the aliens,' deliberately confusing friend and enemy. Finally, the Zygons use force, but they do so out of sight while professing a commitment to peace, and only once they are confident this will bring them a swift victory.

The cliffhanger between 'Invasion' and 'Inversion' is also reminiscent of two of the most controversial incidents related to Russian foreign policy – or, given Gerasimov's 'battle for the narrative', possibly not related to Russian foreign policy – in recent years. Bonnie's attempt to shoot down a plane carrying the President of the Earth is reminiscent of the fates of Polish Air Force Tu-154, a plane carrying the decidedly anti-Putin Polish president which crashed mysteriously in 2010, and Malaysia Airlines Flight 17, which was shot down in 2014 by pro-Russian separatists based in Ukraine.

In sum, the Zygon invasion is a highly political battle in the sense that it is presented with many of the tropes of a clash of civilisations and because it is fought in a way which reflects the politicised strategies employed by Gerasimov's forces in Ukraine.

Perfect treaties and impossible peace

How does the Doctor respond to the threat of non-linear war? In order to understand the Doctor's intervention, it is necessary to revisit 'the most perfect treaty of all time', agreed between humanity and the Zygons in 'The Day of the Doctor'. The treaty agreed in 'The Day of the Doctor' is drawn up by two sides who understand what is at stake, but who have no idea which side they are on. In this sense the negotiation takes place behind something akin to a Rawlsian 'veil of ignorance'. John Rawls famously proposed the 'veil of ignorance' as part of a thought experiment in his *Theory of Justice* and subsequently applied it to international relations in *The Law of Peoples*.[13] In essence, Rawls's argument is that true principles of justice, principles on which social harmony can be built, can be justified by appealing to a thought experiment known as the 'original position'. In general terms, Rawls argues that in a situation where we knew that we lived in a world of class inequalities but were denied knowledge of our individual characteristics, rational human beings would accept two general principles relating to freedom and equality on the basis that they were just, irrespective of their social position.

Turning to 'The Zygon Invasion'/'The Zygon Inversion', Moffat owes a debt to a different tradition of political thought. While the Zygons and UNIT fight, the Doctor plays games. The notion of games runs throughout the serial. The rebel Zygons' slogan 'Truth or Consequences', as Clara points out, is a reference to a US game show. Indeed, Clara's knowledge of the game comes from another game: Trivial Pursuit. The Doctor also introduces the Osgood boxes in the style of a game show host, and the notion of a game involving boxes is reminiscent of the TV show *Deal or No Deal*. In essence, the Doctor's strategy is to get behind the non-linear war and expose what is really at stake. He uses the insights of game theory, as applied to the Hobbesian state of nature, to show that while warfare may be asymmetric, death is equally horrifying to both sides.

The Doctor, like a latter-day Thomas Hobbes, reminds Zygons and humans of the terrible consequences of war. Like Hobbes, the Doctor knows that a state of war is a state of radical insecurity in which there is the constant fear of death and no possibility of justice:

> When you fire that first shot, no matter how right you feel, you have no idea who's going to die! You don't know whose children are going to scream and burn! How many hearts will be broken! How many lives shattered! How much blood will spill ...

Hobbes makes a similar argument in his 'Review and Conclusion' to *Leviathan*. Having set out his arguments on human nature, the 'Naturall Condition of Mankind'[14] and the contract that establishes peace, he ties his theory to a specific victim of a specific war. Writing about the English Civil War, he gives the example of Sidney Godolphin, a man of great virtue. In terms of 'clearness of judgement, and largeness of fancy; strength of reason, and graceful elocution; a courage for the war, and a fear for the laws,' Hobbes writes, Godolphin, 'my most noble and honoured friend, was the most virtuous man of his age'. And yet, Hobbes continues, 'hating no man, nor hated of any, [he] was unfortunately slain in the beginning of the late civil war, in the public quarrel, by an undiscerned and an undiscerning hand.'[15] War, Hobbes says, claims lives indiscriminately. War does not save the innocent or punish the vicious; the violence of war is 'undiscerning'. War robs us of all that we hold most dear. It kills noble people who would, in different circumstances, be admired and respected by all.

The Doctor's method, the 'scale model of war', owes much to Hobbes's twentieth-century commentators. David Gauthier's *The Logic of Leviathan* first noted the similarity between Hobbes's 'theorems for peace' and game theory – a philosophy of rational decision making developed in the 1950s by Merrill M. Flood, Melvin Dresher and Albert W. Tucker for the RAND Corporation.[16] Game theory is a mathematical way of modelling the rationality of choices by considering a matrix of their likely outcomes. Gauthier introduces the terminology of game theory during his discussion of Hobbes's attempt to generate peace; as for Hobbes, all people need to make a binary choice: peace or war.[17] This insight was developed in Gregory S. Kavka's *Hobbesian Moral and Political Theory* and Jean Hampton's *Hobbes and the Social Contract Tradition*, which applied more sophisticated versions of game theory to Hobbesian arguments for peace. Kavka, for example, using complex mathematics derived from game theory, argues that over many iterations of war and peace games, peace is the more rational choice.[18]

The Doctor's thinking is similarly iterative. Having lived through the many battles of the Time War, the Doctor has experienced war in all its terrible permutations. Consequently, he has determined that it is always better to seek peace, that war should only ever be the last resort, an insight that Hobbes calls the 'law of nature'. The Osgood Box game is iterative, and is designed to allow Zygons and humans to understand the consequences of war and peace without having to go through the horror that the Doctor has experienced. The Doctor sets out his reasoning in the following terms:

> You call this a war? This funny little thing? This is not a war! I fought in a bigger war than you will ever know. I did worse things than you could ever imagine. And when I close my eyes I hear more screams than anyone could ever be able to count! And do you know what you do with all that pain? Shall I tell you where you put it? You hold it tight till it burns your hand, and you say this. No one else will ever have to live like this. No one else will have to feel this pain. Not on my watch!

Having reached the end of his game and ended the war, the Doctor decides not to wipe Bonnie's memory, to ensure that she can learn from the game, a game which the Doctor reveals has been played 15 times before.

The other secret to peace that the Doctor reveals is forgiveness. Again, the Doctor and Hobbes are on the same page. Hobbes's fifth and sixth laws of nature, laws conducive for peace, relate to forgiveness and the limits of punishment. The radical argument is that for the sake of future peace, sometimes the crimes of the past must be let go.

The Doctor's logic here is not restricted to his encounter with the Zygons. In 'Flatline' too, the Doctor opines that conflict kills indiscriminately, and that war should only ever be a last resort. While the conflicts that the Doctor finds himself involved in are often novel, his position, a position based on a commitment to preserving all life, is as old as Anglophone political thought.

'Don't be a warrior, be a Doctor'

New *Who* has been written and produced during the seemingly endless 'War on Terror'. While this war poses almost no physical threat to Western citizens, it threatens a deeper, more insidious loss. The 'War on Terror' threatens the loss of the soul, the loss of the essence of what we are as nations and who we are as individuals. These are the existential threats that the Twelfth Doctor faces. In his adventures, he has to choose whether he is a warrior or a doctor.

We encounter the Twelfth Doctor out of sequence. Our first glimpse of him is in the heat of battle on the last day of the Time War. 'The Day of the Doctor' establishes important truths which are foundational to Capaldi's first two seasons. First, and counter to established lore, Gallifrey stands. As a result, and at the prompting of the Curator, the Twelfth Doctor continues the journey 'home, the long way round'. Second, the affinity between the War Doctor (John Hurt) and his other incarnations is closer than it first seemed. At the end of 'The Name of the Doctor' (2013) and at the end of 'The Night of the Doctor' (2013), the War Doctor appears to be the realisation of the 'Dark Doctor', a Doctor who has abandoned morality and uses his considerable gifts to wage war rather than seek peace. However, the War Doctor, like his other incarnations, carries no gun; in fact, he carries no weapon at all. Like his other selves, he wrestles with the morality of his actions, and rather than burning Gallifrey he – with the help of his other selves – brings about its salvation.

The identity of the Twelfth Doctor is one of the underlying themes of series eight. The Eleventh Doctor is a good man, a good man who goes to war, but a good man nonetheless. The Doctor's identity as a good man was underlined in 'The Day of the Doctor' by the opening quote from Marcus Aurelius, and moments of self-description contained in the episode. After nearly 2,000 years the Eleventh Doctor knows himself.

The Twelfth Doctor appears to have lost this certainty about his identity. Clara acknowledges the problem at the end of 'Deep Breath', admitting, 'I don't think I know who you are any more.' The Doctor picks up the theme in 'Into the Dalek', asking: 'Am I a good man?' Indeed, the Doctor asks the question in the context of his adventure aboard the *Aristotle*, surely a nod in the direction of the *Nicomachean Ethics*, a treatise on virtue and the art of being a good man.

The Doctor and the sergeant

Having established the question, Capaldi's first season looks for answers through interactions between the Doctor and various soldiers: Captain Quell (David Bamber), a former soldier with 'the fight knocked out of him'; the 'ancient soldier driven by malfunctioning tech' who is mistaken for a Mummy; the Sheriff of Nottingham's (Ben Miller) Knights; Danny Pink (Samuel Anderson) and his toy soldier, the Skovox Blitzer, 'Doctor Oswald'; UNIT's officers; 'Rusty' the malfunctioning Dalek; the crew of the Aristotle; and Missy's (Michelle Gomez) cyber army.

The primary way in which the Doctor's identity as a soldier is explored in Capaldi's first full season is through a contrast with Danny Pink, who, like *Sherlock*'s Dr Watson, has fought in the 'War on Terror' and therefore provides a link between the fictional world of *Doctor Who* and the real wars of our time. The exploration is extended in series nine through a contrast with Davros and his 'children', and finally through the mystery of the 'hybrid'.

'The Caretaker' establishes some of the essential facts about Danny Pink's soldiering career. According to a fellow teacher, Pink was a sergeant and had five years' military experience in the UK and Afghanistan. Two aspects of his service in Afghanistan are discussed in the show: first that he dug 23 wells, second that he had inadvertently killed a child. His well-digging is far from fanciful. The activity roots Danny Pink's fictional history in the reality of British activities in Afghanistan. In late 2005, 521 members of the Specialist Team Royal Engineers (Water Development) were deployed in Afghanistan to develop a water infrastructure for the Provincial Reconstruction Team and Forward Operating Base and the British military base, Camp Bastion in Helmand Province. By 2009 the STRE had sunk 28 boreholes, most of which were dug in 2008.[19] From this it seems reasonable to assume that Danny Pink was in Afghanistan around 2008, and in all likelihood for some time before. There were also several reports of British soldiers shooting and killing Afghan children in early 2009.[20]

In several episodes in series eight the Doctor and Danny Pink joust over what it means to be a solider. When the Doctor first meets him, he is dismissive in the extreme. He assumes that, as a former soldier, Pink must be a PE teacher, and struggles to come to terms with Danny's role as a maths teacher. This is all the more surprising when you consider that Pink's history as a solider is revealed in the context of a discussion of his technical prowess. In 'The Caretaker', Adrian, the English teacher (Edward Harrison), explains, 'of course, Danny Pink, here's your man Mr Smith. Five years' military experience, here and Afghan. So, electrics, boilers ... if you need a hand ...' Yet the Doctor assumes that Pink's career as a soldier must make him a halfwit. The Doctor makes his disdain for the former soldier clear in his discussion with Clara, calling her relationship with Danny a 'boyfriend error', asking: 'Why would you go out with a soldier? Why not get a dog or a big plant?' This disdain is part of a broader contempt for soldiers. In 'Death in Heaven' the Doctor refuses to salute Colonel Ahmed (Sanjeev Bhaskar), and writes off the entirety of military history as the product of self-inflicted concussion. Yet for all the Doctor's disdain, the Doctor shows many of the characteristics of a soldier. In 'Mummy on the Orient Express', he readily slips into the patter of a general, referring to the ancient soldier as 'son'. Again, in 'The Zygon Invasion', the Doctor seems comfortable swaggering into UNIT HQ issuing the instruction 'At ease.'

Danny Pink spots the Doctor for what he is, a 'blood-soaked old general' who is bound to choose tactical advantage over moral conviction. For Pink, the Doctor is a 'typical officer who has to keep those hands clean'. Pink is right: time and again the Doctor shows a bewildering lack of humanity in conflict situations. In 'Mummy on the Orient Express', for example, Perkins (Frank Skinner) reminds the Doctor of the human tragedy they have just witnessed. The exchange is revealing:

> PERKINS: A man just died in front of us. Can we not just have a moment?
> THE DOCTOR: No. No, no, no. We can't do that. We can't mourn. People with guns to their heads, they cannot mourn. We do not have time to mourn.

At the end of the episode the Doctor recapitulates his strategic approach to his battle with Gus (John Sessions), again demonstrating that, like a general or a military surgeon, he thinks in terms of triage:

> I didn't know if I could save her. I couldn't save Quell, I couldn't save Moorhouse. There was a good chance that she'd die too. At which point, I would have just moved on to the next, and the next, until I beat it. Sometimes the only choices you have are bad ones. But you still have to choose.

By the end of the series the contrast between the Doctor and Danny Pink has thrown up the following contrasts. First, the Doctor behaves like a general, making apparently heartless strategic decisions in the interests of the greater good. Pink, on the other hand, was a sergeant who got his hands dirty rather than making major decisions. Second, as noted in 'In the Forest of the Night', Danny Pink's experience as a soldier has led him to reject one kind of adventure for another:

> I was a soldier. I put myself at risk. I didn't try too hard to survive, but somehow, here I am. And now I can see what I nearly lost. And it's enough. I don't want to see more things. I want to see the things in front of me more clearly. There are wonders here, Clara Oswald. Bradley saying please, that's a wonder. One person is more amazing, harder to understand, but more amazing than universes.

The Doctor, by contrast, continues to thrive under fire, and remains committed to the life of a cosmic hobo, as evident in 'Death in Heaven': 'I am an idiot, with a box and a screwdriver. Just passing through, helping out, learning.' The Doctor has yet to settle down – the implication in 'Mummy on the Orient Express' is that the Doctor is not the kind of person who comes 'round to people's houses for dinner'.

Yet at a deeper level the two soldiers are similar. The similarity between the Doctor and Danny Pink is referenced obliquely in 'The Magician's Apprentice' when the Doctor reveals that he has been spending his time in Dark Ages Essex digging a well and giving 'some top-notch maths tuition in a fun but relevant way', in so doing taking a leaf out of Pink's book. While both can behave like soldiers, neither identifies as one. Danny Pink only speaks like a soldier ironically, to show his dislike for the military aspects of the Doctor's character, and when pushed the Doctor rejects the 'soldier' title. What is more, they are both motivated by love. This, in turn, leads them to deplore some of the things they have had to do – indeed, Danny's killing of a child in Afghanistan is a microcosm of the Doctor's horror at his own willingness to sentence billions of children to death on the last day of the Time War.

'They've worked on you, haven't they, son?'

Modern warfare creates political dangers for the individual and the state, dangers that are explored in series eight and nine of *Doctor Who*. The soldier from a 'forgotten war' that the Doctor encounters in 'Mummy on the Orient Express' is a metaphor for the danger facing all soldiers, a danger that the Doctor himself has had to face. On recognising the Mummy's true nature, the Doctor says:

> They've worked on you, haven't they, son? They've filled you full of kit. State-of-the art phase camouflage, personal teleporter [...] And all that tech inside you, it just won't let you die, will it? It won't let the war end!

Being a soldier was not simply a job for this unfortunate warrior; being a soldier has transformed him, dehumanised him, turning him into a creature that is all too easy to mistake for a zombie.

This danger has long been recognised. It is worth remembering that Capaldi's first full season was made in 2014, a century after the start of World War I. The physical fate of the Mummy recalls the psychological fate of so many soldiers who fought between 1914 and 1918. Erich Maria Remarque's 1929 novel *All Quiet on the Western Front* focuses on this very danger. Remarque's story shows how continual horror, fear, destruction, seeing friends die and the remorseless mechanised killing of World War I affected young soldiers. Rather than turning them into heroes, the novel shows how it ruined young men, destroying their capacity to hope and their ability to love, and robbing them of their humanity. The novel indicates that even those who survived were destroyed psychologically by the physical and mental torment they were forced to endure. Remarque's novel leads to the bleak conclusion that the survivors became a lost generation, unable to find peace.[21]

Remarque was not alone in conceiving the Great War in this way. Artists such as Otto Dix and Georg Grosz demystified the experience of German soldiers. Grosz's *Made in Germany* (1919) is a portrait of a German soldier. Rather than looking noble and invincible, the soldier appears fat, apelike and grotesque. Dix's etching *Stormtroopers Advancing Under Gas* (1924) presents German soldiers as monstrous. Their gas masks transform their faces, the masks' glazed eyes looking like the orbits of skulls. The devastated landscapes of Dix's trenches, replete with mutilated corpses and cowering soldiers, look like hell.

The ultimate danger of modern war, then, is not destruction of the body, but loss of the soul: the transformation of humans into dehumanised killers. Indeed, when peace came, some longed to be back in the trenches, and viewed mechanised killing as the pinnacle of their existence. This is a real danger. While Dix, Grosz and Remarque depicted the true horror of war, others glorified it. Ernst Jünger's novels, to take one example, celebrated butchery on the Western Front, describing the trenches as a kind of paradise in which men were at one with each other, and at one with nature. His books describe acts of slaughter in graphic sensual detail. For Jünger true men can only know peace when they are surrounded by destruction and devastation, because war is the true fulfilment of masculine nature.[22]

The Mummy is not the only soldier who has lost his soul due to perpetual warfare; the Daleks are the show's prime example of a creature which has been transformed by the dehumanising effect of war. The Doctor makes this clear at the beginning of series nine, describing the genesis of the Daleks thus:

> Davros is the child of war, a war that wouldn't end. A thousand years of fighting, till nobody could remember why. So Davros, he created a new kind of warrior, one that wouldn't bother with *that* question. A mutant in a tank that would never, ever stop. And they never did [...] How scared must you be to seal every one of your own kind inside a tank?

Davros, himself the child of endless war, understands their love of conflict. For Davros and his creatures, the moment at which the 'hunter and prey [are] held in the ecstasy of crisis' is the moment at which life is at its purest.

This danger is not merely moral; the psychological impact of war also has political consequences. It is no accident that the generation after World War I (in Italy and Germany, at least) embraced fascism. Moreover, this danger is not restricted to interwar Europe. In fighting 'extremism', in continuing the 'Global War on Terror', Western powers resort to reprehensible methods, and in so doing, Western governments – with at least the tacit support of their populations – engage in acts of war which will necessarily entail the deaths and maiming of civilians, and commit appalling acts of sadistic torture such as hundreds of hours of continual sleep deprivation, 'rectal feeding' and waterboarding in secret concentration camps such as Detention Site Cobalt.[23]

At home, the 'War on Terror' has justified the extension of state power and the growth of military spending; it has led to advocates of peace being branded as traitors ('terrorist sympathiser[s]', to quote David Cameron),[24] and to the manipulation of truth. George Orwell summarised the political consequences of the psychology of modern warfare in the following way in *Nineteen Eighty-Four*:

> ... such acts as raping, looting, the slaughter of children, the reduction of whole populations to slavery, and reprisals against prisoners which extend even to boiling and burying alive, are looked upon as normal, and, when they are committed by one's own side and not by the enemy, meritorious.[25]

The terrible irony is that wars that are fought to advance democratic values are used over time to normalise and celebrate appalling cruelty and the restriction of rights. Indeed, contemporary war hysteria must be one of the reasons for the popularity of Donald Trump's advocacy of torture, the targeting of terrorists' families and the partial ban on Muslim migration to the US.

The potential of war to dehumanise has been recognised again and again in new *Who*. Cass's comments in 'The Time of the Doctor' that it is impossible to tell the difference between the Daleks and the Time Lords indicates that even Time Lord culture cannot withstand the logic of war. The corruption of Time Lord culture is also clear in

'Hell Bent': Rassilon, having led the Time Lords through the Time War, has apparently used fear of the Hybrid to imprison the Doctor in a 'torture chamber' for four and a half billion years, and then to justify the extra-judicial murder of the Doctor and those who stand with him – including children.

However, the Doctor and Danny Pink are similar in that they have not succumbed to the corrupting influence of war. Neither Pink nor the Doctor are prepared to see people die unless there is absolutely no alternative, and when they use force both men are affected by their actions. This is clear from the contrast between the Doctor and Missy. Missy kills for fun, or because she is 'bananas'. The Doctor is a very different kind of warrior. Fighting is against his nature; he only ever fights as a last resort, and always for peace.

Conclusion: 'Words are his weapons'

The Doctor understands the corrupting nature of war. His actions in 'Heaven Sent'/'Hell Bent', exiling Rassilon and the High Council, are a Christlike purging of the temple. Indeed, the parallels to Christ, the 'prince of peace', are heightened by the recurrent use of the phrase, borrowed from Luke 4:23, 'Physician, heal thyself.' The Doctor returns to Gallifrey not as a warrior but as a healer. He also returns to heal himself by bringing back Clara, because the Doctor, unlike the Daleks, cannot be whole without love. The Doctor carries no weapon because, as Rassilon notes, 'Words are his weapons.' Words are his weapons, because without words, as Hobbes reminds us, 'men would not have [...] peace – any more than lions, bears, and wolves do'.[26]

Davros once accused the Doctor of turning people into weapons, but series eight and nine show something more complex. Clara does not become a weapon, she does not even become a warrior. Clara becomes a Doctor, on her own journey to Gallifrey 'the long way round'. Starting a life of adventure, she will have to think strategically, even coldly to create peace, but she will never be cruel or cowardly and if she is, she will make amends. Series nine ends with Clara rededicating herself to the promise of the Doctor, where, in the series ten episode 'Thin Ice' he is reluctant to admit to his new companion Bill (Pearl

Mackie) that, in his centuries of existence, he has taken lives and with the idea of him as warrior re-emphasised later in that series in 'Empress of Mars'.

Notes

1 Carl von Clausewitz, *On War*, trans. M. Howard and P. Paret (Oxford, 2007), p. 252.
2 See Robin Bunce, 'The Evil of the Daleks', in Courtland Lewis and Paula Smithka (eds), *Doctor Who and Philosophy: Bigger on the Inside* (Chicago, IL, 2010), pp 339–50.
3 For critiques of Huntington's thesis see, for example, Richard Bonney, *False Prophets: The 'Clash of Civilizations' and the Global War on Terror* (Oxford, 2008).
4 Samuel P. Huntington, 'The clash of civilizations?', in James F. Hoge (ed.), *The Clash of Civilizations? The Debate* (New York, 2010), p. 1.
5 Ibid., p. 2.
6 Ibid., p. 79.
7 Natan Dubovitsky, 'Without sky', quoted in Peter Pomerantsev, 'Non-linear war', *London Review of Books* [blog] (28 March 2014). Available at https://www.lrb.co.uk/blog/2014/03/28/peter-pomerantsev/non-linear-war/ (accessed 1 July 2017).
8 Ibid.
9 Peter Pomerantsev, 'Putin's Rasputin', *London Review of Books* xxxiii/20 (October 2011), pp. 3–6. Available at https://www.lrb.co.uk/v33/n20/peter-pomerantsev/putins-rasputin (accessed 1 July 2017).
10 For an analysis of the dispersal policy see Gary P. Freeman, *Immigrant Labor and Racial Conflict in Industrial Societies: The French and British Experience, 1945–1975* (Princeton, NJ, 2015), p. 151.
11 A 'NO COLOUREDS' sign appears in 'Remembrance of the Daleks' (1988), rooting the programme in the context of the prevalent racism of the time. For details of the prevalence of this kind of sign in London see Christopher Griffin, *Nomads under the Westway: Irish Travellers, Gypsies and Other Traders in West London* (Hatfield, 2008), p. 89.
12 For an analysis of the Gerasimov doctrine see Mark Galeotti, '"Hybrid war" and "little green men": how it works, and how it doesn't', in Agnieszka Pikulicka-Wilczewska and Richard Sakwa (eds), *Ukraine and Russia: People, Politics, Propaganda and Perspectives* (Bristol, 2015), pp. 149–56. Available at http://www.e-ir.info/wp-content/uploads/2015/03/Ukraine-and-Russia-E-IR.pdf (accessed 1 July 2017); Roger N. McDermott, 'Does Russia have a Gerasimov doctrine?', *Parameters* xlvi/1 (2016), pp. 97–105.

13 John Rawls, *A Theory of Justice* (Cambridge, 1971) and idem, 'The law of peoples', in Steven Shute and Susan Hurley (eds), *On Human Rights: The Oxford Amnesty Lectures* (New York, 1993).

14 Thomas Hobbes, *Leviathan*, ed. Richard Tuck (Cambridge, 1996), p. 86.

15 Ibid., p. 484.

16 For some of the original work on Game Theory see A. W. Tucker, 'The mathematics of Tucker: a sampler', *The Two-Year College Mathematics Journal* xiv/3 (1983), pp. 228–32.

17 David P. Gauthier, *The Logic of Leviathan: The Moral and Political Theory of Thomas Hobbes* (Oxford, 1969), p. 79.

18 Gregory S. Kavka, *Hobbesian Moral and Political Theory* (Princeton, NJ, 1986); Jean Hampton, *Hobbes and the Social Contract Tradition* (Cambridge, 1986). For a discussion of Kavka and Hampton's work on Hobbes see Robin Bunce, *Thomas Hobbes* (London, 2009), pp. 89–91.

19 Edward P. F. Rose and J. D. Mather (eds), *Military Aspects of Hydrogeology* (London, 2012), p. 251.

20 See, for example, Ali Daya, 'Afghan father says his baby dies in coalition raid', RAWA [website]. Available at http://www.rawa.org/temp/runews/rawanews.php?id=1022#ixzz4a6e1zJFk (accessed 1 March 2017).

21 Erich Maria Remarque, *All Quiet on the Western Front* (London, 1929).

22 Ernst Jünger, *Storm of Steel* (1920). This memoir of Jünger's experiences on the Western Front is his best-known work. For an account of Jünger's work more generally see Eric D. Weitz, *Weimar Germany: Promise and Tragedy* (Princeton, NJ, 2013), pp. 338–40.

23 Dominic Rushe, Ewen MacAskill, Ian Cobain, Alan Yuhas and Oliver Laughland, 'Rectal rehydration and waterboarding: the CIA torture report's grisliest findings', *Guardian* (11 December 2014). Available at www.theguardian.com/us-news/2014/dec/09/cia-torture-report-worst-findings-waterboard-rectal (accessed 1 March 2017).

24 Nicholas Watt, 'David Cameron accuses Jeremy Corbyn of being "terrorist sympathiser"', *Guardian* (2 December 2015). Available at www.theguardian.com/politics/2015/dec/01/cameron-accuses-corbyn-of-being-terrorist-sympathiser (accessed 1 March 2017).

25 George Orwell, *Nineteen Eighty-Four* (London, 1955), p. 191.

26 Hobbes, *Leviathan*, p. 24.

5

'CHAP WITH WINGS THERE, FIVE ROUNDS RAPID'

UNIT and the Politics of *Doctor Who*

Eric Leuschner

For a live-action television programme that spans more than fifty years to have recurring characters is quite a feat. *Doctor Who* is a rare example in which the show's eponym has been played by numerous actors but remains the same character. UNIT, and by association its most identifiable character Brigadier Alistair Gordon Lethbridge-Stewart ('the Brigadier', played by Nicholas Courtney), metonymically standing for UNIT and encapsulating most of the organisation's characteristics, has appeared with all but one of the classic television Doctors. The Sixth Doctor (Colin Baker) is the only one not to have a UNIT or Brigadier story; even the First Doctor (William Hartnell/Richard Hurndall) encounters the Brigadier and UNIT ('The Three Doctors', 1972–3, 'The Five Doctors', 1983, as well as being seen in the flashback scenes in the Fifth Doctor serial 'Mawdryn Undead', 1983). Even more astonishing is to see the Brigadier appear as a Cyberman in the Twelfth Doctor episode 'Death in Heaven,' three years after Nicholas Courtney's death.[1] With all the changes incurred as the series was rebooted in 2005, it is remarkable that this one character and organisation is a tie connecting the new and classic series. However, UNIT – the acronym standing first for 'United Nations Intelligence Taskforce' and later 'Unified Intelligence Taskforce' – also serves as a long-standing political cipher in the *Doctor Who* universe, representing for the most part the militaristic agenda of government as well as a vision of a coordinated, worldwide governmental entity, a vision that is often misplaced and misinformed in *Doctor Who*, particularly as it asserts a military-alien complex.

'We're not exactly spies': classic UNIT

First appearing in the 1968 Second Doctor (Patrick Troughton) serial 'The Invasion', UNIT was formed in the wake of the Yeti incident four years earlier in the London Underground ('The Web of Fear', 1968). The Doctor and Jamie (Frazer Hines) are delighted when they discover that Colonel Lethbridge-Stewart, now promoted to Brigadier, who had been in charge during the Yeti incident, is behind unidentified military personnel who have taken them:

> BRIGADIER: I've been in charge of an independent intelligence group that we call UNIT. That's United Nations Intelligence Taskforce.
> JAMIE: You mean you're like a world secret police?
> BRIGADIER: Not quite. We don't actually arrest people, just investigate them.

It is later revealed that UNIT is an international organisation with its central command in Geneva, although it is able to have direct control of a British missile base at Henlow Downs Defence Base. The Brigadier heads the British arm of UNIT – composed of seconded troops from the British army, navy and air force – which is well provisioned, employing cargo planes, helicopters and ground troops armed with machine guns, grenades and bazookas. UNIT is introduced, at first unidentified, in the second episode of 'The Invasion' as the Doctor and Jamie are followed by a mysterious black car containing men in dark suits after they investigate International Electromagnetics. Adding to the *mise en scène* is Don Harper's sinister electronic music as the Doctor and Jamie are cornered in an alleyway. Echoing the earlier scenes of the Company, shots are often dark and rely on odd close-ups, suggestive of film noir and setting the initially unidentified UNIT in espionage thriller terms.

While the details of UNIT uniforms change from series to series, the general intent in the classic series is to reflect standard British Army uniforms.[2] The chain of command is distinct, though, as the Brigadier reports to Major-General Rutlidge in the Ministry of Defence. Befitting his personality, the Second Doctor has an easy relationship with the Brigadier, breaking into a broad smile when first meeting. The relationship is easy perhaps because the Brigadier (and UNIT) can be both militaristic and 'British'. Before explaining the 'cloak and dagger stuff', the Brigadier asks Sergeant Walters to 'lay on some tea'. Later, trying to comfort Zoe (Wendy Padbury), he says, 'Don't look so worried. Fancy a cup of tea?'[3] At other times, he easily spouts military jargon and commands. The Second Doctor appears willing to call upon the military support at various times in the serial, and, of course, UNIT's involvement is necessary to defeat the Cyberman invasion.

UNIT and the Brigadier next appear in the Third Doctor's (Jon Pertwee) debut 'Spearhead from Space' (1970), as a continuity link for the regeneration. The first episode opens with a UNIT tracking station then cuts to the Brigadier's office. Except for the brief appearance of the Third Doctor falling face first out of the just-materialised TARDIS, the Brigadier is the familiar connection for viewers. Interviewing Liz Shaw (Caroline John) as a scientific advisor, the Brigadier objects to her characterising UNIT as 'security work': 'We're not exactly spies here at UNIT [...] We deal with the odd, the unexplained, anything on Earth, or even beyond.' Since the Cyberman invasion, the Brigadier has pushed to emphasise the scientific side and recognises the need for a scientific advisor. He tells Liz that 'there is a remote possibility that outside your cosy little world other things could exist'. However, to reassert the military role, he orders the guards posted to the TARDIS to be issued with live ammunition. The soldiers' shocked response suggests that UNIT has not recently engaged in actual military combat. General Scobie (Hamilton Dyce) is assigned to the Brigadier as a liaison with the regular army, and the Brigadier notes to Liz that he has 'got to keep in with him'.

The Third Doctor acts much more dismissively of the Brigadier and UNIT than did his previous incarnation. At first, he is driven by his curiosity about the meteorite fragments and more concerned with getting access to the TARDIS; it is only later that he finds himself stranded on Earth. When the Brigadier agrees to return the TARDIS key if he helps the investigation, he retorts, 'Then go away and let Miss Shaw and I get on with our work. There's a good fellow.' Intently focused on the fragments, the Doctor does not even look up at the Brigadier as they speak. At the end of the episode, although stuck on Earth, he turns businesslike with the Brigadier, who is drinking cups of tea with Liz Shaw, in order to 'discuss terms'. He calls Earth 'this little planet of yours', and when he requests a similar car to the one he borrowed, the Brigadier can only reply, 'Oh, very well,' an exasperated phrase often muttered by the Brigadier in response to the Doctor.

Because he is stranded on Earth, the Third Doctor is most closely identified with UNIT. Throughout the Third Doctor's tenure, he maintains a friendly yet detached (and sometimes condescending) attitude toward UNIT and the Brigadier. He plays his role as 'scientific advisor' seriously yet with an alien affect. In part this may have to do with the role of UNIT. Andrew Cartmel, *Doctor Who* script editor from 1987 to 1989, describes the sharp contrast between the Doctor's eccentric personality and the seriousness and normality of UNIT as an 'inspired stroke'.[4] The contrast begins to develop with the Third Doctor; in the next serial 'Doctor Who and the Silurians' (1970), the Doctor is summoned by a message: 'Miss Shaw and the Doctor will report themselves forthwith to Wenley Moor. Attend a briefing meeting at precisely—' which the Doctor interrupts with, 'My dear Miss Shaw, I never report myself anywhere, particularly not forthwith.' This episode also establishes the political ramifications of UNIT. While the Doctor plans on finding a peaceful resolution, the Brigadier orders the Silurian base to be blown up. The disappointed and frustrated look on the Doctor's face as he watches the explosions evidences the building tension between the two. He replies to Liz Shaw, 'But that's murder. They were intelligent alien beings. A whole race of them. And he's just wiped them out.' The Doctor pins the blame directly on the Brigadier in this scene, which foreshadows the destruction of the Sycorax in the Tenth Doctor (David Tennant) debut 'The Christmas Invasion' (2005).

The final serial of Pertwee's first season, 'Inferno' (1970), offers an intriguing view of the political ramifications of UNIT. Like *Star Trek*'s 'Mirror, Mirror' (1967) alternative universe, the serial has the Doctor transported to a parallel world where the ostensibly good organisation is transformed into a fascist-leaning militaristic organisation. There UNIT is the British Republican Security Force (RSF), the Brigadier is now 'Brigade Leader' (with requisite eyepatch and scar) and Liz Shaw is 'Section Leader'. What this offers is a vision of UNIT gone bad – what happens when admirable motivations are undercut by political machinations and dictatorial control. Whereas earlier the imputation that UNIT was a police force was rejected, the RSF is firmly set in the authoritarian role with tranquilliser darts used to pacify resistance, a Big Brother-like Central Records and 'full authority given by the Defence of the Republic Act, 1943'. On his return to the normal universe, the Doctor notes that the Brigadier exhibits tendencies reminiscent of the parallel-universe Brigadier. The relationship between the Doctor and the Brigadier comes to a head as the Doctor calls the Brigadier a 'pompous, self-opinionated idiot'.

While the Third Doctor continues to work with UNIT and the Brigadier, there is always a love–hate tension, indicating the wariness the Doctor has towards UNIT's political nature. In the first serial of the next season ('Terror of the Autons', 1971), the Doctor again calls the Brigadier an 'idiot' after finding out he authorised the loan of the Nestene energy unit originally seen in 'Spearhead from Space'. The Doctor's internal conflict is shown as he remarks to Jo Grant that 'I knew I should have destroyed that thing, but somehow it would have felt like murder.' Unfortunately, many of the resolutions to Third Doctor stories involve some sort of explosion, caused either by the Doctor or the Brigadier/UNIT. In his defence, the Brigadier is often seen arguing with superiors in the Ministry of Defence, sometimes as a voice of reason but other times as a voice of force. However, the Brigadier's and UNIT's modi operandi are summed up in his command in 'The Daemons' (1971): faced with the gargoyle Bok (Stanley Mason), he orders Private Jenkins (Christian Cooke), 'Chap with wings there, five rounds rapid.'[5] Ultimately, the conflict between a desire for a peaceful end and one that involves violence and destruction dogs the Doctor throughout his adventures, but seems particularly pronounced as the Third Doctor is strongly associated with UNIT. In other serials such as 'The Ambassadors of Death' (1970), 'The Mind of Evil' (1971), 'Day of the Daleks' (1972) and 'The Time Warrior' (1973–4) UNIT plays a security role. For instance, the organisation provides security for the National Space Programme, the World Peace Conferences and scientists. In yet other serials, such as 'The Claws of Axos' (1971) and 'The Green Death' (1973), UNIT assumes an investigative role and often teams up with the Doctor to defeat the monster of the week.

When the Doctor regenerates for the third time following the events of 'Planet of the Spiders' (1974), his relationship with UNIT and the Brigadier is distinctly different. In a post-regeneration haze, the Fourth Doctor (Tom Baker) mutters, 'I tell you, Brigadier, there's nothing to worry about. The Brontosaurus is large and placid ...' Pausing as Harry Sullivan (Ian Marter) enters, he adds, as if pointing directly at the UNIT representative '... and stupid', hearkening back to the Third Doctor's earlier characterisation of the Brigadier as an 'idiot'. Later, but still recovering, he asks the Brigadier, 'Haven't we met somewhere before? No, don't tell me. Alexander the Great! No? Hannibal? No. Ah! Brigadier? Brigadier Alistair Gordon Lethbridge-Stewart.' The association with great military leaders is usually viewed as a compliment, but when seen in the context of the Doctor's relationship with the Brigadier, it can also be seen as an ironic swipe, associating Alexander and Hannibal as conquerors rather than military strategists. The Doctor's eccentric behaviour, as Cartmel describes it, is best seen in the Fourth Doctor's whining at the end of 'Robot' (1974–5): 'The Brigadier wants me to address the Cabinet, have lunch at Downing Street, dinner at the palace, and write 17 reports in triplicate.' The Doctor puts his foot down: 'Well, I won't do it. I won't, I won't, I won't!' The Fourth Doctor is done playing along with UNIT. In a later serial, 1975's 'Terror of the Zygons', it is only after the Brigadier emphasises to the Doctor that people may die if he does not assist that he concedes to help:

BRIGADIER: This is an emergency.
THE DOCTOR: Oil an emergency? It's about time the people who run this planet of yours realised that to be dependent upon a mineral slime just doesn't make sense. Now, the energising of hydrogen.
BRIGADIER: Doctor, the destruction of these rigs is a complete mystery. Do you want more men to die?

THE DOCTOR: No. Very well. When do we start?

Invoking 'the people who run this planet of yours' suggests the emphasis of the Doctor's alien-ness that is characteristic of the Fourth Doctor. When depth charges are exploded over the Zygon ship, the Doctor comments, 'Sounds like the Brigadier.' But it is the Doctor who sets the ship to self-destruct in the end:

THE DOCTOR: Was that a bang big enough for you, Brigadier?
BRIGADIER: Nicely done, Doctor.

The character of UNIT remains relatively unchanged in the few Fourth Doctor serials that feature UNIT. 'The Android Invasion' (1975) does offer an interesting twist with the reveal that UNIT soldiers have been replaced by androids in the village of Devesham and the Space Defence Station there, but is later exposed to be a fake setting, being a testing site for a Kraal invasion. A compromised UNIT is a device only used in a limited fashion in the original programme. The Fifth Doctor (Peter Davison) sees the Brigadier retired in 'Mawdryn Undead' so it is technically not a UNIT story, and the Sixth Doctor (Colin Baker) never encountered UNIT or the Brigadier, except in the thirtieth anniversary special *Dimensions in Time*. UNIT returns with the Seventh Doctor (Sylvester McCoy) and marks a distinctive alteration in appearance. While UNIT personnel wore camouflaged fatigues in 'Terror of the Zygons', the depiction of UNIT in 'Battlefield' (1989) is of a much greater militarised organisation as well as a more internationalised one. The light blue berets, signifying more of a United Nations control, as well as officers and enlisted personnel with international-sounding names (Brigadier Bambera, an African woman, played by Angela Bruce, and Sergeant Zbrigniev, played by Robert Jezek) and Czechoslovakian troops commanded by a Czech officer, Major Husak (Paul Tomany), as part of the UNIT contingent, suggest the widening of the scope of UNIT as a global organisation. In this serial as in many of the later episodes of the revived series, UNIT is shown in active combat situations, again employing heavy armament. For the first time, UNIT troops are seen wearing Kevlar helmets. The Seventh Doctor's attitude toward UNIT is captured in several opening comments:

PETER: The military use the area as a firing range. Never understood why.

THE DOCTOR: Blowing the occasional chunk out of the earth keeps them amused.

ACE: It's a missile convoy.

THE DOCTOR: A nuclear missile convoy.

ACE: How do you know?

THE DOCTOR: It has a graveyard stench.

The dismissive tone of the Doctor may reflect the change known as the 'Cartmel masterplan', which was to have added more mystery and a darker mood to the Doctor during Sylvester McCoy's incarnation. Faced with the Destroyer at the climax of the serial, the Brigadier reports that he can order an air strike immediately, but understands that, as usual, conventional weapons will have no effect. In the end, military force does resolve the situation as the Brigadier shoots the Destroyer with Ace's (Sophie Aldred) silver bullets. Discovering the Brigadier's body in the rubble, the Doctor calls him yet another name, this time 'You stupid, stubborn, pig-headed numbskull,' an update on the Third Doctor's 'idiot'. The sentiment, though, here is of a great loss, as the Doctor claims it should have been him to make the sacrifice. Of course, the Brigadier is alive and replies to the Doctor, 'Nonsense ... You don't think I'd be so stupid as to stay inside, do you?' David Layton sums up the classic Doctors' relationship with UNIT:

> He runs into constant philosophical conflict with its leader Brigadier Lethbridge-Stewart, generally over the value of the military. Despite his repeated characterisations of the military as 'clumsy' and heavy handed, and his ironic remarks about their 'shoot first' and nationalistic mentality, the Doctor often finds that he needs UNIT.[6]

'A modern UNIT for a modern world'

When the series was revived in 2005, UNIT made a cameo in the Ninth Doctor episode 'Aliens of London' (2005), but it is with the Tenth Doctor debut, 'The Christmas Invasion' (2005), that UNIT evolves into something quite different from its classic format. Reflecting an upped ante militarism, its soldiers now wear tactical vests, black jumpsuits, red (not light blue) berets, and in combat Kevlar helmets with night-vision goggles. The red beret is often associated with military police units, but may also be identified with special operations forces. Instead of military vehicles, they arrive in black SUVs. Unlike the Army-barracks look of UNIT HQ in the Third Doctor period, the organisation's new base, now located underneath the Tower of London, is high-tech and highly secret. For the first time, UNIT possesses weaponry that distinguishes it from the regular military. In 'The Sound of Drums' (2007), the *Valiant* is introduced as an *Avengers*-styled helicarrier, and UNIT has the authority to take over from a nation's military. There is no longer the sense that troops are seconded, or borrowed, from a nation's military force: they are in fact part of an independent organisation. Martha Jones (Freema Agyeman), now working for UNIT, announces the transformation:

> MARTHA: You've been on board the *Valiant*. We've got massive funding from the United Nations, all in the name of Home World Security.
>
> MACE: A modern UNIT for the modern world.

They also possess alien technology (through Torchwood in 'The Christmas Invasion', 2005), and Prime Minister Harriet Jones (Penelope Wilton) orders its use to destroy the Sycorax ship in the name of defence. Again, the Doctor is caught in the middle of competing needs; again he asserts that the act was 'murder'. The modern UNIT also has the ability to destroy the planet with the Osterhagen Project, a network of 25 strategically placed nuclear warheads that can only be triggered by a combination of special keys activated at multiple stations around the world. This ultimate fail-safe is established in the name of 'world security', 'to be used if the suffering of the human race is so great, so without hope, that this becomes the final option'.

Without the Brigadier, a string of determinedly militaristic yet ineffective commanding officers stand in for him, including Colonel Crighton (David Savile), Colonel Ahmed (Sanjeev Bhaskar), Major Blake (Chu Omambala), Colonel Mace (Rupert Holliday Evans) and Lieutenant General Sanchez (Michael Brandon). The 'modern' relationship between the Doctor and UNIT is encapsulated in an exchange with Colonel Mace in 'The Poison Sky' (2008):

MACE: Latest firing stock. What do you think, Doctor?
THE DOCTOR: Are you my mummy?
MACE: If you could concentrate. Bullets with a rad-steel coating. No copper surface. Should overcome the cordolaine signal.
THE DOCTOR: But the Sontarans have got lasers. You can't even see in this fog. The night vision doesn't work.
MACE: Thank you, Doctor. Thank you for your lack of faith. But this time, I'm not listening. Attention, all troops. The Sontarans might think of us as primitive, as does every passing species with an axe to grind. They make a mockery of our weapons, our soldiers, our ideals. But no more. From this point on, it stops. From this point on, the people of Earth fight back, and we show them. We show the warriors of Sontar what the human race can do. Trap One to Hawk Major. Go, go, go. [...] It's working. The area's clearing. Engines to maximum.
THE DOCTOR: It's the *Valiant*.
MACE: UNIT Carrier Ship *Valiant* reporting for duty, Doctor. With engines strong enough to clear away the fog.
THE DOCTOR: Whoa, that's brilliant.
MACE: Getting a taste for it, Doctor?
THE DOCTOR: No, not at all. Not me.
MACE: *Valiant*, fire at will.

The modern manifestation of UNIT relies heavily on the technology of warfare. There is a thin line between military, police, secrecy and politics, which UNIT attempts to straddle. By this point, they have become something quite different from how they started – with the original goal of investigating unknown or extraterrestrial occurrences. Perhaps due to this, the Doctor's dismissive attitude is more overt than even with the Fourth Doctor. Ironically, because the Doctor and UNIT are so intertwined, their evolution is likely due in part to him. The Doctor often specifically describes himself as 'defender of the Earth', and UNIT has positioned itself in that role as well. David Layton, in *The Humanism of Doctor Who*, suggests that there is a 'simplification in this analogical approach that creates a good military/bad military state of mind [...] So long as the military is *our* military, fighting on *our* side to protect *us*, then it appears to be safely in its place.'[7] However, when Martha threatens Davros with using the Osterhagen key on Earth (2008), the Doctor asserts that 'That's never an option.' The unstated motivation or cause of the new Doctor's perspective is undoubtedly his experience in the Time War, where he had to become directly involved in the conflict. He has his own 'Osterhagen' experience with 'the Moment' that, in 'The Day of The Doctor' (2013), destroys both the Time Lords and the Daleks, the consequence being that he must live burdened with the guilt of his actions. In the case of Martha, the irony of the situation is that, as Davros points out, the Doctor takes ordinary people and 'fashions them into weapons', as Martha is ready to sacrifice herself. Martha, a medical student when she first meets the Doctor, foreshadows later developments of UNIT. After leaving the TARDIS, Martha joins UNIT and, now Dr Martha Jones, is named the medical director of UNIT's Project Indigo. Her scientific and medical background plays a role as she asserts that she joined UNIT so that she could change it by working from within, adding a more caring side to the military organisation. Her attempts do not appear successful, as they instead culminate in the Osterhagen project.

With the Eleventh Doctor (Matt Smith), UNIT transforms yet again. On the one hand, UNIT troops in 'The Power of Three' (2012) appear even more beefed up, still wearing black uniforms, tactical vests and helmets with goggles, but also now sporting body armour. Their 'assault' on Amy and Rory's house, with weapons at the ready, is depicted in paramilitary/SWAT-like terms, one soldier announcing 'Ultimate force available.' On the other hand, after breaking down the door, the troops step aside to let a new 'commanding officer' in: Kate Stewart, the Brigadier's daughter (Jemma Redgrave):

> KATE: All these muscles, and they still don't know how to knock. Sorry about the raucous entrance. Spike in Artron energy reading at this address. In the light of the last twenty-four hours, we had to check it out, and the dogs do love a run out. Hello. Kate Stewart, head of scientific research at UNIT. And with dress sense like that, you must be the Doctor. I hoped it would be you.

THE DOCTOR: Tell me, since when did science run the military, Kate?

KATE: Since me. UNIT's been adapting. Well, I dragged them along, kicking and screaming, which made it sound like more fun than it actually was.

While the Doctor had been (and contractually still is) 'scientific advisor' to UNIT during the Third Doctor period, science has played little role in UNIT since. In the Tenth Doctor episode 'Planet of the Dead' (2009), Malcolm Taylor (Lee Evans) was introduced as a scientific advisor but was the stereotypical absent-minded professor. However, Taylor also represented the problems inherent in combining science and military, as he argued with Captain Erisa Magambo (Noma Dumezweni), first introduced in 'Turn Left' (2008),[8] about closing the wormhole before the Doctor can escape. At times in the series, military needs conflict with scientific inquiry ('shoot first, ask questions later'), but in this episode the tension lies between the idea of defence of the whole and the safety of the individual:

TAYLOR: Transmit that, and the wormhole should close.

MAGAMBO: Then do it.

TAYLOR: Well, after the Doctor's come through, obviously.

MAGAMBO: I'm sorry. Believe me. That wormhole constitutes a major threat, and I have a duty to every man, woman and child on this planet. It's got to be closed immediately. That's an order.

TAYLOR: No, no, no, no. No, we can't just abandon him. He's the Doctor. How many times has he saved our lives? I won't let you, ma'am. I simply won't.

MAGAMBO: Right now, soldier.

Ultimately, Taylor's role as a UNIT soldier, albeit not in uniform, has established him as one who must follow orders. His decision is fortunately deferred as the Doctor is able to escape the wormhole moments later, after which Taylor gleefully follows orders: 'Yes, sir. My pleasure, sir.' When the UNIT troops are able to take down a stingray, Captain Magambo observes, 'I don't believe it: guns that work.'

But the introduction of Kate Stewart is something different and complements the Eleventh Doctor's personality and relationship with UNIT. Where the Tenth Doctor is tense and dismissive of UNIT, the Eleventh is more happy-go-lucky, reminiscent in a way of the Second Doctor. UNIT HQ, still beneath the Tower of London, is more a scientific base than a military one. Personnel in civilian clothes, not military uniforms, staff the base. The Doctor appears genuinely pleased to see Stewart in charge and appreciates the humour of her comments to Amy as they enter the base: 'I've got officers trained in beheading. Also ravens of death.' At the end of the episode, Kate Stewart gives a kiss on the cheek to the Doctor ('My! A kiss from a Lethbridge-Stewart. That is new') and the Doctor, in contrast to every Doctor before, salutes her. In 2013's 'The Day of the Doctor' the Eleventh Doctor revels in his role as scientific advisor, telling Clara that 'I work for them ... This is my job,' and later orders Osgood (Ingrid Oliver): 'Now, I want this stone dust analysed. And I want a report in triplicate, with lots of graphs and diagrams and complicated sums on my desk, tomorrow morning, ASAP, pronto, LOL. See? Job.' However, the scientific side of new UNIT also possesses a collection of artefacts known as the Black Archive ('the dark little storage facility for forbidden alien tech', as Zygon Bonnie later describes it in 'The Zygon Inversion') with the 'highest security rating on the planet'. It is TARDIS-proof and Doctor proof – because the Doctor would not approve; even the staff have their memories erased after each shift. Inside the Black Archive, UNIT has gathered alien technology including a Dalek gun, a Cyberman head, a Mir helmet, a Sontaran blaster, a space-time telegraph and a vortex manipulator. Like the warehouse in *Raiders of the Lost Ark* (1981), the Black Archive contains crate upon crate, labelled in this case with the UNIT seal. The Black Archive contains alien technology so powerful that UNIT has established security protocols reminiscent of the Osterhagen Project, including a nuclear warhead 20 feet below the archive itself. The Doctors' (War Doctor, Tenth and Eleventh) facial expressions on hearing Clara mention the Black Archive clearly show his disdain. As with the Osterhagen Project, the parallels with the Moment are clear. The Doctor recognises the political ramifications of 'alien technology plus human stupidity' or, writ larger, plain political stupidity engendered by militarism – it all comes down to pushing the 'big red button'.

The Black Archive parallels the Omega Arsenal of the Time Lords on Gallifrey, 'where all the forbidden weapons are locked away'. At the end of the Time War only the Moment is left. The War Doctor first asks, 'How do you work? Why is there never a big red button?' and later, the Moment obliges by manifesting the interface as one ('You wanted a big red button'). The idea is not new for the series. As John and Michelle Cordone point out,

> the idea of someone or some group having to make a decision with such drastic consequences mirrors the mentality of the Cold War, which was at its apex at the time [of the show's creation] [...] an era of tit for tat politics and mutual assured destruction. Cold and calculated decision were continuously made that would affect all of humanity.[9]

The Cordones point to a casual conversation in 1988's 'Remembrance of the Daleks' about a world without sugar, which would likely negate the need for a significant percentage of historical slave labour and the Doctor's decision in 1975's 'Genesis of the Daleks' to destroy the Daleks before they are even created. It is a moral and ethical question; it is also a political question. In 'The Day of the Doctor', the Doctor stops Kate from initiating the nuclear protocol and a peace treaty is arranged. The experience allows the Doctor(s) to revisit the Moment on Gallifrey and rewrite history and his own timeline. He discovers a way to save Gallifrey and no longer presses the button. The episode reveals that all along the Doctor has been plagued by the guilt of making that decision.

The politics of UNIT and the Twelfth Doctor

Cartmel notes that the 1970s 'was the era of international organiza-tions, preferably accompanied by a snappy acronym. NATO, UNICEF, the World Health Organization (WHO), and the UN in all its myriad forms, loomed large in the post-war mind.'[10] In the Capaldi era, UNIT continues to occupy this role. In 'Death in Heaven', the Doctor is brought on board *Boat One*, UNIT's aeroplane for the President of Earth, which in itself speaks to the constantly increasing scope of

UNIT. However, by the 2010s, UNIT had become not so much part of a military-industrial complex, but instead a military-alien complex, with the Black Archive and the connection to Torchwood. There is a direct link between the scientific sector and the military – as the Doctor warns in 'The Day of the Doctor' when Kate Stewart is prepared to detonate the nuclear warhead underneath the Black Archive: 'Science leads, Kate. Is that what you meant? Is that what your father meant?'

The Twelfth Doctor, then, inherits a UNIT that remains militarised (the uniforms and equipment of UNIT troops are consistent with the recent appearances), rife with protocols but still led by the scientific side. The Twelfth Doctor's view of the military is established as tense, but he did in fact respect the Brigadier and would have saluted him. As noted in the previous chapter, in the Zygon two-parter the Doctor has created the Osgood boxes in the wake of the events in 'The Day of the Doctor' as a way of ensuring that the ceasefire treaty between the Zygons and humans remains intact; significant here, however, is that opening the human box would supposedly either release gas that will kill all the Zygons, as the enemy within, or would detonate the nuclear warhead under the Black Archive, mentioned above, killing everyone in London. The Zygon box, meanwhile, would either identify all Zygons or ensure that they remain in human form. The Osgood Box, though empty, becomes another part of the military-alien complex and recalls the moral, ethical and ultimately political problems of The Moment, and after the Doctor has made an impassioned speech that the choice is not a game he rearms the box – and the military-alien complex – by erasing Kate's memory.

UNIT returns at the end of the 2016 Christmas special, 'The Return of Doctor Mysterio', to mop up the alien threat with SWAT-like combat troops, as seen in earlier series. Their appearance is somewhat remark-able for the fact that the episode is set in New York City, reinforcing UNIT's international influence.[11] The Doctor's strong connection to UNIT is indicated by his passing remark that UNIT appears on the scene quickly, 'almost as if they've been tipped off'. Although UNIT does not appear in Capaldi's final series and is only briefly alluded to in 'The Pyramid at the End of the World', the reveal that one of the UNIT soldiers has been swapped by the Shoal of Winter Harmony portends a later return of UNIT, but a UNIT that has been compromised, this time for real (as opposed to the earlier instance in 'The Android Invasion').

The mind-swapping now turns on end the familiar appropriation of alien technology by UNIT; instead, the alien is appropriating UNIT.

Conclusion: a great big threatening button which should never, ever, ever, be pressed

Whether Twelfth Doctor executive producer Steven Moffat consciously followed through with the continuity from Russell T Davies's 'great big threatening button' from 'The Christmas Invasion' and the mutually assured destruction of the Osterhagen project, or if he was just employing a more common trope, it could be argued that 'the big red button' is yet another story arc in the Moffat era, connecting the earlier manifestations to the Black Archive, Osgood box and ultimately the Moment. With the first two instances, there exists a direct connection to UNIT and its ever-increasing militarisation over the years. Interestingly, the change to Kate Stewart as a scientific leader of UNIT from the militaristic leadership of the Brigadier and his replacements from the ranks provides UNIT with seemingly much more political power as it becomes the custodian of technology that it can only lock away. The political ramifications of this are clear, with talk of nuclear weapons and the fear of nuclear codes falling into the wrong hands being a very real and present danger. Examining the depiction of UNIT from a historical perspective reveals how *Doctor Who* not only satirises but also reflects the political choices faced today. How one defines 'political' and which elements of the text are analysed, such as the changing depiction of UNIT, may reveal ways in which *Doctor Who* does and continues to promote ideological and political work.

Notes

1   This chapter limits itself to the television programme. UNIT and the Brigadier appear numerous times in comic adventures, books and audio dramas. *Recall UNIT: The Great T-Bag Mystery*, a play written by and starring *Doctor Who* actor Richard Franklin, was performed in 1984.
2   The website 'UNIT Uniforms' (http://unituniforms.blogspot.com) provides a visual history of the different uniforms worn by UNIT from 1968 to 'The Zygon Inversion'.

3 Maura Grady and Cassie Hemstrom argue that 'nostalgia for empire has been foundational to *Doctor Who*'. Grady and Hemstrom situate *Doctor Who* in a post-colonial context, defined by 'rising tensions about declining British power and the overt retreat of empire' (p. 125). In the case of UNIT, the tropes of the British cup of tea and stiff upper lip hark back to a bygone era. See Maura Grady and Cassie Hemstrom, 'Nostalgia for empire, 1963–1974', in Gillian I. Leitch (ed.), *Doctor Who in Time and Space: Essays on Themes, Characters, History and Fandom, 1963–2012* (Jefferson, NC, 2013), pp. 125–41.

4 Andrew Cartmel, *Through Time: An Unauthorised and Unofficial History of Doctor Who* (New York, 2005), p. 95.

5 This phrase has become so closely identified with the Brigadier that Nicholas Courtney titled his autobiography *Five Rounds Rapid!* The phrase returns to *Doctor Who* when the Brigadier's daughter, Kate Stewart, utters it after shooting Norlander, the Zygon who took the form of the sheriff in Truth or Consequences in 'The Zygon Inversion'.

6 David Layton, *The Humanism of Doctor Who: A Critical Study in Science Fiction and Philosophy* (Jefferson, NC, 2012), p. 276.

7 Ibid.

8 The UNIT of the parallel world of 'Turn Left' appears no different from that of the regular world, unlike the mirror universe of 'Inferno', despite the changes in London caused by the Doctor's absence.

9 John Cordone and Michelle Cordone, 'Who is the Doctor? The meta-narrative of *Doctor Who*', in Christopher J. Hansen (ed.), *Ruminations, Peregrinations, and Regenerations: A Critical Approach to Doctor Who* (Newcastle upon Tyne, 2010), p. 9.

10 Cartmel, *Through Time*, p. 93.

11 The American/United States arm of UNIT was last seen in 'The Stolen Earth' (2008).

6

HEAVEN SENT?

The Afterlife, Immortality and Controversy in the Steven Moffat/Peter Capaldi Era

Andrew Crome

The presence of the afterlife, in a variety of different forms, has been one of the more surprising aspects of the Moffat/ Capaldi era of *Doctor Who*. From series eight's focus on the computerised post-death world of the Nethersphere to the titles of series nine's final episodes ('Heaven Sent'/'Hell Bent'), potential afterlives have rippled through Capaldi's tenure as the Doctor. While *Doctor Who* has always raised questions about the nature of death and the possibility of post-mortem survival, this focus on the afterlife has recently proven a source of controversy. This chapter examines questions of the afterlife and death in the Capaldi era as one way of exploring the intersection between Christianity and the media in twenty-first-century British television. In dealing with these themes, *Doctor Who* is open to multiple readings, raises questions about the positioning of potentially controversial religious issues in the television landscape and highlights the importance of canonical consistency between its narratives.

'Wherever it is people go when they die': the ambiguous afterlife

Television programmes based around death and the afterlife are not a new phenomenon, but the number of dramatic narratives exploring these themes has increased markedly from the turn of the millennium, both in Europe and in the United States.[1] The popularity of these topics is, to some extent, unsurprising. Art and literature have always imaginatively explored life after death, as the continuing influence of Dante's images of hell testifies.[2] These media depictions of life after death can be conservative Christian ones;[3] alternatively, texts may challenge orthodox Christian views or, as we shall see, be open to multiple readings, appealing to a broader audience. Popular culture portrayals of the afterlife might include ideas drawn primarily from Christianity, but these may be combined with concepts from Buddhism and alternative religions. Elements of different media may merge with a variety of more traditional and alternative beliefs to form a personal religious bricolage.[4]

Representations of the afterlife present particular problems for *Doctor Who*. Whereas programmes such as *Supernatural* can establish post-death worlds as part of their diegesis, *Doctor Who* has more than fifty years' worth of pre-existing mythology to contend with. As David Layton has argued, the programme has often celebrated its humanistic roots, and movement away from these can be controversial.[5] To establish an afterlife within *Doctor Who* might imply that the series is disavowing its traditional critique of attempts to transcend death, as well as abandoning a 'humanistic' position. While the consistency of the programme's humanism can be questioned,[6] controversy has arisen at points when it appears to adopt a pro-religious position.

It is important to note that *Doctor Who*'s humanism is more unstable than Layton argues. Claims that the Doctor represents a 'Christ figure', made by both popular and academic commentators, provide evidence for the possibility of religious readings of the programme.[7] While generally inviting humanist interpretations, and occasionally openly criticising religion,[8] in general *Doctor Who* has displayed a degree of ambiguity on religion that allows for both pro- and anti-religious readings. The programme's ambiguity on the subject demonstrates its polysemic nature, allowing viewers to find their own beliefs reflected in the text.[9] Even *Torchwood*, which celebrated its opposition to conserv-ative values (including religious belief), was more ambivalent about the afterlife than it first appeared to be. While the opening scenes of its first episode featured a briefly resurrected man's terrified realisation that there was no afterlife, Jim Clark has argued that the programme later suggests some kind of hellish post-death existence.[10]

The vision of 'heaven' presented in series eight of *Doctor Who* per-fectly illustrates the programme's ambiguous treatment of religion. Although the portrayal of the afterlife was arguably the most explicit attack on religious belief since *Doctor Who*'s return in 2005, this cri-tique was inherently unstable. Firstly, criticism was combined with philosophical arguments that could be used to support belief in an afterlife. Secondly, any concerns about the programme's presentation of heaven were overtaken by larger controversies that touched both on fans' primary concerns and on wider public shibboleths surround-ing discussion of death. This allowed for flexibility in interpretation.

Series eight's portrayal of heaven begins in 'Deep Breath', when the episode's antagonist reveals his aim is 'to find the promised land'. While the Doctor dismisses this idea out of hand, the final scene finds his vanquished foe in a garden, identified by Missy (Michelle Gomez) as 'Paradise. Welcome to heaven.' A similar motif is repeated throughout the series, as the appearances of Missy and 'heaven' come together to constitute an ongoing arc. A dead marine is welcomed 'to heaven' in 'Into the Dalek'; robots seek the 'promised land' in 'Robot of Sherwood'. In 'The Caretaker', Missy's assistant Seb (Chris Addison) informs a deceased police officer that they are now in 'The afterlife. The Promised Land.'

The complete revelation of the nature of this 'heaven' comes in the series's penultimate episode, 'Dark Water'. The afterlife is the 'Nethersphere'; a piece of Time Lord technology that allows minds to be uploaded into a vast database.[11] Missy, a female regeneration of the Master, and a proxy God, has collected these minds in order to download them into corpses converted into Cybermen. The concept of an afterlife is a ruse designed to persuade humans to treat their dead with reverence and provide a stock of corpses and minds for the Cybermen. In an offhand comment in the following episode, the Doctor reveals that Missy seeded the concept of heaven in human consciousness in the distant past in order to fulfil her plan. Missy, as befits her character, delights in the fact that she has deceived humanity: 'The Nethersphere. You know, it's ever so funny, the people that live inside that think they've gone to heaven.'

This appeared to be a clear-cut criticism of religious belief, consistent with Layton's emphasis on the humanist nature of the programme. The 3W Institute, the company controlling the Nethersphere, were based in St Paul's Cathedral, perhaps symbolically demonstrating that science had superseded religion.[12] This concept of heaven as a tool of social control is a science-fiction intensification of the Marxist critique of religion. Here, even the souls of those who think they have reached heaven become capital, stored for the later benefit of imperialistic and depersonalised overlords. The raising of the dead as Cybermen acts as a parody of the final resurrection, which occurs towards the end of the Book of Revelation.[13] Humanity's apocalyptic rising 'to glory' here destroys individuality and personal distinctions, adopting the critical viewpoint that equates apocalyptic longing with a desire for a totalitarian erasure of difference.[14] Yet at the same time, the show portrays the Nethersphere as 'real': the people contained within maintain their personalities and individual identities. They also appear to preserve, to some extent, their external relationships, although there remains a firm line between the worlds of the living and the dead.[15]

This afterlife is also a place of possible redemption. Throughout series eight, Clara's (Jenna Coleman) love interest, Danny Pink (Samuel Anderson), has flashbacks from his time as a soldier in Iraq. In the Nethersphere he is able to meet and attempt reconciliation with the child that he accidentally killed. In Christian Haunton's examination of the afterlife in cinema, he notes that the presence of opportunities for change in the afterlife represents the major difference between filmic and religious depictions of the concept.[16] Although it is true that Christianity generally teaches that personal transformation needs to occur prior to death, heaven is usually depicted as a place of reconciliation. As Christopher Deacy has pointed out, popular culture representations often fail to highlight this concept of heaven as a place of restored relationship.[17] The Nethersphere, in emphasising the redemptive potential of the afterlife, paradoxically supports an important Christian image of heaven while seeming to deny it. This ambiguity contributes to the polysemic nature of the text, providing supports for both humanistic and more conventional religious read-ings of the episode.[18]

Likewise, the episode also includes philosophical supports for the concept of the afterlife. While Danny Pink is initially sceptical of his post-mortem location, Seb provides support for his new ontological status:

> Imagine babies in wombs could talk to other babies in other wombs. What would they say? What would they think life was like if they could talk among themselves? [...] They'd think that life was nine months long. Then, boom, trapdoor opens, out you fall, gone for ever. Never hear from those guys again. Nothing at the end of the cord [...] This isn't really an afterlife. It's just more life than you were expecting.

In this way, the series arc was able both to provide a critique of the afterlife and to offer possible support for those who believed. The programme's religious critique was softened by philosophical sup-ports for faith.

It is interesting to compare this presentation of the afterlife with its portrayal in *Doctor Who*'s 2016 spin-off *Class*, which develops a number of key narrative points built upon the concept. The first series's story arc focuses upon the question of whether the 'Cabinet of Souls', a device that houses the Rhodian afterlife, will be weaponised to destroy the race that has massacred all but one of that species. The Doctor's presence in the first episode sees a reiteration of the parent series's position on the afterlife; for the Time Lord, the Cabinet is 'just bedtime stories for children to make death less scary'. Yet in reality, the Cabinet contains both the souls of deceased Rhodians and the potential to weaponise them. *Class* repeatedly emphasises the power of souls and the possibility of an afterlife as both a positive and neg-ative force. The penultimate episode in the series, 'The Metaphysical Engine' introduces the idea that all possible afterlives exist if there is sufficient belief in them: 'Everything in the universe is conserved. Everything, even belief. Get millions of creatures believing something strongly enough for long enough, and even space responds.'

Class's position on the afterlife reflects the greater willingness to take belief and the existence of supernatural worlds seriously that

Laura Feldt has recently argued is a staple of contemporary young adult fantasy.[19] This is perhaps unsurprising given *Class* showrunner Patrick Ness's background in this genre, but demonstrates a major divergence from the denial of the afterlife in *Doctor Who* and the hellish darkness imagined in *Torchwood*. While it may matter little to an individual viewer's enjoyment of either *Doctor Who* or *Class* whether the two series share a position on the possibility of the afterlife, their divergence provides further evidence of the difficulty of maintaining a consistent mythology within larger narrative universes across a franchise.

'If you've had a recent loss ... this will be disturbing': death, public-service broadcasting and the sacred

As well as offering an ambiguous critique of the afterlife, series eight's presentation of heaven was also subsumed by other areas of controversy, such as the gendering of Time Lords. The choice of a female Master provided canonical confirmation that Time Lords could change gender at regeneration.[20] Much of the controversy surrounding the episodes within *Doctor Who* fandom focused upon the significance of Missy as a female Master, particularly as it reopened the possibility of casting a female Doctor.[21] That the episode dealt with one of the longest-running controversies in *Doctor Who* fandom acted as a way of drawing fan focus away from the depiction of the afterlife. Where individual fans may have been concerned about the religious implications of the story arc, fan and mainstream press debate could focus instead on the importance of Missy's appearance for the future of the programme.

General viewers also focused on another concern. The popular Christian view of heaven has seen it as a place of disembodied existence. The soul separates from the body, which perishes at death and fades away.[22] Theologically this can be problematic, as several parts of the Bible discuss a resurrection of the body prior to the final judgement, and the creation of a new heaven and new earth that suggests embodied experience.[23] Where 'Dark Water' caused controversy was in its suggestion that a connection between the body and mind/soul continued after death. As Seb told Danny, 'you're still connected to your old body in the old world. You're still going to feel what it feels.' This had serious implications for the treatment of the dead. Disembodied voices pleaded with the living not to cremate them, while those who had left their bodies to science were heard screaming in agony as they were dissected.

'Dark Water' generated more complaints than any other episode since *Doctor Who*'s revival in 2005.[24] Media reports of the complaints were interesting for the way in which they perceived objections to the content. The *Daily Mail*, for example, suggested in its article header that viewers were upset 'about *Doctor Who* – a children's show – dealing with [the] afterlife'.[25] This suggested a general religious objection that the show had strayed into territory that was not only off-limits for popular television, but also particularly unsuitable for children. Other publications focused on the implied criticism of cremation as the reason for the offence, especially the possibility that the programme might offend the recently bereaved and those who were terminally ill.[26]

Given the BBC's view of *Doctor Who* as a key 'reputational asset', it is unsurprising that they were quick to respond to complaints.[27] Their official response used two strategies. First, they emphasised their commitment to warning viewers of potentially upsetting material. Ofcom requires that 'clear information about content that may distress some children should be given, if appropriate, to the audience' on pre-watershed programmes.[28] While there was no warning prior to 'Dark Water', the BBC's response insisted that a notice of the disturbing content had nonetheless been broadcast: 'The scene in which a character reveals 3W's unconventional theory about the afterlife was preceded by the same character warning the Doctor and Clara several times that what they were about to hear could be distressing.'[29] This claim, which transforms a diegetic warning to characters into a public-service warning to viewers, provides an example of the way in which a broadcaster's attempted defence of material can detract from the effectiveness of artistic decisions. In the episode, Dr Chang (Andrew Leung) plays the Doctor and Clara a recording of a voice begging not to be cremated. He repeatedly warns them that 'If you've had a recent loss, this might be ... this *will be* disturbing' and that 'If you'd rather not hear these words, there's still time.' Diegetically these warnings make sense – Clara *has* just experienced the loss of Danny Pink. Yet acting paratextually, the BBC's statement transforms Dr Chang's warning to Clara and the Doctor into a fourth-wall-breaking caution to viewers, creating a distancing effect from the narrative.

The BBC's second strategy was to claim subtly that the complainants had misread the episode:

> When the Doctor does hear these claims, he immediately pours scorn on them, dismissing them out of hand as a 'con' and a 'racket'. It transpires that he is correct, and the entire concept is revealed to be a scam perpetrated by Missy.[30]

However, this is not what the episode suggests. While the afterlife itself may be 'a con', the dead really do remain conscious. Danny Pink continues to feel the cold of the freezer where his body is stored, while there is nothing to suggest that the screaming of dissection victims or the pain of the cremated is not genuine. The dead may be experiencing these things through a computer simulation, but the feelings nonetheless appear real to them. As Matt Hills has noted, post-transmission broadcaster-produced paratexts can serve to maintain an 'on brand' message.[31] They can also operate as a means of disciplining the viewer, reiterating what producers or broadcasters see as the 'correct' reading of the programme.[32] In this case, the broadcaster's response was to inform upset viewers that they had misread the text, a position that both attempted to overwrite complaints and potentially undermined artistic decisions taken by the production team.

The anger over the treatment of bodies (and the BBC's response) suggests that death and the treatment of the dead continue to be viewed as a category of the 'sacred'. Although the term is often used as a synonym for 'religion', the 'sacred' need not refer to a distinctly religious category. Following Gordon Lynch, it can instead denote 'what people collectively experience as absolute, non-contingent realities which present normative claims over the meaning and conduct of social life'.[33] The sacred is therefore not a singular category. Societies can hold a number of different sacred forms concurrently that exist in hierarchical relationships to one another.[34] The 'Dark Water' controversy touched on two of these: first, the idea that children should be protected from disturbing content about death, and second, that society should not risk offending the recently bereaved, or disrespect the recently deceased, through questioning the morality of cremation.

The reaction to 'Dark Water' therefore reveals something important about the hierarchy of the sacred in contemporary British life. As Lynch notes, breaches of the sacred require some form of response and restitution in order to return to the status quo: in this case via the BBC's official statement.[35] However, a breach of the sacred can also vividly reveal the hierarchy of values operating at any given moment within society. That concerns over the treatment of the dead and protection of children took precedence over portrayals of the afterlife suggests, on the one hand, the declining importance of religion, as these areas of the 'secular sacred' assumed precedence over the presentation of heaven.[36] On the other hand, they also demonstrate a continued concern with areas of life traditionally addressed by religion: comfort in death, and responsibility for protecting the child. That many see the BBC as having a duty to perform these roles is not necessarily surprising given its place within wider British culture and its public-service commitment. Indeed, as viewers fund the BBC through the licence fee, any breach of this commitment may generate particular discontent for those who feel some degree of indirect complicity in the broadcaster's actions.[37]

Nonetheless, viewer responses to 'Dark Water' demonstrate the way in which media can begin to take on roles previously associated with organised religion in terms of protecting children and providing comfort in the face of death. It is possible to interpret media adopting these functions as a symptom of what Stig Hjavard has described as the 'mediatisation of religion'.[38] Yet this is not a simple case of the broadcaster performing religious roles. The controversy over 'Dark Water' emerged during discussions leading up to the renewal of the BBC Charter in 2016: a political context in which questions of the role of the public-service broadcaster and the role of high-budget popular drama within the BBC's remit led to an atmosphere of heightened scrutiny around its output.[39] The controversy therefore erupted at a point at which discussions of the BBC's societal position were part of a broader political debate. It is therefore important that any apparent 'mediatisation' of religion be read within its wider political and media context, rather than as an example of broadcasters straightforwardly 'replacing' religion.

'She died, Doctor': death and the sacred in series nine

Just as societies and individuals have their own categories of the sacred, so too do popular narratives. Large narrative worlds are based on ideas of internal consistency and the maintenance of certain moral norms.[40] As in the real world, breaches of these categories can constitute a profanation of the sacred. The acceptance of death, along with the dangers of prolonging life beyond its natural boundaries, acts as one of these shibboleths in the *Doctor Who* universe. As Courtland Lewis has noted, the programme has shown 'an acute awareness of the dangers of living forever'.[41] The horror of the Master's (Peter Pratt) form after he exceeds his regeneration limit in 'The Deadly Assassin' (1976), the desperation of the immortal Mawdryn's (David Collings) quest for death in 1983's 'Mawdryn Undead' and Borusa's (Philip Latham) fate to be forever frozen in stone after seeking immortality in 1983's 'The Five Doctors': all emphasise the danger of seeking to escape death. The theme continued in the revived series – Professor Lazarus's (Mark Gatiss) attempts to live indefinitely are the work of 'a vain old man who thought he could defy nature' (2007), while the Doctor's plan to rewrite history by saving Captain Adelaide Brooke (Lindsay Duncan) in 'The Waters of Mars' (2009) is frustrated when she commits suicide in order to preserve the 'correct' historical record. Similarly, Captain Jack Harkness's (John Barrowman) immortality is portrayed as being both unnatural and a curse – a theme that is explored in more depth in *Torchwood*. As Sarah-Jane Smith (Elisabeth Sladen) concludes in 2006's 'School Reunion': 'Pain and loss, they define us as much as happiness or love. Whether it's a world, or a relationship, everything has its time. And everything ends.'

For all its controversy, series eight's finale emphasised the importance of accepting death as a natural part of life. Danny accepts his death in rejecting the chance to rejoin Clara when offered the chance, instead sending the boy that he had shot back to the world of the living. In doing so, he completes his redemptive arc and confirms his heroic characterisation. In the 2014 Christmas special 'Last Christmas', Clara continues to struggle with Danny's death. Under the influence of carnivorous 'Dream Crabs' she inhabits a fantasy world in which Danny has survived and their relationship has continued. Although this fantasy is comforting, it is also deadly. Clara can only survive if she accepts Danny's death and moves on. Death, as the dream world Danny reminds her, is natural.

Series nine's approach to death and the afterlife initially appeared to follow this pattern. For example, the Daleks are revealed to be functionally immortal, a horrific fate as 'they still age, poor loves. Over time, the body breaks down, rots, liquefies.' The main examination of immortality in the series comes through the character of Ashildr (Maisie Williams), introduced in 'The Girl Who Died', a young Viking girl whom the Doctor brings back to life through alien technology. Although Clara initially views this as an act of mercy, the Doctor immediately doubts the wisdom of his action. Immortality is 'everybody else dying [...] Just possibly, I have made a terrible mistake. Maybe even a tidal wave.' The following episode, set in seventeenth-century England, provides evidence that the Doctor's fears are justified. Ashildr's unending life is filled with heartbreak as she watches her lovers and children age and die while she continues to live. She disavows meaningful relationships due to their impermanence; her self-reliance and isolation are demonstrated in renaming herself simply 'Me'. Again, the Doctor reaffirms the importance of death for meaningful life: 'People like us, we go on too long. We forget what matters ... We need the mayflies. See, the mayflies, they know more than we do. They know how beautiful and precious life is because it's fleeting.'

Doctor Who's standard position on death and immortality initially seemed to be reinforced by the lead-in to the series finale, 'Face the Raven'. Ashildr's ruthlessness and ambivalence towards the Doctor is demonstrated when she places human lives at risk in order to deliver him to forces seeking his capture. Her plan backfires after the Quantum Shade she has placed on Rigsy (Joivan Wade) is transferred to Clara, guaranteeing her death. The Shade, a 'kind of spirit' that requires a soul for satisfaction, acts as a metonym for death itself. It is inescapable in the end: 'You can pass it on, but you can't cheat it.' The Doctor's uncharacteristic threat to punish Ashildr ('I will rain hell on you for the rest of time') demonstrates his attachment to Clara, but also provides her with the opportunity to reinforce the programme's affirmation of the necessity of death. Her final act is to 'Die right. Die like I mean it', an action that is both an assertion of personal responsibility and a brave acceptance of the inevitability of her fate.

The Doctor's refusal to accept Clara's death is initially unsurprising. His close attachment to his companions and propensity to either transgress the self-imposed limits on his behaviour (e.g. 'The Waters of Mars', 2009) or withdraw from the world (e.g. 'The Snowmen', 2012) without them is well established in the post-2005 series. The Doctor's response in 'Heaven Sent' and 'Hell Bent', however, goes beyond previous reactions to loss. Clara's death drives his reaction. Placed in a personal prison of his worst fears which (in another reference to the afterlife) the Doctor suggests might be hell, she serves as his inspiration to escape through enduring billions of years of painful death and resurrection.[42] Her loss drives his decision to cheat death by removing a 'time-locked' Clara from her time stream the moment before she dies. This is a dangerous choice, with the Doctor told that he has 'broken every code [he] ever lived by' and that his actions threaten to splinter time itself. At several points in the narrative, the show reinforces its standard position on death. Both Clara and Ashildr challenge the Doctor's right to deny them a dignified death, and the Doctor accepts that having his memory wiped of Clara is a 'necessary' punishment.

All of this is undermined by the episode's conclusion. Clara will return to Gallifrey to die, but will take 'the long way round', travelling with Ashildr in a stolen TARDIS until she has exhausted the possibilities of life. This not only undermines the series's general position on immortality, but also confuses the central narrative theme of series nine, in which the danger of Clara becoming too like the Doctor is repeatedly emphasised. In her final scenes, Clara literally becomes a second Doctor – fleeing Gallifrey to travel the universe in a stolen TARDIS.

This compromise, which prolongs Clara's life, suggests that the programme struggled to steer a middle course between the desire for a happy ending and the maintenance of the wider mythos's commitment to condemning immortality. The Doctor's hubris results in the removal of his memory of Clara (a symbolic death), while her failure to return to Gallifrey to die avoids repeating the downbeat conclusion of series eight. 'Dark Water' had drawn criticism for failing to protect young viewers from disturbing material on death. 'Heaven Sent' avoids this in its coda, but in the process undermines the consistency of the programme's own position on immortality.

This can be partially understood by the nature of *Doctor Who*'s position in the market. The programme's coding as 'family television' presumes that it will contain material that will be broadly suitable for the child audience.[43] This requires a certain minimisation of themes that might be deemed distressing for the child viewer, such as death, violence and sexual content. While *Doctor Who* is marketed for a family audience in the UK, in the United States and other territories it is generally sold as genre television. The attempt to balance these two positions is apparent in official interviews with the production team. While Moffat told *Variety* that he saw *Doctor Who* 'as a children's show', at the same time he reinforced *Doctor Who*'s genre credentials in giving the interview at an Italian comic convention.[44] Appearances of producers and stars at events such as ComicCon further reinforce the show's status as genre television. Up until 2011, *Torchwood* operated intertextually as a way of dealing with issues considered either too 'mature' or 'dark' to appear in its parent programme,[45] a position that was appropriated by *Class*.[46] With *Torchwood*'s continued hiatus, and international marketing of *Doctor Who* as a high-concept science fiction series, 'darker' themes surrounding death increasingly came to the fore during the Capaldi era. Clara's survival allowed for the show to meet its remit of producing material suitable for the child audience, while her death in 'Face the Raven' simultaneously permitted producers to emphasise their use of darker themes. The danger with this approach is that it risks undermining the overall cohesiveness of the textual universe – in other words, profaning the sacred categories of the programme's structuring mythology. This is not the same thing as the intra-franchise inconsistency between *Class* and *Doctor Who* discussed above. Rather, it is the undermining of a central position which risks introducing a potentially destabilising inconsistency into the world of the programme. Should this modification result in a severe breach of the programme's own sacred categories, fan rejection may result.[47] In such cases, official paratexts can then renarrate the established position of the franchise to emphasise producer consistency. Like the BBC statements on 'Dark Water', they serve as official attempts to heal a breach in the sacred. For example, *Doctor Who Magazine* warned of catastrophic consequences for the universe should Clara not return to Gallifrey to die, while emphasising the programme's 'remarkable consistency' on the topic.[48] The approach in this chapter has therefore differed from that of Richard Hewett, who argued that Capaldi's older age was appropriate for dealing with the theme of immortality.

Afterword

Examining the presentation of death and the afterlife in the programme allows us to see how potential controversy can be avoided both by story decisions (in the ambiguous presentation of the afterlife) and by post-broadcast paratexts. These responses demonstrate something of the 'sacred' in contemporary British society, as discussions of the fate of the dead are deemed inappropriate for a 'family' television programme. However, as series nine's reluctance to accept Clara's death shows, attempts to provide happy endings can risk undermining the programme's own 'sacred' categories. In the end, the confused representations of death and the afterlife in *Doctor Who* and its spin-offs reflects the confusion and uncertainty about these concepts in contemporary societies. Fear of death and attempts to prolong life compete with worries about the potential horrors of living too long; doubts about an afterlife mingle with vague hopes of a future place of reward, rebirth or chance to atone for failure. In this respect, while *Doctor Who*'s representation of death and the afterlife may be inconsistent, it nonetheless reflects the confused state of modern Western speculation on the hereafter.

Notes

1   There have been many examples of afterlife-based television produced in Europe. There was the French drama *Les Revenants* (Canal, 2012–present), while UK programmes like *Sea of Souls* (BBC/Carnival Films, 2004–7), *Afterlife* (Clerkenwell Films, 2005–6) and *Apparitions* (BBC, 2008) deal with the paranormal and the BBC's *In the Flesh* (2013–14) explored the tensions caused by 'recovering' zombies in a Lancashire village. Prior to the turn of the millennium there was also the series *Springhill* (Granada, 1996–7). British programmes dealing explicitly with religion included *The Second Coming* (ITV, 2003). US programmes such as *Dead Like Me* (Showtime, 2003–4), which featured the recently deceased re-employed as grim reapers, or *Pushing Daisies* (ABC, 2007–9), which focused on the central character's ability to restore the dead to

life, joined *Six Feet Under* (HBO, 2001–5), where the living and the dead mingled in and around a funeral parlour. Since 2010, an explosion of post-death content has been produced in the United States. This ranges from series with significant portions set in heaven (e.g. *Dominion* [Syfy, 2014–15]) or hell (e.g. *Constantine* [NBC, 2014–15], *Lucifer* [Fox, 2015–present]), to those which focused on the return of the dead, either as zombies (e.g. *iZombie* [CW, 2015–present], *The Walking Dead* [AMC, 2010–present]) or as part of mysterious mass revivals (e.g. *The Returned* [A&E 2015], a remake of *Les Revenants*). The most popular and long-lasting of these shows has been *Supernatural* (WB/CW, 2005–present), which has featured repeated visits to heaven and hell in the course of its decade-long run.

2   See Nick Havely (ed.), *Dante's Modern Afterlife: Reception and Response from Blake to Heaney* (Basingstoke, 1998).

3   James Y. Trammell, 'Watching movies in the name of the Lord: thoughts on analyzing Christian film criticism', *Journal of Media and Religion* xi/3 (2012), pp. 113–26.

4   Greg Garrett, *Entertaining Judgment: The Afterlife in Popular Imagination* (New York, 2015), pp. 1–7; Lynn Schofield Clark, *From Angels to Aliens: Teenagers, the Media, and the Supernatural* (New York, 2003).

5   David Layton, *The Humanism of Doctor Who: A Critical Study in Science Fiction and Philosophy* (Jefferson, NC, 2012).

6   See for example Francis Bridger, 'Book review: *The Humanism of Doctor Who: A Critical Study in Science Fiction and Philosophy*, by David Layton', *Implicit Religion* xviii/4 (2015), pp. 579–81.

7   For examples from popular commentary see, for example, small group Bible studies based on *Doctor Who* in Matt Rawle, *The Salvation of Doctor Who: A Small Group Study Connecting Christ and Culture* (Nashville, TN, 2015), or the comments of clergy quoted in Jonathan Wynne-Jones, 'The church is ailing – send for *Dr Who*', *Daily Telegraph* (4 May 2008). Available at http://www.telegraph.co.uk/news/newstopics/howaboutthat/1925338/The-church-is-ailing-send-for-Dr-Who.html (accessed 22 February 2017). For more academic commentary, see for example Dee Amy-Chin, 'Davies, Dawkins, and deus ex TARDIS: who finds God in the Doctor?', in Christopher J. Hansen (ed.), *Ruminations, Peregrinations, and Regenerations: A Critical Approach to Doctor Who* (Newcastle upon Tyne, 2010), pp. 22–34; Ruth Deller, 'What the world needs ... is a Doctor', in Courtland Lewis and Paula Smithka (eds), *Doctor Who and Philosophy: Bigger on the Inside* (Chicago, IL, 2010), pp. 239–49.

8   Examples of direct criticism of religion can be seen, for example, in 'The Face of Evil' (1977) and 'The God Complex' (2011). Religious controversy has also surrounded allegedly Christic portrayals of the Doctor. See, for example, Adam Sherwin, 'Christians protest as Doctor Who is portrayed

as "messiah"', *The Times* (21 December 2007). Available at http://www. thetimes.co.uk/tto/arts/tv-radio/article2441741.ece (accessed 23 February 2017).

9 Line Nybro Petersen, 'Renegotiating religious imaginations through transformations of "banal religion" in *Supernatural*', *Transformative Works and Cultures* 4 (2010). Available at http://journal.transformativeworks. org/index.php/twc/article/view/142/145 (accessed 28 February 2017).

10 Jim Clark, '"The resurrection days are over": resurrection from *Doctor Who* to *Torchwood*', *Journal of Religion and Popular Culture* xxvii/1 (2015), pp. 36–7.

11 In itself an idea drawn from cyberpunk literature. See, for example, Iain M. Banks, *Feersum Endjinn* (London, 1994) and *Surface Detail* (London, 2010); Greg Egan, *Permutation City* (London, 1994); Robert Sawyer, *The Terminal Experiment* (London, 1995). *Doctor Who* employs a similar idea in the virtual world depicted in 'Forest of the Dead' (2008), although not all inhabitants are aware that they are deceased.

12 It is possible to make too much of this point. The primary reason for the use of St Paul's Cathedral is to recall intratextually the iconic scene from 'The Invasion' (1968), mentioned in the Introduction to this collection, in which Cybermen march down the steps of the cathedral.

13 Revelation 20:11–15. This is a general resurrection of all humanity. A first resurrection of 'the righteous' takes place in Revelation 20:5–6.

14 Lee Quinby, *Millennial Seduction: A Skeptic Confronts Apocalyptic Culture* (Ithaca, NY, 1999); Gwendolyn Audrey Foster, *Hoarders, Doomsday Preppers, and the Culture of Apocalypse* (Basingstoke, 2014), pp. 44–59.

15 Kelton Cobb has argued that contemporary afterlife film might suggest that the firm division between the worlds of the living and the dead, established as a result of the Protestant reformation's abolition of purgatory, is being undermined in popular culture. See Kelton Cobb, *The Blackwell Guide to Theology and Popular Culture* (Malden, MA, 2005), p. 289.

16 Christian Haunton, 'Images of God in the movies', in William L. Blizek (ed.), *The Continuum Companion to Religion and Film* (London, 2009), p. 259.

17 Christopher Deacy, *Screening the Afterlife: Theology, Eschatology and Film* (Abingdon, 2012), pp. 102–9.

18 Cornel Sandvoss, *Fans: The Mirror of Consumption* (Cambridge, 2005), pp. 123–52. Sandvoss goes further than polysemy, and posits that the text can become 'neutrosemic' in terms of its openness to interpretation.

19 Laura Feldt, 'Harry Potter and contemporary magic: fantasy literature, popular culture, and the representation of religion', *Journal of Contemporary Religion* xxxi/1 (2016), pp. 101–14.

20 This had already been confirmed in a throwaway comment in 2011's 'The Doctor's Wife'. However, 'Dark Water' was the first time that a significant recurring character had changed gender.

21 See, for example, '"A woman will eventually play Doctor Who": sci-fi show's writer Steven Moffat says a female star will take on the role of the famous timelord', *Daily Mail* (5 December 2014). Available at http://www.dailymail.co.uk/tvshowbiz/article-2862743/A-woman-eventually-play-Doctor-Sci-fi-s-writer-Steven-Moffat-says-female-star-role-famous-timelord.html#ixzz4Seoka6Vr (accessed 12 December 2016).

22 Deacy, *Screening the Afterlife*, pp. 40–3.

23 For example Daniel 12:1–4, 1 Corinthians 15 and Revelation 20.

24 Rob Leane, '*Doctor Who*: Dark Water got the most complaints in 10 years', Den of Geek [website] (13 March 2015). Available at http://www.denofgeek.com/tv/doctor-who/34532/doctor-who-dark-water-got-the-most-complaints-in-10-years (accessed 9 December 2016).

25 Alasdair Glennie and Matt Grimson, 'BBC receives more than 100 complaints about "disturbing" *Doctor Who* episode that features people feeling the pain of being CREMATED', *Daily Mail* (6 November 2014). Available at http://www.dailymail.co.uk/news/article-2823307/Dr-episode-Dark-Water-prompts-complaints-BBC-dark-themes-concerning-afterlife-cremation.html (accessed 9 December 2016).

26 Matilda Battersby, 'BBC defends *Doctor Who* episode "Dark Water" following more than 100 complaints', *Independent* (5 November 2014). Available at http://www.independent.co.uk/arts-entertainment/tv/news/bbc-defends-doctor-who-episode-dark-water-after-complaints-9841379.html (accessed 9 December 2016).

27 Catherine Johnson, 'Doctor Who as programme brand', in Matt Hills (ed.), *New Dimensions of Doctor Who: Adventures in Space, Time and Television* (London, 2013), pp. 107–9.

28 Ofcom, *The Ofcom Broadcasting Code* (2013), p. 9. Available at https://www.ofcom.org.uk/__data/assets/pdf_file/0005/100103/broadcast-code-april-2017.pdf.

29 Battersby, 'BBC defends *Doctor Who* episode "Dark Water"'.

30 Ibid.

31 Matt Hills, *Doctor Who: The Unfolding Event – Marketing, Merchandising and Mediatizing a Brand Anniversary* (Basingstoke, 2015), p. 39.

32 Paul Booth, *Playing Fans: Negotiating Fandom and Media in the Digital Age* (Iowa City, IA, 2015), pp. 94–9.

33 Gordon Lynch, *The Sacred in the Modern World: A Cultural Sociological Approach* (Oxford, 2012), p. 29.

34 Ibid., pp. 54–86.

35 Ibid., pp. 105–8.

36 Kim Knott, Elizabeth Poole and Teemu Taira, *Media Portrayals of Religion and the Secular Sacred: Representation and Change* (Farnham, 2013), pp. 1–13.

37 See the discussion of viewer responses to the BBC's refusal to air a DEC appeal for Gaza in Lynch, *The Sacred in the Modern World*, pp. 107–9.

38 Stig Hjarvard, 'The mediatisation of religion: theorising religion, media and social change', *Culture and Religion* xii/2 (2011), pp. 119–35.

39 Most clearly seen in questions raised about the BBC's dramatic output during the charter review. See Department for Culture, Media and Sport, *BBC Charter Review: Public Consultation* (2015). Available at https://www.gov.uk/government/uploads/system/uploads/attachment_data/file/449830/DCMS_BBC_Consultation_A4__1_.pdf (accessed 23 December 2016).

40 Mark J. P. Wolf, *Building Imaginary Worlds: The Theory and History of Subcreation* (New York and Abingdon, 2012), pp. 43–64.

41 Courtland Lewis, 'Why Time Lords do not live forever', in Andrew Crome and James McGrath (eds), *Time and Relative Dimensions in Faith: Religion and Doctor Who* (London, 2013), p. 1.

42 The Doctor's prison is perhaps better compared to purgatory than to hell, as he will be released when he has completed a predetermined task (see Garrett, *Entertaining Judgment*, pp. 179–84). Whereas in similar purgatorial films employing the time-loop structure the protagonist accepts their task (e.g. *Groundhog Day*, *The Edge of Tomorrow*), here the Doctor refuses to cooperate.

43 Matt Hills, *Triumph of a Time Lord: Regenerating Doctor Who in the Twenty-First Century* (London, 2010), pp. 120–3.

44 Nick Vivarelli, 'Lucca Comics: "Doctor Who" showrunner Steven Moffat on why the reboot is a global hit', *Variety* (31 October 2015). Available at http://variety.com/2015/tv/festivals/doctor-who-steven-moffat-lucca-comics-1201631032/ (accessed 28 February 2017).

45 Clark, '"The resurrection days are over"'.

46 In an interview with *Doctor Who Magazine*, Patrick Ness stated that 'you might be surprised at how dark it gets …' (Benjamin Cook, '*Class* preview', *Doctor Who Magazine* 505 (2016), p. 17). As *Class* director Ed Bazalgette noted, 'we had a licence to shoot things that certainly you couldn't expect for a show that goes out to very much a family audience on a Saturday evening' ('The art of the director', *Doctor Who Magazine* 505 (2016), p. 32).

47 Rebecca Williams, *Post-Object Fandom: Television, Identity and Self-Narrative* (London, 2015), pp. 103–23.

48 Steve Lyons, 'Who wants to live forever?', *Doctor Who Magazine* 499 (2016), p. 17.

7

COMFORT AND JOY?

The Steven Moffat/Peter Capaldi Christmas Specials

David Budgen

n my chapter for the collection of essays *Doctor Who: The Eleventh Hour*, I argued that Steven Moffat's Christmas specials, like Russell T Davies's, existed as stand-alone narratives reflecting the extended audience that tuned in on Christmas Day. Their plot lines functioned outside season-long story arcs appealing to non-regular viewers, with festive themes and guest stars.[1] More recent episodes, however, have diverted from this approach. Instead, Moffat used the Smith and Capaldi-era Christmas specials to deal with the Doctor's grief at the loss of Amy (Karen Gillan) and Rory (Arthur Darvill), to reintroduce the characters of Madame Vastra (Neve McIntosh), Jenny Flint (Catrin Stewart), Strax (Dan Starkey) and Clara (Jenna Coleman), to reintroduce the Troughton-era villain the Great Intelligence, to resolve Clara's trauma after Danny Pink's (Samuel Anderson) death, and to resolve the River Song (Alex Kingston) plot line that had begun in 2008. Indeed, Christmas themes have featured less prominently. This is not to say that the recent Christmas specials entirely forsake tradition. In this chapter, it will be shown that in their engagement with elements of the uncanny, the Twelfth Doctor's festive episodes can still be seen as part of a wider tradition. This adherence to established festive storytelling practices, moreover, can be both unnerving *and* comforting.

In the bleak midwinter: Christmas ghost stories

Tales of the uncanny and the supernatural are strongly associated with the Christmas period. In his attempt to define the uncanny, Nicholas Royle argues: 'The uncanny is ghostly. It is concerned with the strange, weird and mysterious, with a flickering sense (but not conviction) of something supernatural. The uncanny involved feelings of uncertainty, in particular regarding [...] what is being experienced.'[2] Such characteristics could even apply to the season itself. Christmas Day sees once-busy streets deserted. Across the country, families converge in isolated gatherings, their feasting and celebrations juxtaposed with the eerie silence of the world outside. Far removed from the romantic snowbound white Christmases of Hollywood movies, the festive season in Britain is often grey and still, echoing the words of Kazran Sardick (Michael Gambon) in the 2010 *Doctor Who* Christmas special: 'On every world, wherever people are, in the deepest part of winter, at the exact midpoint, everybody stops, and turns, and hugs, as if to say, "Well done. Well done, everyone! We're halfway out of the dark."' Sardick's words embody those aspects of the Christmas period that make the uncanny such an appropriate motif. The brightly coloured Christmas lights contrast with a pervading sense of gloom that envelops the world outside. Of course, one of those lights, a glowing box in the corner of the room, becomes the storyteller around which the family gathers. Frank Collins and Alec Charles both argue that the television set itself, 'that familiar stranger at the heart of one's home', is the 'perfect medium for conveying this state [of the uncanny]'.[3] It is little wonder, then, that this period should so frequently provoke and inspire unsettling and macabre tales.

Catherine Belsey has examined the tradition of winter ghost stories in an early modern context, finding their origins in the pervasiveness of the chilly climate. She writes:

In the long cold evenings, when the soil had been tilled to the extent that climatic conditions permitted, the still predominantly agricultural community of early modern England would sit and while away the hours of darkness with fireside pastimes, among them old wives' tales designed to enthral young and old alike.[4]

For Belsey, the pre-industrial era lent itself to such tales:

The light cast up by our cities makes it easy to forget how very dark the countryside must have been on moonless evenings, and how very long were the winter nights through which travellers were obliged to complete their journeys.[5]

Indeed, Derek Johnston traces the origins of this custom back further, to at least the Middle Ages.[6] The nineteenth century witnessed a reconfiguration of such traditions, partly in response to increasing rates of literacy and the emergence of a new mass readership.[7] Some have seen the publication of Dickens's *A Christmas Carol* in 1843 as the beginning of a trend for festive ghost stories, but as Mark Connelly argues, 'one of the reasons for [Dickens'] success was that he produced an outstanding example of the genre'.[8]

The relationship between the festive season and the supernatural, then, has a rich heritage. In Shakespeare's *Hamlet*, after seeing the ghost of Hamlet's father, Marcellus comments upon the protection offered by the holiness of the night before Christmas:

Some say that ever 'gainst that season comes
Wherein our Saviour's birth is celebrated,
This bird of dawning singeth all night long;
And then, they say, no spirit dare stir abroad,
The nights are wholesome, then no planets strike,
No fairy takes, nor witch hath power to charm,
So hallow'd and so gracious is the time.[9]

Yet for Hamlet the ghost brings knowledge that will lead to madness and death. In Christmas ghost stories, protagonists often seek forbidden knowledge that will bring them either an epiphany or a gruesome demise.[10] This was a recurring theme in the BBC's *A Ghost Story for Christmas* strand, broadcast throughout the 1970s. These were often adaptations of stories by M. R. James, and many of these tales saw protagonists haunted, and even killed, after they pursue hidden treasure and knowledge. As Brian Cowlishaw argues, 'If James' antiquarians would only let sleeping ruins lie, they would remain safe.'[11]

The success of these adaptations led to the appearance of further supernatural tales throughout the Christmas period. Examples included Nigel Kneale's 'The Stone Tape' (BBC, 1972), the later episodes of the anthology series *Dead of Night* (BBC, 1972) and an adaptation of Sheridan Le Fanu's *Schalcken the Painter* (BBC, 1979). In 1987, Danny Huston's *Mister Corbett's Ghost*, a TV movie based upon the children's novel by Leon Garfield, saw an apothecary's apprentice wish his employer dead, only to be haunted by his master's corpse. Semi-regular *Doctor Who* writer Mark Gatiss has attempted to revive the Christmas ghost story on several occasions. Elements of the genre were present in *Crooked House* (BBC, 2008). In 2013 he adapted another James story for the BBC, 'The Tractate Middoth'.

The appearance of the uncanny and associated literary motifs in the Doctor's festive adventures is therefore unsurprising. As John Tulloch and Manuel Alvarado argue, science fiction has a 'tendency [...] towards the unsettling, destabilising qualities of Gothic Fantasy and the uncanny'.[12] From the robotic Pilot Fish in Father Christmas costumes in 'The Christmas Invasion' (2005) to the mysterious Christmas present that appears under the tree in 'The Doctor, the Widow and the Wardrobe' (2011), the writers have unsettled audiences with that sudden sense of the *unheimlich*, or instead that the scene they are watching is strangely familiar. The form this takes is not always sinister. Writing in the *Guardian*, Mark Lawson drew a connection between *Doctor Who* and the Christmas ghost story: 'If Dickens effectively invented the British Christmas', he suggested, 'it is Moffat who has perfected the *Doctor Who* story that honours its top-of-the-tree timeslot by invoking the ghosts of the season: Father Christmas, Frank Capra and Dickens himself.'[13] Nevertheless, throughout the series's history, a sense of disquiet has figured prominently, and such imagery pervades the Twelfth Doctor's adventures.

The Twelfth Doctor and the uncanny

Almost every episode of the Moffat/Capaldi era of *Doctor Who* has been infused with a sense of ominous dread. Peter Capaldi's first episode, 'Deep Breath', sees the Doctor wrestle with a sense of the uncanny almost immediately. His new face reminds him of something long-forgotten but familiar, and yet to be fully revealed. The theme continues throughout the rest of the series. 'Listen' draws upon childhood fears of monsters lurking under the bed. Seemingly borrowing from the plot of David Robert Mitchell's 2014 film *It Follows*, itself a play on James's 'Casting the Runes', 'Mummy on the Orient Express' sees passengers relentlessly stalked by a creature only visible to its victims. In 'Flatline', paintings of missing people mysteriously appear in a railway tunnel. In reality, the paintings *are* the people; creatures from another dimension have absorbed their energy and converted them into living 2D images.

'The Magician's Apprentice' opens with a young Davros stranded in a minefield. These 'mines' take the form of actual hands, with a single eye in the centre of each of their palms. Such imagery evokes memories of Guillermo del Toro's Pale Man in *Pan's Labyrinth* (2006), or the candelabra that guide Belle into the Beast's castle in Jean Cocteau's *La Belle et la Bête* (1946). Detached from human bodies, yet seemingly sentient, the 'handmines' induce a sense of unease in the audience, partly because they resemble the severing of limbs that one might associate with actual landmines. In 'Under the Lake' and 'Before the Flood', the Doctor and Clara are stalked by ghosts on an underwater base in 2119. The Doctor then returns to 1980 and meets some of the living figures whose spectres have been haunting the station. The ninth season also includes the Doctor's interactions with a young Viking girl, Ashildr (Maisie Williams). The Doctor saves her life, but curses her with immortality. Embittered, she reappears in several episodes. Her later appearances in a number of historical photographs are uncanny, and reminiscent of the evidence about the Ninth Doctor (Christopher Eccleston) collected by the conspiracy theorist, Clive (Mark Benton), in 'Rose' (2005).

'The Zygon Invasion' and 'The Zygon Inversion' play with the idea of doubles, as the Zygons transform into human doppelgangers. A persistent theme of the episodes, therefore, is the questioning of identity: Clara, Kate Stewart (Jemma Redgrave) and Osgood (Ingrid Oliver) are all mimicked by the Zygons. Evil doubles are common in uncanny works, from Edgar Allan Poe's short story 'William Wilson' (1839) and Fyodor Dostoyevsky's novel *The Double* (1846), to Basil Dearden's *The Man Who Haunted Himself* (1970) and Krzysztof Kieslowski's *The Double Life of Veronique* (1991). The true moment of horror often comes when the protagonist finally comes face to face with their double, though there are many eerie moments as characters notice subtle differences in the behaviour of those who should be familiar. Moffat would employ similar motifs throughout his Christmas episodes.

'Sleep No More' sees writer Gatiss draw upon one of the most famous discussion points of the uncanny, that related to the eponymous character in E. T. A. Hoffman's short story 'The Sandman', who would steal children's eyes to feed to his own children. The episode utilises a 'found footage' format, bookended with commentaries from Reece Shearsmith's Gagan Rassmussen. The Doctor, Clara and a rescue team are hunted by 'Sandmen' – creatures constructed from sleep dust – on a seemingly abandoned space station. An analysis of Hoffman's story was the main focus of Sigmund Freud's 1919 treatise on the subject of the uncanny. The original tale told of Nathanael, a man haunted by a childhood story of the Sandman. This inspires a psychosis that haunts Nathanael throughout his life. Freud noted that the uncanny was manifested in Hoffmann's story largely through the fear of losing one's eyes, which he connected to the fear of castration.[14] 'Sleep No More' draws upon this fear of being blinded. In the final scene Rassmussen disintegrates before the camera, eyes first. In 'Heaven Sent', the Doctor is endlessly stalked by a cloaked wraith around a Gothic castle. Repeatedly dying in order to enable the creation of a new copy of himself, the Doctor becomes trapped in his own nightmare for billions of years. Like Walter Craig (Mervyn Johns) in Dearden's framing sequence of the classic British portmanteau horror film *Dead of Night* (1945), the Doctor seems doomed to relive the same events again and again.[15] The horrific consequences of being trapped in dreams are fundamental to the first festive special of the Capaldi era, 'Last Christmas'.

Dream-worlds and 'Last Christmas'

'Last Christmas' begins after dark, on a snowy Christmas Eve in London. The timing and setting are important. Charles notes that 'setting was at its most unsettling [...] when it juxtaposed the ordinary with the extraordinary'.[16] Moreover, Elizabeth Bronfen observes that 'The ordinary night is [...] uncanny in the sense that it allows us to conceive this irretrievable point of origin [what Bronfen calls an 'earlier state of uninterrupted night'] precisely through those after-effects, which render the time between dusk and dawn strange, dangerous as well as compelling.'[17] Those qualities that imbue the Christmas period with a sense of the uncanny are present at night; like the Christmas season itself, night is the midpoint between two worlds, a recurring end destined eternally to be followed by a new beginning. In the series eight episode 'Listen', the Doctor comments upon the eerie nature of night-time: 'What's that in the mirror, or the corner of your eye? What's that footstep following, but never passing by? Perhaps they're all just waiting, perhaps when we're all dead ... out they'll come a-slithering, from underneath the bed.' The supernatural figure that appears before Clara, however, is less sinister.

Hearing an unexpected noise, she discovers Father Christmas and two elves on her rooftop. The figure of Father Christmas is often subverted in film and television, juxtaposing traditional understandings of the character's jollity with macabre or sinister reinterpretations. In '... And All Through the House', a story in Freddie Francis's anthology-horror *Tales from the Crypt* (1972), Joan Collins is stalked on Christmas Eve by an escaped killer dressed in a Father Christmas costume. Having just murdered her husband, she cannot call the police without revealing her own crime. The tale ends with her young daughter (Chloe Franks) letting the killer in, believing him to be the real Father Christmas. In *The League of Gentlemen* Christmas special (BBC, 2000), the Rev. Bernice Woodall is haunted by a half-remembered childhood memory of a sinister Father Christmas-figure kidnapping her mother. Such imagery is reminiscent of *Tales from the Crypt* or Charles E. Sellier Jr's *Silent Night, Deadly Night* (1984), the poster of which shows Father Christmas's axe-brandishing hand emerging from a snow-covered chimney. Similarly, in the 2015 Christmas special of the sitcom *Not Going Out*, the regular characters were stalked around a deserted department store by a vicious, shotgun-wielding robber dressed as Father Christmas. Kim Newman has argued that such imagery alludes to a truth that many have ignored: 'What nobody except the filmmakers seemed interested in saying was that a lot of children found Santa frightening even before the movies depicted him as an axe-wielding psychopath.'[18] The robotic Father Christmases in Russell T Davies's Christmas specials function in a similar way. In 'Last Christmas', Father Christmas appears to be a more customary, jovial figure – the casting of comic actor Nick Frost supports this – but questions about his existence raise doubts among the protagonists.

The Doctor is immediately suspicious of this manifestation of Father Christmas. Charles has argued that 'the Doctor's talent (as an alien and as an innocent) is to see what is everywhere but what people have chosen not to see, that which has been secreted away.'[19] Moreover, Belsey has noted the importance of scepticism in supernatural tales: 'How many subsequent ghost stories begin with the disbelief of one participant, both legitimating our incredulity and making the evidence to the contrary, when it comes, the more appalling?'[20] Similarly, James stated that in a successful ghost story, 'there must be ordinary level-headed persons – Horatios – on the scene [...] to play the part of the lay observer.'[21] The Doctor experiences a sense of the uncanny through the impossibility of Father Christmas's existence; Father Christmas is a mythical figure whom the Doctor *knows* to be a folkloric (and therefore fictional) creation. Freud discussed such phenomena in his essay, 'The Uncanny': 'an uncanny effect is often and easily produced when the distinction between imagination and reality is effaced, as when something we have hitherto regarded as imaginary appears before us in reality'.[22] Faced with the living embodiment of a figure he is certain does not exist triggers a feeling that something is out of place. Father Christmas is both familiar *and* a figure worthy of doubt. This response draws upon more traditional fears. Belsey argues, for example, that after the Reformation, 'although there were no ghosts, demons might yet impersonate them to win us to our harm'.[23] Hamlet's father is a case in point. Throughout 'Last Christmas', the Doctor and Father Christmas bicker as the former attempts to solve the riddle of the latter's existence and to ascertain whether he represents help or harm. Indeed, Father Christmas functions as a warning to the Doctor and Clara. He is a manifestation of their subconscious designed to help them fight parasitic Dream Crabs; his very fictitiousness is intended to alert the protagonists to the truth – that they are trapped in a dream.

In its use of dreams, 'Last Christmas' appears to reference a number of screen sources. Joseph Ruben's *Dreamscape* (1984), for example, saw scientists developing technology capable of projecting a test subject into other people's dreams. More recently, Christopher Nolan elaborated on this theme in *Inception* (2010), a heist movie in which spies steal industrial secrets from the subconscious of their sleeping targets. Such ideas were also present in a Christmas episode of one of *Doctor Who's* 1960s contemporaries: *The Avengers* (ITV/ABC, 1961–9). In 'Too Many Christmas Trees' (1965) John Steed (Patrick Macnee) and Emma Peel (Diana Rigg) find themselves the target of telepathic thieves who steal the secrets of agents in a process resulting in the agents' deaths. The episode opens in Steed's dream. He walks through a forest of cardboard Christmas trees until he finds, in a clearing, a mysterious present, similar to the uncanny gift in 'The Doctor, the Widow and the Wardrobe'. He is then beckoned by a sinister Father Christmas figure.

'Last Christmas', then, uses familiar motifs, and could even be read as a festive homage to Nolan's cerebral blockbuster. In particular, *Inception* used the concept of dreams within dreams; the further into the target's dreams they travel, the easier it is for Cobb's (Leonardo DiCaprio) team to steal information. These deeper dreams, however, are difficult to escape from, and the line between dream and reality becomes increasingly blurred. The protagonists of 'Last Christmas' are also trapped in deep dream-layers, in which waking up does not necessarily mean that they are awake. Similar ideas were used in the US science-fiction series *The X-Files* (Fox, 1993–). In 'Last Christmas' the protagonists are kept in a dream state while alien entities digest their brains. In 'Field Trip' (1999), FBI agents Mulder (David Duchovny) and Scully (Gillian Anderson) become trapped in a cave after inhaling fungal spores while searching for missing hikers. The spores cause their victims to hallucinate their escape and the continuation of their normal lives; in reality their bodies are being slowly digested. A Christmas episode of *The X-Files* repeated the motif in a more frivolous manner. In 'How the Ghosts Stole Christmas' (1998), spirits attempt to persuade Mulder and Scully to re-enact their own suicide pact. At the episode's denouement, the seemingly mortally wounded agents, after having apparently shot each other, realise they have been hallucinating and emerge from the sinister Gothic mansion unscathed. In all of these examples, dreams become prisons, used against characters to keep them docile and unaware of a creeping danger. As the Doctor notes, the Dream Crabs have 'weaponised our dreams against us'. To escape, they need to physically and metaphorically awaken.

Other aspects of 'Last Christmas' demonstrate the influence of earlier sources. Setting the story at a North Pole scientific research station conjures memories of *The Thing from Another World* (1951), or its remake, *The Thing* (1982). The season one *X-Files* episode 'Ice' (1993) utilised a similar setting. The bodies in the sickbay, faces hidden by the feasting Dream Crabs, are clearly reminiscent of *Alien* (1979) and its sequels. In Ridley Scott's science-fiction slasher movie, Kane (John Hurt) becomes a host for the 'facehugger', a creature that attaches itself to victims' faces in order to impregnate them with an alien egg. This becomes a joke in 'Last Christmas'. When audiences might reasonably question the story's similarity to *Alien*, Professor Albert (Michael Troughton) reaches the same conclusion:

PROFESSOR ALBERT: They're a bit like facehuggers, aren't they?
THE DOCTOR: Face... Huggers?
PROFESSOR ALBERT: You know. *Alien*. The horror movie, *Alien*.
THE DOCTOR: There's a horror movie called *Alien*. That's really offensive. No wonder everyone keeps invading you.

The connection with *Alien* and *The Thing from Another World* is deliberate. Moffat uses the growing sense of recognition to set up a punchline for a joke at the episode's conclusion. After her encounter with the Dream Crab, Shona (Faye Marsay) groggily awakes in her living room on Christmas morning. There she finds a list, her itinerary for the day. She had intended to watch *The Thing from Another World*, *Alien* and *Miracle on 34th Street* (1994), a film about the questioning of Father Christmas's existence: her plans for a movie marathon have shaped the structure of the dream throughout the episode. Royle defines the uncanny as 'a peculiar commingling of the familiar and unfamiliar. It can take the form of something familiar unexpectedly arising in a strange and unfamiliar context, or of something strange and unfamiliar unexpectedly arising in a familiar context'.[24] For the audience of

'Last Christmas', the bringing into focus of the hidden meaning is not necessarily uncanny; it provokes wry laughs, rather than trepidation. Actual uncanny motifs, however, are still present.

Uncanny repetition plays a role in 'Last Christmas'. Royle suggests that a sense of the uncanny 'might arise from the seemingly mechanical repetition of a word'.[25] Moffat has used such techniques frequently, most famously in the gas-masked child's cry of 'are you my Mummy?' in 'The Empty Child' and 'The Doctor Dances' (2005). The characters at the research station all reply to questions about their past with variations upon the phrase, 'it's a long story'. When the Doctor and Clara recognise this, it provides them with proof of their captivity. In 'The Uncanny', Freud notes: 'what is novel can easily become frightening and uncanny', but that 'something has to be added to what is novel and unfamiliar in order to make it uncanny'.[26] The Doctor, however, *always* engages with the 'novel and unfamiliar', thereby rendering it familiar. James recognises the importance of familiarity in enhancing a sense of dread:

> Let us be introduced to the actors in a placid way; let us see them going about their ordinary business, undisturbed by forebodings, pleased with their surroundings; and into this environment let the ominous thing put out its head, unobtrusively at first, and then more insistently, until it holds the stage.[27]

In trying to solve the mystery of the research station, the Doctor is going about his business as normal, but the sudden awareness of the repeated phrase renders the situation uncanny and reveals the truth. This technique has been used throughout the post-2005 *Doctor Who* revival. References to 'Bad Wolf' and Harold Saxon pepper the first and third series. There is then a realisation – usually in the penultimate episode – that these have been harbingers of greater threats: the Daleks and the Master. Similarly, a scene in 'Last Christmas' shows the Doctor and Clara remembering each use of the key phrase, bringing its importance to the forefront. This epiphany marks the point at which the episode shifts from the unfamiliar into the territory of the uncanny.

The dream setting of 'Last Christmas' also allows Moffat to respond to a traumatic event in the preceding series: the death of Danny Pink in 'Dark Water'. In 'Last Christmas', Clara engages with her loss within the dreams provoked by the Dream Crabs. A sense of the uncanny is not always connected to a feeling of fear, as Royle has suggested: 'The uncanny can be a matter of something gruesome or terrible [...] [b]ut it can also be a matter of something strangely beautiful, bordering on ecstasy ('too good to be true'), or eerily reminding us of something.'[28] The Dream Crabs make their victims feel safe and happy: Clara feels comfortable because Danny is still alive and her sorrow is lifted. Clara and Danny share Christmas Day together in a state of bliss, cocooned in Clara's living room, though uncanny intrusions are used to warn Clara of this unreality. Spotting a mysterious blackboard with her name written in chalk, Clara erases the word. Each word she wipes is replaced with a new one, spelling out the phrase 'You are dying.' The camera tracks back to reveal a hallway covered in blackboards, all repeating the same phrase. Clara has been subdued with an illusion that overrides her grief. Bringing that truth into focus will allow her to wake up. In the dream, she must accept Danny's death, which she already knows to be true. As James noted of apparitions, 'the ghost should be a contemporary of the seer. Such was the elder Hamlet and such Jacob Marley.'[29] In a similar sense, Danny serves to warn Clara of the threat.

In all of these representations, the dream world represents entrapment and danger. The protagonists' hallucinations shield them from an awareness of their predicament, sheltered from the outside world like the Christmas audiences watching them. The unrealities they inhabit are both familiar and unfamiliar. To save themselves, they need to become aware of the illusion; only by waking can they escape the dangers they face. Importantly, these dreams take on a semblance of reality. Distinguishing between waking states and dreaming has been a recurring theme in *Doctor Who*. 'Silence in the Library' (2008) begins from the perspective of a small girl who dreams of a deserted library-planet. In reality, she is an illusion, a digital imprint uploaded to a computer program. Later, the consciousness of River Song and other victims of the carnivorous Vashta Nerada are uploaded to the library's database, existing forever in a serene digital afterlife. If these imagined realities prefigure the dream-layers of 'Last Christmas', the fate of River Song sets up the events of Capaldi's second Christmas special, 2015's 'The Husbands of River Song'.

Memory and mourning: 'The Husbands of River Song'

'The Husbands of River Song' initially appears to contain few uncanny elements. It is an exercise in respite in the wake of a particularly macabre preceding series, which had examined the curse of immortality, witnessed the death of Clara and seen the Doctor repeatedly die in 'Heaven Sent'. Greg Davies's performance as King Hydroflax is deliberately humorous and overblown, and fitting for a broad Christmas audience. Issuing threats after decapitation, he evokes memories of the Black Knight (John Cleese) in *Monty Python and the Holy Grail* (1975), or Tony Harrison (Noel Fielding) in the BBC sitcom *The Mighty Boosh* (2004–7). There are also some eerie facets to the episode. Hydroflax's mysterious hooded bodyguards are not unlike the wraith that stalked the Doctor in 'Heaven Sent'. River plots to sell the Halassi Androvar to a representative of the Shoal of the Winter Harmony, creatures able to separate their heads diagonally into halves. Moreover, the name of the Shoal's representative has diabolical connections: Scratch has often been used as a synonym for the devil, particularly in Faustian tales such as Washington Irving's 'The Devil and Tom Walker' (1824) and Stephen Vincent Benét's 'The Devil and Daniel Webster' (1936). Given the setting for the deal aboard a starship, *Harmony and Redemption*, whose crew and passengers are all intergalactic villains and war criminals – 'where genocide comes to kick back and relax' – River has entered into her own transaction with the devil. Indeed, it is here that Moffat introduces stronger elements of the uncanny and connects the episode more closely to more unsettling Christmas traditions.

If one feature of the uncanny is the sudden awareness of something unfamiliar and frightening in a setting of comfort and safety, Moffat uses such a device aboard the *Harmony and Redemption*. The Doctor and River feel safe in their meeting with Scratch; River has deliberately chosen the restaurant as a public space. The revelation, then, that all of the other patrons are fellow members of the Shoal renders the situation uncanny, for both the protagonists and the audience. As Charles notes, 'The most dangerous and terrifying monsters are the ones which are so obviously under our noses that we fail to notice them.'[30] As River and the Doctor focus on each other, the attention of the viewer is directed at them. The sudden revelation of the Shoal's presence, then, has a jolting impact. A seemingly safe space is revealed to be anything but. This sense of the *unheimlich*, however, is brief, and the tone quickly becomes comic. Indeed, it is at this point that River finally realises her mysterious companion is actually the regenerated Doctor. Again, recurring phrases become important in this epiphany. The Doctor's repetition of River's catchphrase, 'Hello, sweetie', brings the truth into focus.

The episode's conclusion brings closure to River Song's story after her first appearance in 'Silence in the Library', which ends with River's death and resurrection in a digital afterlife within the computer CAL. The introduction of River just before her death means that every subsequent appearance of the character becomes uncanny. River's other catchphrase, 'spoilers', is an acknowledgement of this. As Rosemary Jackson suggests, 'Frightening scenes of uncanny literature are produced by hidden anxieties concealed within the subject, who then interprets the world in terms of his or her apprehensions.'[31] River is an uncanny figure because she reminds the audience and the Doctor of mortality. Her fear of spoilers emanates from a deeper understanding that the Doctor – a centuries-old time traveller – knows her fate.

Like a character in one of James's stories, River is an archaeologist haunted by her proximity to a knowledge that should remain undisturbed. In this sense, the episode begins to function as a take on more familiar storytelling customs associated with the festive season. Gabriel Moshenska has argued of James's characters, and in particular the archaeologist protagonists, that 'in their desire for knowledge or possession of the past they awaken malign supernatural forces that pursue them, often to their death'.[32] This is certainly the case for River: her quest for treasure leads her to perilous encounters with sinister forces. Moshenska notes that for James's archaeologists, 'the artefact [functions] as bait in a supernatural trap'.[33] He continues, 'There is a recurring theme that presents archaeological investigation or excavation, and the revelation of the material past in general, as sacrilegious acts that incur a harsh punishment.'[34] It is this bait that leads River to the Library, where she receives her punishment. The foreknowledge of her demise means that River can even be seen as a ghostly figure; the audience has already witnessed her death in her first appearance in the series. This truth hides in plain sight of the viewer. As Belsey has observed, 'Ghosts suspend the rules of logic just as they break the laws of nature [...] A ghost is always radically out of time, as well as out of place.'[35] In life and in death, this is true of River.

The series nine episode 'Heaven Sent' evokes similar macabre thoughts. The Doctor's opening narration reflects upon the inevitability of death:

> As you come into this world, something else is also born. You begin your life, and it begins a journey towards you. It moves slowly, but it never stops. Wherever you go, whatever path you take, it will follow – never faster, never slower, always coming. You will run; it will walk. You will rest; it will not. One day, you will linger in the same place too long; you will sit too still or sleep too deep. And when, too late, you rise to go, you will notice a second shadow next to yours. Your life will then be over.

Similarly, Charles argues that the Vashta Nerada 'represent the shadow of death which we already feel within us'.[36] For River, the Doctor becomes that second shadow. Writing on the subject of early modern ghosts and spirits, Belsey has discussed the prominence of a figure known as a 'fetch', 'a wraith who returns to summon the living'.[37] Variations of such creations appear frequently throughout *Doctor Who*. The Quantum Shade in 'Face the Raven', for example, emerges to take the lives of those who have been sentenced to death; its appearance is an ominous and eerie forewarning of their demise. In 'The Husbands of River Song' it becomes clear that the Doctor is the fetch. The Doctor's encounters with River often reflect on their first meeting in the Library and his knowledge of her eventual fate. In 'Forest of the Dead', moments before she sacrifices her life, River reflects upon the uncanny nature of her relationship with the Doctor:

> Funny thing is, this means you've always known how I was going to die. All the time we've been together, you knew I was coming here. The last time I saw you, the real you, the future you, I mean, you turned up on my doorstep, with a new haircut and a suit. You took me to Darillium to see the Singing Towers. What a night that was. The Towers sang, and you cried. You wouldn't tell me why, but I suppose you knew it was time. My time. Time to come to the Library.

The future Doctor is fully aware of the events leading up to River's death, and it imbues their meetings with a melancholic sense of the uncanny.

Indeed, time travel creates opportunities for the experience of the uncanny: characters in such tales are constantly trying to avoid bumping into their older or younger selves. Whereas in folklore and Gothic literature meeting a doppelganger is likely to herald a character's death, in time-hopping science fiction such meetings could bring about a paradox, perhaps even the destruction of the universe. As a time traveller, River shows an awareness of other characters' fates. When Flemming questions how River knew the *Harmony and Redemption* would crash, she replies gleefully, 'I'm an archaeologist from the future. I dug you up!' Though this line is delivered humorously – it is, after all, a Christmas episode – it exemplifies one of the most unsettling aspects of time travel within *Doctor Who*. River's knowledge of the later incarnations of the Doctor in 'Silence in the Library'/'Forest of the Dead' radically shifts his placement in time. In almost every episode, he is a figure of the present; the audience watches his adventures as they happen. But River's presence locates him firmly in the past: these events have already occurred. River has knowledge, for example, of the future of Donna Noble (Catherine Tate) and the tragedy that awaits her. Her statement to Flemming, then, is a turning point in the episode, because it raises the issue of fate. After the Doctor and River defeat Hydroflax and his followers, the comic tone diminishes.

Christmas spirit: from 'The Return of Doctor Mysterio' to 'Twice upon a Time'

2016 saw *Doctor Who* go on hiatus, so the Christmas special of that year directly followed 'The Husbands of River Song'. There is little sense of Christmas in 'The Return of Doctor Mysterio'. Writing in the *Telegraph*, Michael Hogan described it as the 'most family-friendly Christmas special for five years', but beyond its short prologue, it barely acknowledged the season.[38] *Radio Times* reviewer Patrick Mulkern recalled that Moffat had remarked to him of the episode, 'It'll be a relief to you, it's got virtually no Christmas in it at all!'[39] Aside from a few scenes in which characters have awkward encounters with body-snatching aliens masquerading as seemingly familiar colleagues, creepiness is also not at the forefront of the episode, played for laughs.

Season ten, however, makes frequent use of the unsettling uncanny. In 'The Pilot', new companion Bill (Pearl Mackie) discovers a mysterious puddle in which her reflection is not quite right. This *unheimlich* likeness is reminiscent of Anthony Horowitz's *Dramarama* (ITV, 1983–9) episode 'Back to Front' (1989), in which a young boy discovers his reflection is actually a sinister double from a reversed world. Like Heather (Stephanie Hyam) in 'The Pilot', its eyes express the other-worldliness of the reflection. 'Knock Knock' functions as a fairly typical but effective haunted house story, while the lumbering, corpse-filled spacesuits of 'Oxygen' conjure memories of 'Silence in the Library'. In 'World Enough and Time', Bill watches the Doctor and Missy (Michelle Gomez) on a glowing television screen, their movements rendered imperceptible by a distortion that means time flows faster on the spaceship's lower levels. They become ghosts of a past that is moving increasingly further away from her. The events of this episode witness the deaths of Missy and Bill (who is later resurrected by Heather), and the beginning of the regeneration process for the Doctor. These events form the basis for the next Christmas special, 'Twice upon a Time' (2017).

'Twice upon a Time's' title and prologue invoke memories of Christmas storytelling. It opens with an excerpt of 'The Tenth Planet' (1966) and captions reading 'Previously on Doctor Who' and '709 episodes ago …' The First Doctor's (William Hartnell) face dissolves into David Bradley's as the new First Doctor, and the image shifts from black and white to colour. The First Doctor begins to regenerate. Having refused to complete the regeneration process, he moves over the snowy landscapes of the South Pole, and happens upon the Twelfth Doctor. Their bemusement is compounded by the appearance of a British World War I captain (Mark Gatiss). Again, uncanny imagery – the arrival of the captain is heralded by the freezing of time; snowflakes hover in mid-air in scenes that are at once uncanny and festive – is unobtrusive and not the main focus. Time has stopped because the captain was supposed to die in the trenches. Like Squadron Leader Peter Carter (David Niven) in Powell and Pressburger's *A Matter of Life and Death* (1946), he is given a second chance of life through a technical error. Humans of the distant future have discovered a way to travel through time and upload the consciousness of people to glass avatars at the moment of their deaths. They then live on in a digital afterlife, much like River Song and the patrons of the Library. Having missed the captain, they attempt to correct the error.

The humanoid avatars are uncanny presences: their sudden appearances are unheralded; their faces are expressionless, but resemble those of real people; they are signifiers of impending death. Indeed, the episode can be seen as a Christmas ghost story, albeit a comforting one. The Doctor is reunited with Bill, whom he has last seen transformed into a Cyberman. Her consciousness has been uploaded to the database; she maintains her personality, but, in a moment of uncanniness, is unable to recall how she travelled to the Doctor's location. At the end of the episode, the Doctor is able to say goodbye to Clara and Nardole (Matt Lucas). In a further uncanny echo, the captain is revealed to be an ancestor of Brigadier Lethbridge-Stewart, another ghost from the Doctor's past. These are kindly spirits, then, who reappear to convince the Doctor to regenerate, and reject a permanent death. Like Scrooge on his journey with the Ghost of Christmas Past, the jaded Twelfth Doctor revisits his former companions – and his former iterations in one sequence – who convince him to embrace his present.

There are uncanny aspects to the landscape in the episode. The Western Front acts as an uncanny space, an alien landscape in the fields of France and Belgium. As George Mosse remarked, 'the surrounding landscape was more suggestive of the moon than the earth, as heavy shelling destroyed not only men but nature.'[40] The World War I setting also enabled the retelling of another traditional Christmas story, as the Doctor uses his knowledge of the Christmas truce to save the captain's life. The Doctor presents the truce as an almost supernatural event: 'for one day, one Christmas, a very long time ago, everyone just put down their weapons, and started to sing. Everybody just stopped. Everyone was just kind.' The truce is depicted as a miracle, in which battle-hardened soldiers are suddenly overcome by a sense of festive brotherhood, though soldiers had often negotiated short truces in order to gather the dead and wounded. Whatever the truth behind the events of Christmas 1914, in 'Twice upon a Time' they aid in the resetting of the story. For Mosse, wartime interpretations of the season often focused upon 'the Christian spirit descend[ing] into the dugout to heal and purify'.[41] Thanks to the Doctor, the captain's life begins again, and the decision is justified when he immediately calls for aid for an enemy combatant. The Doctor too is purified by his encounter. His former companions resolve his feelings of fatigue, preparing him to embrace his regeneration and begin anew, just as the First Doctor (Hartnell) regenerates into the Second (Patrick Troughton) in a black-and-white clip from 1966 and just as audiences would emerge from the Christmas season into the New Year.

Conclusion: The Twelve Days of Christmas

Christmas episodes often mark a period of transition in the series, and Moffat regularly used the sense of the uncanny to bring characters through these evolutions. The events of 'Last Christmas' enable Clara to come to terms with her grief for Danny, while 'The Husbands of River Song' sees the Doctor alone again after the departure of Clara. Grumpy and isolated in these episodes – a sign on the TARDIS at the beginning reads 'Carol singers will be criticised' – the Doctor reunites with River, only to realise that this will be their final encounter before her rendezvous with the Vashta Nerada. But, if the Twelfth Doctor's tenure is defined by themes of loss and an awareness of mortality, these are then subverted into something positive. As Charles argues of Moffat's earlier episodes:

> Moffat's narratives suggest that if we have nothing to fear but fear itself, then by confronting that fear, by exposing ourselves to that uncanny moment of self-recognition and physical revelation, we can turn that fear back upon itself: fear shall grow afraid, doom will crack and shatter, and death itself shall die.[42]

The Doctor's final evening with River sees the fruition of her earlier account of their last meeting in 'Forest of the Dead'. The Doctor recognises this, and prepares for her fate by giving her a sonic screwdriver infused with the digital imprint that will allow the Tenth Doctor to save her. By the end of 'The Return of Doctor Mysterio', the Doctor seems sparkier. As Nick Setchfield noted, 'He used to need flash cards to deal with human feelings. Now he's doling out relationship advice.'[43] In this sense, the message is brought into line with the spirit of the Christmas season. As Lawson remarked in the *Guardian*, 'the Doctor is now as much a part of mid-winter tradition as all the other figures from whom Moffat borrows'.[44] In their repeated appearances and their structure, the Christmas specials function as an extension of traditional Christmas cultures of storytelling. Part of *Doctor Who*'s success can surely be ascribed to its place within a recurring tradition that stretches back to those early modern firesides in the depths of winter.

Notes

1   David Budgen, 'Halfway out of the dark': Steven Moffat's *Doctor Who* Christmas specials', in Andrew O'Day (ed.), *Doctor Who: The Eleventh Hour – A Critical Celebration of the Matt Smith and Steven Moffat Era* (London, 2014), pp. 89–105.

2   Nicholas Royle, *The Uncanny* (Manchester, 2003), p. 1.

3   Alec Charles, 'The crack of doom: the uncanny echoes of Steven Moffat's *Doctor Who*', *Science Fiction, Film and Television* iv/1 (2011), p. 3; Frank Collins, 'Monsters under the bed: Gothic and fairy-tale storytelling in Steven Moffat's *Doctor Who*', in O'Day (ed.), *Doctor Who: The Eleventh Hour*, p. 31.

4   Catherine Belsey, 'Shakespeare's sad tale for winter: *Hamlet* and the tradition of fireside ghost stories', *Shakespeare Quarterly* lxi/1 (2010), p. 4.

5   Ibid., p. 20.

6   Derek Johnston, *Haunted Seasons: Television Ghost Stories for Christmas and Horror for Halloween* (Basingstoke, 2015), pp. 23–5.

7   Ibid., p. 25.

8   Mark Connelly, *Christmas: A History* (1999; London, 2012), p. 163.

9   William Shakespeare, *Hamlet* (1.1.181–7).

10 For more on Shakespeare and such literary traditions see Johnston, *Haunted Seasons*, p. 27.

11 Brian Cowlishaw, quoted in Gabriel Moshenska, 'M. R. James and the archaeological uncanny', *Antiquity* lxxxvi/334 (2012), p. 1199.

12 John Tulloch and Manuel Alvarado, *Doctor Who: The Unfolding Text* (London, 1983), p. 140.

13 Mark Lawson, '*Doctor Who*: The Return of Doctor Mysterio review – Capaldi takes Manhattan!', *Guardian* (26 December 2016). Available

at https://www.theguardian.com/tv-and-radio/2016/dec/26/doctor-who-the-return-of-doctor-mysterio-review-capaldi-takes-manhattan (accessed 3 March 2017).

14 Sigmund Freud, 'The uncanny', in Albert Dickson (ed.), *The Penguin Freud Library*, vol 14: *Art and Literature* (London, 1985), p. 352.

15 David Pirie describes *Dead of Night* as 'the most important English supernatural thriller prior to the late 1950s'. David Pirie, *A New Heritage of Horror: The English Gothic Cinema* (London, 2008), p. 16.

16 Charles, 'The crack of doom', p. 2.

17 Elisabeth Bronfen, 'Night and the uncanny', in Jo Collins and John Jervis (eds), *Uncanny Modernity: Cultural Theories, Modern Anxieties* (Basingstoke, 2008), p. 52.

18 Kim Newman, *Nightmare Movies: Horror on the Screen Since the 1960s* (London, 2011), pp. 132–3.

19 Charles, 'The crack of doom', p. 9.

20 Belsey, 'Shakespeare's sad tale', p. 3.

21 M. R. James, 'Ghosts – treat them gently!', in idem, *The Haunted Dolls' House and Other Ghost Stories*, ed. S. T. Joshi (London, 2006), p. 262.

22 Freud, 'The uncanny', p. 367.

23 Belsey, 'Shakespeare's sad tale', p. 9.

24 Royle, *The Uncanny*, p. 1.

25 Ibid.

26 Freud, 'The uncanny', p. 341.

27 M. R. James, 'Introduction to *Ghosts and Marvels*', in idem, *The Haunted Dolls' House*, ed. Joshi, p. 248.

28 Royle, *The Uncanny*, p. 2.

29 James, 'Ghosts – treat them gently!', p. 262.

30 Charles, 'The crack of doom', p. 7.

31 Rosemary Jackson, *Fantasy: The Literature of Subversion* (London, 1981), pp. 64–5.

32 Moshenska, 'M. R. James and the archaeological uncanny', p. 1195.

33 Ibid., p. 1196.

34 Ibid., p. 1197.

35 Belsey, 'Shakespeare's sad tale', p. 5.

36 Charles, 'The crack of doom', p. 12.

37 Belsey, 'Shakespeare's sad tale', p. 23.

38 Michael Hogan, '*Doctor Who*, The Return of Doctor Mysterio review: the happiest, most heroic Christmas special in years', *Daily Telegraph* (25 December 2016). Available at http://www.telegraph.co.uk/tv/0/doctor-return-captain-mysterio-review-happiest-heroic-christmas/ (accessed 3 March 2017).

39 Patrick Mulkern, '*Doctor Who* Christmas special review: a beautifully packaged hour of uplifting escapism', *Radio Times* [website] (22 December 2017). Available at http://www.radiotimes.com/news/2017-

12-22/doctor-who-christmas-special-review-a-beautifully-packaged-hour-of-uplifting-escapism/ (accessed 25 February 2018).

40 George Mosse, *Fallen Soldiers: Reshaping the Memory of the World Wars* (Oxford, 1990), p. 5.

41 Ibid., p. 76.

42 Charles, 'The crack of doom', p. 21.

43 Nick Setchfield, '*Doctor Who* Christmas special review: charm, imagination and wit: these are the show's superpowers', *GamesRadar+* [website] (25 December 2016). Available at http://www.gamesradar.com/doctor-who-christmas-special-review/ (accessed 27 February 2017).

44 Lawson, '*Doctor Who*: The Return of Doctor Mysterio'.

PART THREE

PROMOTIONAL DISCOURSES

8

'PLEASE WELCOME THE TWELFTH DOCTOR'

The Paratextual Branding of Peter Capaldi's Tenure

Matt Hills

On Sunday, 4 August 2013, Peter Capaldi was announced as playing the Twelfth Doctor in BBC TV's science fiction series *Doctor Who*. Like David Tennant before him, Capaldi had long been a fan of the programme. But unlike Tennant, a young Capaldi had actually tried to take over the running of the *Doctor Who* Fan Club, a predecessor of the *Doctor Who* Appreciation Society.[1]

In a sense, Capaldi's tenure did not begin with the first episode fully featuring him as a new Doctor ('Deep Breath'), nor even with 'The Day of the Doctor' in November 2013, in which he had a brief cameo. Instead, it could be said that the 'Capaldi era' very much began *paratextually*, with the broadcast of *Doctor Who Live: The Next Doctor* on 4 August 2013, followed by official promotional activity such as The World Tour (see Paul Booth's following chapter). I therefore want to focus on how publicity paratexts work around *Doctor Who*'s televised episodes to smooth out and otherwise manage the transitions and 'eras' of this unusually long-running programme.

In order to explore such issues, my chapter will be divided into three sections. Firstly, I will introduce some recent shifts in paratextual theory, and how this approach can be utilised to better understand *Doctor Who*'s 'periodisation'.[2] Secondly, I will address how *Who* is promoted via what might be called *dominant official paratextual activities* (e.g. hype and marketing), utilising a logic of the media event aligned with social media's 'digital flows'.[3] *Doctor Who Live: The Next Doctor* absolutely fits into this category; so too does the reveal of Bill Potts (Pearl Mackie) as a new companion in 2016's 'Friend from the Future'. Cover-feature magazine interviews with Peter Capaldi in the mainstream UK press also form an 'old media' part of these event-building promotional strategies, along with *Radio Times*'s cover stories.

Thirdly, I will broaden the scope of my analysis, considering the Capaldi era not only through dominant paratextual practices but also via more marginal and exceptional examples that have glanced across Peter Capaldi's tenure. These include 'fakes', such as the supposed pilot for a new BBC TV programme which actually covered for *Doctor Who Live: The Next Doctor*; paratextual 'glitching' where professional journalists self-reflexively draw attention to how *Who* is promoted, and their role in these processes; and Peter Capaldi's left-wing politics, which he has displayed in specific interviews. I will conclude by thinking about the transition out of the Twelfth Doctor's era, and how audience/journalistic paratexts focused on the possible gendering of the Thirteenth Doctor ahead of the announcement that the Doctor would be played by a woman. It should be noted from the outset that paratexts generally tend to operate at national-cultural levels, being created afresh as TV texts circulate through different national markets. Given this fact, I will focus on UK-oriented paratexts such as the national press, broadcasting and commercial fan magazines (although some of these, e.g. *Doctor Who Magazine*, certainly have a limited international circulation, while San Diego Comic-Con is widely reported in the UK and its news circulates internationally via social media). First, though, how did Capaldi's tenure begin back in 2013? And how can paratextual theory help us to understand the brand management of a BBC flagship programme such as *Doctor Who*?

Framing *Who*: paratextual developments and demarcations

Paratextual analysis argues that in an era of 24/7 social media live-ness,[4] the bits of hype and marketing that circulate around TV texts have become both increasingly important and increasingly ordinary. These orbiting satellites of promotion have been dubbed paratexts, with the term covering spoilers, teasers, trailers, posters and the like.[5] Extending such analysis, I have suggested that fans tend to be 'para-textual completists', keeping track of interviews with stars, official press releases and announcements of teaser trailers.[6] Being a *Doctor Who* fan in 2017 can mean reading fairly detailed previews in the fan blogosphere a few days ahead of a new episode, then encountering clues and hints as those granted access to BBC previews start to circulate titbits of information online. Consuming *Who* as a fan occupies the time before, after and between episodes. And it is this everyday hype that paratexts can enable us to study. Jonathan Gray and Amanda Lotz have argued that paratexts work like 'game-pieces in a game of interpretation', with official industry paratexts trying to 'set limits for interpretation around a program' by emphasising certain meanings over others, while fandom typically 'toggles, underplays, or amplifies certain dynamics in either a show or its industry-created paratexts' by way of seeking to complicate industrially preferred meanings.[7] Indeed, this was how paratextual analysis became established in TV Studies, via the notion that paratexts seek to delimit textual interpretations for audiences.

More recently, and since *Doctor Who: The Eleventh Hour* included a chapter on 'official, industry-created or licensed paratexts [...] *which precede[d] the broadcasting of Moffat's Doctor Who*' during Matt Smith's time as the Doctor,[8] paratextual analysis has arguably entered a distinctive second phase. Here, the focus is no longer on how paratexts frame textual meanings, but instead on the diversity of ways in which paratexts can operate, for instance by referencing other paratexts – just as the 'iconic' promotional poster for 'World Enough and Time' cites and reworks the key image for 'The Day of the Doctor' – or by collat-ing arrays of paratexts together under a specific banner such as a TV anniversary.[9] Scholarship has also further investigated the relationship between paratexts and brands, with Melissa Aronczyk arguing that in our current 'promotional culture [...] paratext overcomes text'.[10] By this, Aronczyk means that

> Brand positioning [...] assembles and organizes cultural elements into temporary relationships according to strategic principles [...] Audiences may make meanings from this assemblage [...] but the meanings elicited *redound to the paratext, not the text*. The meaning and value created does not enhance the legitimacy of the text but rather accrues to the benefit of the brand.[11]

Following such an argument, it makes far more sense that Peter Capaldi's tenure would be announced so far in advance of his full textual 'unveiling' as the Twelfth Doctor. After all, in the interval between *Doctor Who Live: The Next Doctor* (August 2013) and the series eight TV premiere of 'Deep Breath' (September 2014), Capaldi's casting as the Doctor bore no relationship to textual meanings (with the brief exception of his tightly framed appearance in the 50th anniversary special). Instead, the Twelfth Doctor and speculation over his costume and characterisation redounded entirely to the paratext of *Doctor Who*'s programme brand.[12] Similarly, pre-16 July 2017 speculation over the Thirteenth Doctor's gender was less about delimiting specific textual meanings and much more about seeking to position the *Who* brand as forward-looking/progressive rather than dated and reactionary.

Thinking about paratexts as bids to (re)shape a brand means that fans are increasingly responding to paratexts as texts in their own right,[13] for example when merchandising is felt to be problematic. As Suzanne Scott has observed of *Star Wars: The Force Awakens* and its initial lack of Rey toys – leading to the #wheresrey hashtag and fan activism – paratexts can 'function to codify gendered franchising discourses, even in the midst of a franchise's attempt to adopt more progressive representational strategies'.[14] As I will go on to explore towards the end of this chapter, in the case of Peter Capaldi's transition into the Thirteenth Time Lord incarnation, the reverse may also be true: audience/journalist paratexts were often ahead of the programme itself in relation to the Doctor's regendering.

But there is an additional consequence to re-theorising paratexts as brand-oriented rather than straightforwardly text-oriented: paratexts can play a key role in smoothing over moments of considerable textual transition and brand 'refreshing', such as the introduction and departure of a Doctor. Paul Booth has examined how *Doctor Who* has been read by generations of fans via a periodisation into different eras,[15] dictated either by the lead actors[16] or by script editor–producer production teams as well as elements of production design.[17] Booth argues that where

> periodisation becomes the lens through which all *Doctor Who* is interpreted, then that [...] reductively facilitates a specific reading of the corpus – a reading itself based on periodisation as the totalising principle. Focusing on periodisation in *Doctor Who* makes periodisation a central, connective tissue across the text [...] Thus, periodisation always-already brings with it a disciplining procedure; periodising [...] reinforces what fans may think of a particularly favoured era.[18]

He also notes that periodisation is not simply a way of reading *Doctor Who*; it is also a process through which the fan community can 'create strata in order to self-actualise. The positioning of individual membership in any fandom depends on the relationship with others' organisational principles, highlighting the impact of periodisation on viewers as well.'[19] Yet by using Derridean theory, Booth does not connect *Who*'s periodisation to the operation of brand-focused paratexts, instead tending to see the programme's division into distinct eras as an imposition of fan interpretations/identities.[20] I would argue that this fannish division of *Doctor Who* into phases relies on paratexts – partly those of credits sequences through which the contributions of production personnel can be identified or debated, but also those paratexts that are more distant from the TV text yet seek to manage and hold together the *Who* brand as it is retooled.[21] Thus it is not just the case that audiences and scholars 'must articulate the binary between continuity and fragmentation' to 'see *Doctor Who* as *both* a continuous programme split into fragmented parts *and* as a series of fragments cohered to a whole at the same time'.[22] Brand-oriented paratexts also play a vital role in cementing this articulation, working to maintain a programme brand's coherence even while it threatens to pull apart. And it is this paratextual assuaging of change – this capacity to paratextually gloss brand incoherence – that I will consider in the next section. More specifically, I will focus on dominant logics of brand-benefiting paratexts: the event or reveal as a moment of promotion that runs in excess of merely inflecting TV textuality.

Covering *Who*: paratextual nowness and newness

Peter Capaldi's casting formed the highlight of *Doctor Who Live: The Next Doctor*. By staging this reveal within glitzy live TV, the BBC generated an instant of brand progression where, as Celia Lury has observed, brands typically develop via 'an ongoing process of [...] differentiation and [...] integration'.[23] This involves a series of gaps or intervals 'organized so as to produce branded products as [...] different [...] as new or up to date [...] sometimes even as an event'.[24] In the case of this *Doctor Who Live* episode, it was most certainly an event logic that predominated; as I have noted elsewhere, in 'terms of new *Who*'s rebrandings, these intervals are usually constituted as events, as moments where the show is "updated" by a new cast, new logo, new title sequence, new-look TARDIS or Daleks'.[25] But the announcement of a new Doctor is surely foremost among such bids for value based on immediacy and having to 'be there' at the broadcast moment.

Capaldi's own *Doctor Who* fandom immediately formed one narrative circulating around his assumption of the programme's title role: a fan letter he had written to the *Radio Times* in the 1970s, praising its 1972/73 tenth-anniversary special, was featured in the live reveal. And as Capaldi was initially introduced on *Doctor Who Live* he noticeably and deliberately struck a William Hartnell-like pose by clutching at his lapels. (Hartnell had played the First Doctor back in 1963 as a crotchety grandfather-like figure.) Blogging for *Who Watching*, Andrew O'Day picked up on Capaldi's fannish reference to the Hartnell era, suggesting that 'perhaps in *Who* circles we can use "lapel-tugging" as a new synonym for being Doctorish and maintaining continuity'.[26] As such, Capaldi's wholly paratextual phase as the Twelfth Doctor began by citing the programme's early history, working to reassure fans that, at a time of significant textual change, continuity would be observed, and hence that the transition from Matt Smith would be smoothed out 'as a series of fragments cohered to a whole'.[27]

Capaldi's 'lapel-tugging' may have been barely perceptible to more casual fans – or at least it might not have been readable as especially significant. But for fans recalling 1960s *Who*, Capaldi's seemingly spontaneous, enthusiastic gesture acted as a commemoration of the First Doctor: 'paratextual memory [...] potentially maintains an "authentic" fan self-narrative in terms of "having been there" at times of broadcast, and performs a "good" fan identity [...] Paratextual memory is testified to throughout fandom, as it distinguishes fans from other audiences.'[28]

Paratextual memory was similarly invited by Capaldi's later costume choices: the red lining of his coat strongly resembled a cape worn by Jon Pertwee as the Third Doctor and infamously featured in promotional/publicity images from the 1970s. The very first photograph of Capaldi and Jenna Coleman filming series eight together also knowingly imitated an image of the Third Doctor and Jo Grant (Katy Manning), aligning Peter Capaldi's arrival with the period of the programme that he had been a fan of, and linking his portrayal of the Twelfth Doctor to the Third and First Doctors. In fact, attempts at stitching the Whoniverse together into a coherent whole migrated from paratextual framing to textual centrality as Capaldi's time in the programme came to an end, with 'lapel-tugging', or an intratextual invocation of William Hartnell's performance, giving way to David Bradley's appearance as the First Doctor in Capaldi's final story. What had previously been a paratextual acknowledgement of Peter Capaldi's *Who* fandom thus became part of a textual 'gift' to him from outgoing showrunner Steven Moffat,[29] as both the Mondasian Cybermen and a recast First Doctor were featured in 'The Doctor Falls'. This movement from paratext to text indicates that what had initially worked to paratextually smooth out the transition in *Doctor Who*'s periodisation could (and would) go on to become an identifying marker of Capaldi's tenure as the Doctor. As such, 'lapel-tugging' became more than simply synonymous with maintaining programme continuity. The meeting of First and Twelfth Doctors involved 'references to the show's own past via diegetic rewritings', as the Time Lord's very first incarnation was 'put in different circumstances [...] reflecting a continuity-laden attempt to both elide and highlight periodisation. Such a revelation/ revision requires a shift in the conception of all *Doctor Who* knowledge, highlighting both the connectivity and periodisation of the show.'[30] Uniting the First and Twelfth Doctors on screen just as each apparently neared their own diegetic regeneration provided a textual event – a multi-Doctor cliffhanger designed to spark and inspire fan speculation between the end of series ten (1 July 2017) and 'Twice upon a Time' some six months later. This 'fan novum' or reworking of established *Who* lore on the part of Steven Moffat seemingly exploited gaps in classic *Doctor Who* to craft new interpretations of the programme's hyperdiegetic past.[31]

Back before Capaldi had fully appeared in the role, though, another significant spike in press/fan activity occurred in January 2014 when his costume was revealed via an official BBC image. Design guru Stephen Bayley's reading of this promotional image emphasised Peter Capaldi's choice of a Crombie coat and boots:

> Why does Peter Capaldi, in character as the twelfth Doctor and striking a memorable pose that he will surely soon regret, look like an ageing mod? [...] Are we having a mod revival? Is the Doctor going to summon up the sensibility of 1966 among us all? The art-school-educated Capaldi was born in 1958, so the question is not beyond his personal experience, nor his intellectual range.[32]

Relatedly, Peter Capaldi's first interview after he had started filming as the Doctor, with the *Sunday Times* magazine, also stressed both the Twelfth Doctor's costume and Capaldi's age – once again para-textually relating him to the First Doctor, played by William Hartnell from 1963 to 1966:

> In the translucent flesh, he looks a good 30 years younger than Hartnell, thanks largely to the fact that he gave up alcohol years ago (and Hartnell liked a drink). But he's still old enough that the BBC has a chiropractor on speed dial. More awkwardly, he's old enough to be Clara's father. This regeneration lark can have disturbing Freudian implications.[33]

Journalist Matt Rudd's piece is particularly concerned with the transformation from Capaldi-as-actor to Capaldi-as-character, and its accompanying photo shoot therefore illustrates Peter Capaldi getting into costume, beginning with him in civvies (T-shirt and jeans) and ending as he strikes a strongly Doctorish pose in full regalia. Rudd writes about the shift in Capaldi's body language, and how once he has donned the Twelfth Doctor's costume 'his eyes are firing lasers around the studio [...] [H]e's no longer the very relaxed, very happy Glaswegian will-o-the-wisp. He's a full-on Gallifreyan nutjob.'[34]

Emphasising this rapid switch from ordinary self to Time Lord figure validates Capaldi's skilfulness as an actor; his portrayal is 'conjured from a book of thoughts [Capaldi's self-analysis of the role] and half a lifetime of enthusiasm' for *Doctor Who*. Capaldi is depicted as a soft-spoken, thoughtful figure who, once divested of his *Who* costume and returned to his own anonymous outfit, 'leaves quietly, via the stairs, not a Police Box'.[35] The role of the Doctor is also represented as transformative for him professionally, converting him from a jobbing character actor to a fully-fledged celebrity: 'as soon as this happened I had paparazzi outside my house. People spoke to me before and recognised me, but nothing like this.'[36]

In contrast to this broadsheet press coverage, the official *Doctor Who Magazine*'s pre-series eight interview avoided touching directly on the issue of Capaldi's age, instead simply stressing that he is 'a proper fan' who has read the official *Magazine* for as long as he can remember, and who has adorned his binder of scripts with photos of William Hartnell and Tom Baker in costume meeting youngsters.[37] *DWM* also focuses on Capaldi's role as an ambassador for the series, discussing a 'shaky mobile phone recording' on YouTube taken during filming and featuring Capaldi reassuring a young fan who had been upset by Matt Smith's departure.[38] The actor is shown to be taking his responsibilities very seriously, but this, in turn, is rooted in his own awareness, as a 'proper' fan, of 'where *Doctor Who* was born for [him]. It was in [his] childhood.'[39] Discourses of age remain significant here, but not via the more or less implicit ageism of cracks about 'chiropractors' and questions about age-appropriate romance. Instead, *Capaldi's age is mediated through his fandom* by *DWM*: it is his own fannishness from his childhood that gives him a sense of how to relate to today's child fans, and hence renders him an appropriate custodian of the programme's lead role.

However, in mainstream media coverage in the *Guardian*, Capaldi defensively and contrastively positioned his 1970s fan letter to the *Radio Times* as 'the full anorak',[40] seemingly worrying that this para-textual memory would position him as an excessive or extreme fan in the eyes of the general public and the programme's more casual audience. UK press/niche fan magazine paratexts were thus not directly concerned with activating textual meanings and were instead far more preoccupied with what the programme brand of *Doctor Who* might mean for different audiences: Capaldi was firmly 'one of us' in the official *DWM* targeted at fan readers, yet not an 'anorak' in the eyes of *Guardian* readers.

Meanwhile, worries about Capaldi's age in pre-broadcast press coverage continued to focus on the physical demands of filming. *ShortList* justified a question about this by saying, '[n]o offence, but you've a few years on your predecessor', while Capaldi's response was to point out that Matt Smith had been injured during filming – relative youthfulness was no guarantee of this not happening – and that all the 'running up and down corridors' replaced the need to 'do any exercise because you do a lot at work during the day'.[41] *The Big Issue*'s August 2014 interview reiterated similar paratextual framings of Capaldi, even to the point of reproducing a photo from July's *Sunday Times* magazine photo shoot. There is a sense of the actor being paratextually fluent and rehearsed by this point, shuffling bits of paratextual business around and hitting established beats familiar from previous publicity: there's his lapsed teenage fandom before returning to *Who* like 'the prodigal son'; the hope that at least some fans will embrace him as 'their Doctor'; the act of writing to the *Radio Times* as well as for a 1976 fanzine; and being 'absolutely appropriate' in the Doctor-Clara relationship.[42]

Pushing back against ageist framings of Capaldi's casting as the Doctor, the contrast in age between Capaldi and Matt Smith is significantly recontextualised as a positive development by showrunner Steven Moffat, who argues that casting a younger actor had become the default setting for the BBC Wales series:

> you have to watch for the moment [...] when inspiration degrades into reflex [...] You just think, 'Hang on. We're not doing that because it's new any more, or clever, or right. We're doing it because we know it works' – which [...] is sensible, but not [...] interesting.[43]

And the commercial fan magazine *Sci-Fi Now* likewise suggested that Capaldi's casting represented a 'new direction for the show [...] after much of the last year was spent celebrating its history [...] *Doctor*

Who's eighth season feels like an opportunity for a clean break'.[44] The lead character's regeneration has always offered a chance to retool the programme, of course, but Capaldi's age is specifically acknowledged here as part of a rejuvenation and newness for the series, operating as a counter to the programme's ageing where the formula of 'new *Who*' may otherwise begin to feel tired and predictable. Discourses of ageing remain very much present, but they are recoded from Capaldi-as-celebrity to the brand of *Doctor Who*, with an older lead actor authenticating the creative risk-taking of showrunner Steven Moffat and demonstrating the flexibility of *Who*'s format.

Perhaps unsurprisingly, series nine – Capaldi's second year on-screen as the Doctor – was less rampantly promoted and paratextually encircled than his debut. The *Telegraph* magazine ran a cover feature interview, suggesting that although he was 'too gracious to say it [...] Capaldi is definitely tired and homesick [...] He has even developed the same knee complaint that had Matt Smith [...] on crutches at their first meeting.'[45] And by the time of series ten in 2017, Capaldi's tiredness and knee injury – 'they call it Doctor's Knee'[46] – constitutes standardised paratextual fare to be rehashed in Lynn Barber's interview for the *Sunday Times* magazine:

> Eventually Capaldi joins me [...] The first thing that strikes me is that he has aged an awful lot since he played Malcolm Tucker in *The Thick Of It* (he is 58) and that he seems terribly tired, with bloodshot eyes. He explains that he was doing a night shoot until 11:30pm the night before. And they have been filming 12 hours a day for almost nine months, with only a short break for Christmas, so he is pretty exhausted.[47]

Critical paratextual framings thus become especially sticky, being cited and reiterated in press coverage,[48] regardless of whether or not Capaldi is aiming to refine a well-honed and brand-related self-image.

Contra such patterns in journalistic practice (as professional tabloid/broadsheet journalists exaggeratedly perform their independence from BBC brands),[49] practices of official brand management attempt to instal paratextual meanings of newness and nowness. This involves making the launches of series eight, nine and ten into media 'events'. For instance, series eight received a press preview (attended by paying members of the public) in Cardiff's St David's Hall, followed by a same-day London event at the BFI Southbank and, straight after the broadcast of 'Deep Breath', a live-streamed Q & A featuring Peter Capaldi, Steven Moffat and Jenna Coleman. This Q & A was hosted by Zoe Ball, who had previously introduced Capaldi in 2013's *Doctor Who Live: The Next Doctor*. Series nine also had a press/preview screening in Cardiff, albeit on a much smaller scale than Capaldi's first series, while series ten's penultimate episode was accompanied by a live orchestral score at the Wales Millennium Centre, again followed immediately by a live-streamed Q & A, this time with Steven Moffat and Pearl Mackie.

Other paratextual mechanisms for reinforcing an 'event' logic include utilising contemporary norms of industry promotion such as appearing at San Diego Comic-Con.[50] SDCC typically boasts 'exclusive' trailers and production news which can confer status on attending fans. As Anne Gilbert points out, promotion at SDCC can 'use paratexts – previews, exclusive footage, merchandising, interviews, casting announcements – to build fan interest and, ideally, eventual consumption [...] SDCC provides industrial participants [with] the opportunity to introduce influential paratextual material to a particularly receptive fan audience.'[51] But SDCC can also be interpreted as marking out important franchise developments, with Capaldi and Moffat's appearance in 2017 being seen by fan website *Blogtor Who* as offering 'a huge send off' for the two, thus being paratextually cast in a commemorative mode.[52]

A very different kind of media event was used to reveal Pearl Mackie's role as companion Bill Potts. In this instance, Capaldi appeared with Mackie in a specially shot scene entitled 'Friend from the Future' which was eventually, in an edited and reshot version, incorporated into episode one of 2017's series ten, 'The Pilot'. But the initial version received its TV premiere in the half-time break of the 23 April 2016 FA Cup semi-final between Everton and Manchester United, prompting the *Daily Telegraph* to ponder 'how much crossover there is between Whovians and football fans'.[53] Being 'announced live'[54] incorporated this unusual *Doctor Who* paratext into a televisual mode of sporting liveness rather than invoking the 'shiny floor show' genre that had characterised Capaldi's announcement. And although it represents a twist on the exact kind of 'event' logic that BBC Wales's *Doctor Who* has tended to paratextually trade on, the FA Cup nevertheless conveys connotations of Britishness, forming part of a 'national conversation' and resonating with the BBC's values:

> Michelle Osborn, head of communications for BBC One and BBC Drama explains [...] 'It's about BBC One being the home of big live events and real moments that brings the nation together. That is a core role that BBC One [has] [...] that it can bring the nation together for big moments.[55]

Thus, although 'Friend from the Future' and *Doctor Who Live: The Next Doctor* may seem to be very different instances of UK TV entertainment – a recorded drama scene versus a live chat show-style programme; an announcement amid Saturday football versus a one-off Sunday night 'Special' – both perform the dominant paratextual and brand-management aim of providing 'moments' of nowness and newness. Both are self-consciously produced TV 'events', designed for press take-up and online dissemination as pop cultural news stories. For instance, announcing that *Doctor Who Live* would unveil the Twelfth Doctor only two days before its broadcast, on Friday, 2 August, the BBC's online/social media team and communications and marketing then collaborated to release 'a drip feed of announcements, including guest confirmations for the show',[56] while Capaldi himself participated in a last-minute photo shoot with Rankin, meaning that an official portrait of the actor was ready for release immediately after the live reveal programme. Indeed, this photograph was widely used in the UK press the following day, including on a number of newspapers' front pages. The success of *Doctor Who Live: The Next Doctor* was measured not just through its audience ratings of 6.9 million but also in social media terms: 'the BBC Doctor Who website crashed, with over 800m tweets sent in total around #doctorwho and #petercapaldi, while 89.4 per cent of all conversation on Twitter during the programme transmission was about the show.'[57] The 16 July 2017 reveal of the Thirteenth Doctor was more akin to Pearl Mackie's announcement as Bill – this time featuring a specially shot sequence after the men's Wimbledon final rather than during FA Cup coverage – and it carried exactly the same 'event' logic. By virtue of being embedded in one of the BBC's broadcasting crown jewels, the governmentally 'listed' sporting event of a Wimbledon final, the reveal was once more deployed to shore up the 'core role that BBC One [has] ... that it can bring the nation together for big moments'. And though the reveal video would go on to be viewed by more than sixteen million people online,[58] it was still a BBC One live broadcast which remained the premier placement for the unveiling. The BBC seemingly anticipated that this news might be controversial in some quarters, and pre-emptively sought to smooth over the transition. The new Doctor was very swiftly paratextually endorsed by Capaldi in an official press release.[59]

Such pre-planned 'real moments' do not account for all the industrial and paratextual strands that have wended their way around and through the Capaldi era, however. Although Peter Capaldi's evocation of paratextual memory, especially via his *Radio Times* fan letter, demonstrated a version of fan authenticity which – along with his 'lapel-tugging' and Pertwee-referencing costume – could reassure fandom that *Doctor Who*'s continuity was safe, an array of more subordinated and exceptional paratextual activities have highlighted occasional glitches in officially endorsed publicity.

Contesting *Who*: paratextual glitching and gendering

Doctor Who Live: The Next Doctor was kept secret until shortly before transmission in August 2013, but it still needed to recruit a live audience of *Who* fans. The result was a highly unusual paratext, as the BBC's audience ticketing website advertised a 'pilot for a show celebrating 50 years of *Doctor Who* [...] The as yet untitled programme is said to be an entertainment show that will include clips from throughout the show's history.'[60] As the Head of Communications for BBC One explained in a post-reveal interview:

> it had been out there for two weeks that we were doing this live show [...] we needed to put it out there on the audience services website, but we disguised it as a [...] show looking at Doctor Who's 50 years, so we knew we would get fans in the mix but we didn't tell them what the show was.[61]

This non-existent pilot TV programme was an *official but fake paratext*; a necessary deception in order for the BBC's planned 'moment' to retain its element of surprise. Although in this case the fake TV pilot worked within dominant paratextual logics of the media event, other unusual paratexts have framed the Capaldi era in more contestatory if not marginal ways.

Some journalistic coverage has focused self-referentially on the professional mechanics of paratextual production itself – and problems or difficulties in this process – rather than treating paratextuality straightforwardly as an entry point into *Doctor Who*'s branding/textuality. Writing in the *Sunday Times Culture*, for example, Martin James made a series eight episode his 'pick of the day' while confessing that he hadn't actually seen it due to an issue with the BBC's previewing site:

> Put 'Doctor Who' into the search box on the website critics use to preview BBC offerings and the response is 'o result – Did you mean Tom Kerridge's Best Ever Dishes?' Clearly, tonight's episode was not available in advance – and we are left wondering if Kerridge [...] has a new recipe for Dalek pie.[62]

In fact, the BBC had taken to listing *Doctor Who* previews under code names in order to prevent them from being found by title-searching alone – perhaps to prevent journalist-fans from watching the programme when they otherwise had no professional requirement to do so, hence cracking down on the possible information flow of pre-transmission spoilers.

Writing for the same publication, but this time in regard to the series ten finale, David Hutcheon also focused on glitches in *Doctor Who*'s paratextual circulation at the *Sunday Times*: 'Is anybody still watching? [...] [T]onight sees the final episode of a 12-part series and not a single person has written [in] [...] to say how good/bad/indifferent Peter Capaldi and Steven Moffat's swansong has been.'[63] Rather than fully buying into the event logic of digital flows, such marginal paratexts instead frame Peter Capaldi's tenure in terms of the BBC's (supposedly problematic) engagement with professional TV critics/journalists, or the public's (again problematic) disengagement with long-established mechanisms of press feedback. The generation of journalistic or audience paratexts itself becomes a central topic, in place of framing the Twelfth Doctor's time on screen or the *Doctor*

Who brand. In another example, Lynn Barber, a senior journalist and multiple winner of British Press Awards, begins one feature interview with Peter Capaldi – meant to promote series ten – in a fully self-referential mode:

> You have to sign the equivalent of the Official Secrets Act to get into the BBC studios in Cardiff where they film *Doctor Who*. You will not photograph, record or discuss anything you see [...] *Doctor Who*, I soon learn, is a cult and I am penetrating to its Holy of Holies. Trouble is, it's a cult I don't belong to, so when the press officer says, in awed terms, that she might be able to let me touch the actual Tardis, I just stare.[64]

Barber performs her professional journalism via rigorous non-fandom, but at the same time she highlights processes of paratextual control that are exerted (or attempted) by BBC Wales. Interviewing Peter Capaldi at Roath Lock Studios means being granted privileged access to the media world, e.g. touching 'the actual' TARDIS, but instead of playing along with this game, Barber highlights its stakes. The suggestion is that journalists may realistically have relatively little professional independence or detachment from *Doctor Who* in this scenario, being required to sign and observe a non-disclosure agreement, as well as potentially being fannishly co-opted via the press officer's promise of a TARDIS trip.

As such, Barber's account of this glitching promotional set visit is very different in tone to Rachel Aroesti's in the *Guardian* which preceded series eight. In the *Guardian*'s smoothly normative rather than contestatory framing of Capaldi's first season, Aroesti narrates her journalistic movement from the 'flagrant mundanity' of Roath Lock to 'the Tardis [...] illuminated by a pillar of burnt-orange vertical strip-lights' as a microcosm for the programme's essence,[65] integrating her personal account with Capaldi's interview: 'It is this relationship between the domestic and the epic', says Capaldi of what appeals to him about the programme. 'The sense that there's a bridge, that a hand can be extended, and you can step from [...] the supermarket car park [...] into the Andromeda nebula or whatever.'[66] Rather than exposing and contesting BBC Wales's attempt to exert paratextual control over the Capaldi era, Aroesti performs her role as a professional journalist by neatly folding together the narrative of her set access and the *Doctor Who* brand as reinforced by its lead actor.

A more extreme celebration of journalistic proximity and access is performed, perhaps unsurprisingly, by a fan-journalist writing for the commercial fan magazine *SFX*. In this instance, Nick Setchfield focuses on the visceral experience of being on set (for filming of series ten's 'Empress of Mars'), repeatedly and almost poetically asking 'How does it feel to step inside *Doctor Who*? It feels like this.'[67] Setchfield conveys the physical details of his privileged entrance into the media world: 'red dust' of the Mars set settles on his shoes, accompanying 'the tell-tale paint-and-glue tang of television make-believe in your nostrils'.[68] There is a sense of the thrillingly momentary and promotional 'event' logic embedded in this account too, as Setchfield narratively stitches together his visit with the situations of Capaldi and Moffat, soon to leave the programme: 'How does it feel to step inside *Doctor Who*? It feels deeply, unmistakably *Doctor Who*. Breathe it in. It doesn't last for-ever. Not even if you're the Doctor. Or the man who tells his stories.'[69] But a sense of fan excitement and privilege colours this account more strongly than Aroesti's, as Setchfield recurrently emphasises that he has moved 'inside' the branded tautology of *Doctor Who* – a domain that can only adequately be described as 'deeply [...] *Doctor Who*'.

This fannish desire for proximity to the fan object is not only present in terms of journalists' set visits, however. Steven Moffat argues in his 2017 interview with Nick Setchfield that 'everyone who reviews [...] *Who* is inside the bubble with us. We very, very rarely hear the voice of the actual audience. I'm not sure we ever hear it, except in audience research.'[70] And yet professional journalists complaining about glitches in BBC previews or reader comments ('is anybody [...] watching?'), as well as refusing to fetishise the 'Holy of Holies' of *Doctor Who*'s sets are, however marginally, seeking to mark out some professional distance from TV's promotional-cultural coverage. Nonetheless, Moffat is largely accurate in his assessment of the fan blogosphere that has emerged around contemporary *Doctor Who*. It is now common for multiple fan websites to preview new episodes in some detail in the week prior to broadcast, as well as subsequently reviewing Peter Capaldi's episodes alongside professional TV critics. Jan Teurlings has referred to this proliferation of enthusiasts' TV (p)reviews as the 'commonification' of TV criticism, while scholars such as Paul Rixon and Sandra Falero have also explored the alleged 'democratisation' of TV reviewing linked to Web 2.0 contexts.[71]

However, fan sites who sign up to gain access to BBC previews of *Doctor Who* do so on the basis that their social media reach is assessed by BBC PR. They also sign up to BBC terms and conditions, including strictly observing detailed instructions on spoilers, and on exactly what can and cannot be discussed pre-broadcast. Fans may, of course, produce highly negative episode reviews (having the same freedom in this respect as professional journalists), but the fan blogosphere is undoubtedly 'inside the bubble' with the *Who* production team in terms of being required to observe professional codes of pre-transmission brand management and information control. Far from constituting a 'democratisation' of TV criticism via fan-created paratexts, the era of the Twelfth Doctor has thus involved a consolidation of professionalised fan-reviewing that is aligned with a (somewhat) privileged blogosphere granted early access to episodes and proximity to the BBC's PR. Rather than a thoroughgoing 'digital participatory culture', in Falero's terms,[72] this is probably better thought of as what Emma Keltie has called 'authorised participation', given that fan-bloggers' previews have to paratextually match up with the BBC's non-spoiler instructions.[73]

If some unusual framings of Capaldi's tenure have involved official fakery and journalistic self-referentiality temporarily disrupting the smooth operation of brand-building, other marginal frames have been explicitly political. Interviewed by *The Big Issue*, for example, prior to his first full appearance as the Doctor, Capaldi discussed the fact that without a student grant he would never have become BBC TV's Time Lord:

> the government paid for you to be educated because they believed it was a civic responsibility. And I certainly would not be here, being Doctor Who, if they hadn't done that [...] So I find it alarming that we live in an age where we don't think, as a society, it is worthwhile paying to help people be educated and become the best they can be.[74]

This left-wing politics was also evident during a charity event in 2014 where Capaldi discussed the fact that he hadn't (at that point) received a Twelfth Doctor-specific sonic screwdriver design. In response to Mark Gatiss's light-hearted comment that this had missed a 'marketing opportunity', Capaldi responded: 'Well I think we should side step [*sic*] the marketing opportunities. I don't think we should be too focused in that direction.'[75] However, Capaldi's anti-commercial exploitation stance has been predominantly submerged in his star *Doctor Who* persona, very much unlike his fan enthusiasm. Whereas performing fandom is evidently a culturally-politically 'safe' move for the programme's lead actor, aligning him paratextually with its dedicated audience and with fellow fans among the production team such as Steven Moffat, expressing an anti-neo-liberal perspective is a far riskier paratextual manoeuvre. At odds with the contemporary branding and merchandising of *Doctor Who*, as well as with neo-liberal positionings of fandom, challenging the merchandising activities of BBC Worldwide appears to be less paratextually acceptable than, say, directly challenging the BBC's scheduling of series nine.[76] Capaldi's expressions of his politics have therefore tended to be sidelined in paratextual framings of 'his' era, although it will be interesting to see whether such elements return to the fore once Capaldi has become a former Doctor and hence is less strongly bound by the need to comply with norms of *Who*'s brand management. By contrast, Capaldi's artistic creativity has been repeatedly emphasised through his drawings and doodles for charity, as well as via his Dalek artwork on *Doctor Who* clapperboards and his design for a 'Paddington Who' figure as part of the Paddington Bear Trail in 2014.[77] Paratextually emphasising Capaldi's creativity represents a further way in which his star persona can be articulated with *Who* fandom, i.e. via fans' productivity as well as via shared affect.

One cultural-political aspect of the Capaldi era which *has* proliferated in fan and journalist paratexts alike is the issue of the Doctor's gender. Unlike contestations of marketing/merchandising *tout court*, though, this question is absolutely of a piece with neo-liberal culture, exploring the matter of how a brand should respond to its audience markets:

While a neoliberal system and its free market approach encourages agency, it is an agency without [...] the questioning of dominant structures that is favoured. Thus, the 'good' fan accepts that he or she can affect the production of media content by establishing himself or herself as part of a visible and vocal market segment – without openly questioning the 'rules' of the free market.[78]

And in an inversion of the *Star Wars: The Force Awakens* situation, where the film text worked to reposition the franchise as significantly female-targeted while merchandising paratexts marginalised its heroine Rey,[79] *Doctor Who* across Capaldi's era *has been more feminist and progressive at its paratextual than textual level.* Paratextual suggestions for a female Doctor dominated fan and press discussions of the Thirteenth Doctor, running ahead of the programme's eventual pro-feminist rebranding. And despite textual hints at the Doctor's capacity to be regendered, this 'regendering, like the Master–Missy transformation, has occurred through the body of a supporting character, not via the traditionally masculine body of the Doctor' throughout the Capaldi era.[80] Both the conclusions to series nine and ten play connotatively with entirely female versions of the conventional Doctor–companion pairing. Clara (Jenna Coleman) and Ashildr (Maisie Williams) represent a Doctor–companion analogue in 'Hell Bent': 'The shifts of tone and the evolving story [...] imply that the series still cannot accommodate an autonomous woman with the experience and assurance to challenge, and match, the Doctor.'[81] Indeed, the Doctor is made to diegetically forget Clara at the point at which she becomes most Doctor-like. The resolution to Bill Potts's series ten narrative is startlingly similar; reunited with 'The Pilot' Heather (Stephanie Hyam), Bill also becomes part of a fantastical, female and universe-hopping duo, yet this time the Doctor believes her to be deceased.

While Peter Capaldi's tenure has formed part of 'one longer-term arc of meaning in the series [...] [i.e.] its privileging of a white male perspective',[82] fan/journalist paratexts following in the wake of Capaldi's announcement that he was leaving the role challenged this textual limit, carrying a greater progressive potential than Lorna Jowett sometimes allows in *Dancing with the Doctor*:

Of course, paratexts of any kind are not necessarily there to support or to subvert gender representations in the 'parent' text. There are obvious reasons why they have proliferated. Even for a public-service broadcaster like the BBC, paratexts help build both programme brands, and audiences for those brands.[83]

But I would argue that paratexts can do more than smooth over transitions in *Doctor Who*'s continuity or periodisation, or marginally highlight glitches in contemporary brand management. Here, they can also anticipate and rehearse moments of brand revitalisation, doing the ground work to recodify 'gendered franchising discourses' and 'acknowledge the diversity of [...] [*Who*'s] audience' in advance of textual regeneration, and ahead of the Thirteenth Doctor.[84] This amounts to a different kind of paratextual smoothing-over, ultimately, *one that prepares and cues audiences to expect the programme brand's updating* rather than only reassuring them that a specific lead actor will cohere with *Who*'s longer history and wider Whoniverse.

Conclusion: paratexts of a 'fanboy dream'

Paratextual framings of the 'Capaldi era' have played an active part in its initiation and conclusion. Capaldi's fandom for 1960s and 70s *Doctor Who*, and the First to Third Doctors, has been paratextually co-opted in order to authenticate his casting in the eyes of long-term fans, even eventually moving into a position of textual centrality thanks to the programme's current paratextual-textual permeability to fanboy identification.[85] As director Rachel Talalay has noted of Moffat and Capaldi's final story featuring David Bradley as the First Doctor: 'It's a fanboy's dream [...] there's a certain absolute fanboy-ness to it.'[86]

While Capaldi's *Who* fandom has been (para)textually embraced as a key facet of his tenure,[87] the actor's own anti-neo-liberal politics have been paratextually marginalised and textually neglected rather than referenced. That is to say, the Twelfth Doctor has frequently acknowledged his Scottishness, as well as Peter Capaldi's distinctive physiognomy, but relatively little sense of Capaldi's politics has made it through into his era's paratexts or texts, with 'Oxygen' standing as a notable exception in series ten thanks to its powerfully anti-capitalist position (indeed, given Capaldi's attachment to the more politicised era of the Third Doctor, it is tempting to ponder whether 'Oxygen' constituted just as much a 'gift' to the outgoing lead as the Mondasian

Cybermen). Instead, the very much pro-neo-liberal brand 'refresh' proffered by a female Thirteenth Doctor has been (para)textually trailed and trialled – via debate surrounding the Master's transformation into Missy, and hopes for the casting – as a way of maintaining the brand value (the newness and nowness) of this Doctor's replacement.

Presenter Zoe Ball introduced Capaldi during *Doctor Who Live* with the words 'Please welcome the Twelfth Doctor, a hero for a whole new generation.' But it is apparent that paratexts have done far more than simply hyping and marketing the Twelfth Doctor between 2013 and 2017, or delimiting the preferred meanings of series eight through to ten's episodes. Above all, the Capaldi era has been marked out by paratextual meanings that redound to the brand identity of *Doctor Who*: a seemingly fan-friendly programme brand at ease with its longer cultural history, as well as open to new unfoldings, new experiments and new gender possibilities. Indeed, it could be said that although the casting of the Thirteenth Doctor, and its revitalising change regarding the Doctor's gender, was textually hinted at across Capaldi's tenure, it also represents a moment that has been paratextually prepared for.

Notes

1   Keith Miller, *The Official Doctor Who Fan Club*, vol. 1: *The Jon Pertwee Years* (Raleigh, NC, 2011), p. 74.
2   Paul Booth, 'Periodising *Doctor Who*', *Science Fiction Film and Television* vii/2 (2014), pp. 195–215.
3   Casey J. McCormick, '"Forward is the battle cry": binge-viewing Netflix's *House of Cards*', in Kevin McDonald and Daniel Smith-Rowsey (eds), *The Netflix Effect: Technology and Entertainment in the 21st Century* (New York, 2016), p. 112.
4   Karin van Es, *The Future of Live* (Cambridge, 2017).
5   Jonathan Gray, *Show Sold Separately: Promos, Spoilers, and Other Media Paratexts* (New York, 2010).
6   Matt Hills, *Doctor Who: The Unfolding Event – Marketing, Merchandising and Mediatizing a Brand Anniversary* (Basingstoke, 2015), p. 13.
7   Jonathan Gray and Amanda Lotz, *Television Studies* (Cambridge, 2012), p. 134.
8   Matt Hills, 'Hyping *Who* and marketing the Steven Moffat era: the role of "prior paratexts"', in Andrew O'Day (ed.), *Doctor Who: The Eleventh*

Hour – A Critical Celebration of the Matt Smith and Steven Moffat Era (London, 2014), p. 183. Italics in original.

9   Hills, *Doctor Who: The Unfolding Event*.

10 Melissa Aronczyk, 'Portal or police? The limits of promotional paratexts', *Critical Studies in Media Communication* xxxiv/2 (2017), p. 113. For more on the relationship between paratexts and brands, see Catherine Johnson, *Branding Television* (London, 2012).

11 Aronczyk, 'Portal or police?', p. 113.

12 Catherine Johnson, 'Doctor Who as programme brand', in Matt Hills (ed.), *New Dimensions of Doctor Who: Adventures in Space, Time and Television* (London, 2013), pp. 95–112.

13 Paul Grainge and Catherine Johnson, *Promotional Screen Industries* (London, 2015).

14 Suzanne Scott, '#Wheresrey? Toys, spoilers, and the gender politics of franchise paratexts', *Critical Studies in Media Communication* xxxiv/2 (2017), p. 139.

15 Booth, 'Periodising *Doctor Who*'.

16 John Tulloch and Manuel Alvarado, *Doctor Who: The Unfolding Text* (London, 1983), p. 97.

17 Reading *Dr Who* via periodization into different eras: Paul Booth, 'Periodising *Doctor Who*', *Science Fiction Film and Television* vii/2 (2014), pp. 195–215. The idea that this periodisation has been dictated by lead actors: John Tulloch and Manuel Alvarado, *Doctor Who: The Unfolding Text* (London, 1983), p. 97. For the idea that script editor–producer production teams and elements of production design have dictated periodisation, see Piers D. Britton, *TARDISbound: Navigating the Universes of Doctor Who* (London, 2011), p. 12.

18 Booth, 'Periodising *Doctor Who*', p. 205.

19 Ibid., p. 206.

20 Ibid., pp. 207–8.

21 Matt Hills, 'Rebranding *Doctor Who* and reimagining *Sherlock*: "quality" television as "makeover TV drama"', *International Journal of Cultural Studies* xviii/3 (2015), pp. 317–31.

22 Booth, 'Periodising *Doctor Who*', p. 197.

23 Celia Lury, *Brands: The Logos of the Global Economy* (London, 2004), p. 8.

24 Ibid., p. 9.

25 Hills, 'Rebranding *Doctor Who* and reimagining *Sherlock*', p. 321.

26 Andrew O'Day, '*Doctor Who* and the tugging of the lapel', Who Watching [website] (2013). Available at https://whowatching.wordpress.com/2013/08/28/doctor-who-and-the-tugging-of-the-lapel/ (accessed 16 June 2017).

27 Booth, 'Periodising *Doctor Who*', p. 197.

28 Matt Hills and Joanne Garde-Hansen, 'Fandom's paratextual memory:

remembering, reconstructing, and repatriating "lost" *Doctor Who*', *Critical Studies in Media Communication* xxxiv/2 (2017), p. 160.

29 Morgan Jeffery, 'Yes – the return of *Doctor Who*'s Mondasian Cybermen WAS a gift to Peter Capaldi from Steven Moffat', Digital Spy [website] (19 April 2017). Available at http://www.digitalspy.com/tv/doctor-who/news/a826323/doctor-who-mondasian-cybermen-peter-capaldi/ (accessed 16 June 2017).

30 Booth, 'Periodising *Doctor Who*', p. 206.

31 The concept of Moffat reworking fan lore is explored in Matt Hills, 'The expertise of digital fandom as a "community of practice": exploring the narrative universe of *Doctor Who*', *Convergence* xxi/3 (2015), pp. 360–74. The concept of new interpretations of the programme's hyperdiegetic past appears in idem, *Fan Cultures* (London, 2002), p. 137; see also Paul Booth and Jef Burnham, '*Who* are we? Re-envisioning the Doctor in the 21st century', in Carlen Lavigne (ed.), *Remake Television* (Lanham, MD, 2014), p. 204.

32 Stephen Bayley, 'Doctor Who and Crombie: Mod mod man with a box', *Independent* (29 January 2014). Available at https://www.independent.co.uk/life-style/fashion/features/doctor-who-and-crombie-mod-man-with-a-box-9091847.html (accessed 1 July 2017).

33 Matt Rudd, 'The Doctor will see you now', *Sunday Times Magazine* (27 July 2014). Available at https://www.thetimes.co.uk/article/the-doctor-will-see-you-now-gwj76873s8z (accessed 1 July 2017).

34 Ibid.

35 Ibid.

36 Ibid.

37 Benjamin Cook, 'The *DWM* interview: Peter Capaldi', *Doctor Who Magazine* 477 (2014), p. 31.

38 Ibid., p. 35.

39 Ibid., p. 32.

40 Rachel Aroesti, 'Peter Capaldi: "I know how to work the Tardis. I've known for a long time"', *Guardian Guide* (16 August 2014). Available at https://www.theguardian.com/tv-and-radio/2014/aug/16/doctor-who-peter-capaldi (accessed 1 July 2017).

41 Andrew Lowry, 'Doctor How?', *ShortList* 335 (7 August 2014), p. 43.

42 Adrian Lobb, 'It's dark and spare, pulled back to something simple', *Big Issue* (11–17 August 2014), pp. 19, 21.

43 Moffat in Andrew Billen, 'Abrasive, difficult, but he's your best friend in the universe', *The Times: Saturday Review* (16 August 2014).

44 Jonathan Hatfull, 'The oncoming storm', *SciFiNow* 96 (2014), p. 25.

45 Chloe Fox, 'Peter Capaldi: "You don't just play the Doctor, you represent him"', *Telegraph* (12 September 2015). Available at https://www.telegraph.co.uk/tv/2015/peter-capaldi-you-dont-just-play-the-doctor-you-represent-him/ (accessed 1 July 2017).

46 Capaldi in Lynn Barber, 'I don't want to spend my life doing *Doctor Who* conventions ... but I'm lucky I have that option', *Sunday Times Magazine* (2 April 2017).

47 Ibid.

48 See also Stephen Armstrong, 'The right stuff?', *Radio Times* (1–7 November 2014), pp. 12–17; Andrew Duncan, 'Who's looking at *Who*?', *Radio Times* (19–25 September 2015), pp. 14–18; Stephen Armstrong, 'Dead man walking?', *Radio Times* (24–30 June 2017), pp. 10–13.

49 Jen Pharo, 'As Capaldi quits and ratings plunge we ask... Doctor Whodunnnit?', *Sun* (1 February 2017).

50 Kyle Anderson, '*Doctor Who* is bringing Peter Capaldi to San Diego Comic-Con', Nerdist [website] (27 May 2015). Available at http://nerdist. com/doctor-who-is-bringing-peter-capaldi-to-san-diego-comic-con/ (accessed 16 June 2017).

51 Anne Gilbert, 'Live from Hall H: fan/producer symbiosis at San Diego Comic-Con', in Jonathan Gray, Cornel Sandvoss and C. Lee Harrington (eds), *Fandom: Identities and Communities in a Mediated World* (2nd edn, New York, 2017), p. 363.

52 Susan Hewitt, 'Peter Capaldi & Steven Moffat to appear at SDCC', Blogtor Who [website] (2 July 2017). Available at https://blogtorwho. com/peter-capaldi-steven-moffat-appear-sdcc/ (accessed 4 July 2017).

53 Michael Hogan, 'Pearl Mackie revealed as new *Doctor Who* companion in season 10 teaser: everything you need to know', *Telegraph* (25 April 2016). Available at http://www.telegraph.co.uk/tv/2016/04/23/doctor-who-pearl-mackie-is-the-new-companion/ (accessed 4 July 2017).

54 Ibid.

55 Stephen Lepitak, 'How they kept it quiet – the BBC PR strategy behind Peter Capaldi being named Doctor Who', The Drum [website] (5 August 2013). Available at http://www.thedrum.com/news/2013/08/05/how-they-kept-it-quiet-bbc-pr-strategy-behind-peter-capaldi-being-named-doctor-who (accessed 16 June 2017).

56 Ibid.

57 Ibid.

58 Rob Leane, '*Doctor Who*: Jodie Whittaker reveal video has 16 million hits', Den of Geek [website] (19 July 2017). Available at http://www. denofgeek.com/uk/tv/doctor-who/50785/doctor-who-jodie-whittaker-reveal-video-has-16-million-hits (accessed 24 July 2017).

59 'Introducing Jodie Whittaker – the Thirteenth Doctor', BBC Media Centre [website] (16 July 2017). Available at http://www.bbc.co.uk/media centre/latestnews/2017/jodie-whittaker-13-doctor (accessed 24 July 2017).

60 Stephen Kelly, 'BBC1 *Doctor Who* pilot asks fans to help celebrate 50 years of the show', *Radio Times* [website] (26 July 2013). Available at http://www.radiotimes.com/news/2013-07-26/bbc1-doctor-who-pilot-

asks-fans-to-help-celebrate-50-years-of-the-show/ (accessed 16 June 2017).

61 Michelle Osborn, quoted in Stephen Lepitak, 'How they kept it quiet'.

62 Martin James, 'Pick of the day: *Doctor Who*', *Sunday Times Culture* (21 September 2014).

63 David Hutcheon, 'Critics' choice', *Sunday Times Culture* (25 June 2017).

64 Barber, 'I don't want to spend my life doing *Doctor Who* conventions'.

65 Aroesti, 'Peter Capaldi: "I know how to work the Tardis"'.

66 Quoted ibid.

67 Nick Setchfield, 'The time of their lives', *SFX* 286 (2017), pp. 42, 52.

68 Ibid., p. 42.

69 Ibid., p. 43.

70 Ibid., p. 44.

71 Jan Teurlings, 'Social media and the new commons of TV criticism', *Television & New Media* xix/3 (2018; published online 28 May 2017). Available at http://journals.sagepub.com/doi/abs/10.1177/1527476417709599 (accessed 14 June 2017); Paul Rixon, *TV Critics and Popular Culture: A History of British Television Criticism* (London, 2011); Sandra M. Falero, *Digital Participatory Culture and the TV Audience: Everyone's A Critic* (Basingstoke, 2016).

72 Falero, *Digital Participatory Culture and the TV Audience*.

73 Emma Keltie, *The Culture Industry and Participatory Audiences* (Basingstoke, 2017), p. 133.

74 Lobb, 'It's dark and spare', p. 21.

75 Cameron K. McEwan, '*Doctor Who*: Peter Capaldi wants another TARDIS ... has to be retro', *Metro* [website] (16 November 2014). Available at http://metro.co.uk/2014/11/16/doctor-who-peter-capaldi-wants-another-tardis-has-to-be-retro-4950782/ (accessed 14 June 2017).

76 Rebecca Lawrence, '"They take *Dr Who* for granted": Peter Capaldi blasts BBC bosses for tampering with the show's family-friendly time slot', *MailOnline* (11 March 2016). Available at http://www.dailymail.co.uk/tvshowbiz/article-3488421/They-Dr-granted-Peter-Capaldi-blasts-BBC-bosses-tampering-s-family-friendly-time-slot.html (accessed 14 June 2017).

77 Harry Ward, 'Paddington Who?', Doctor Who News [website] (3 November 2014). Available at http://www.doctorwhonews.net/2014/11/paddington-who-031114124115.html (accessed 14 June 2017).

78 Henrik Linden and Sara Linden, *Fans and Fan Cultures: Tourism, Consumerism and Social Media* (Basingstoke, 2017), pp. 68–9.

79 Scott, '#Wheresrey?'.

80 Tom Powers, *Gender and the Quest in British Science Fiction Television: An Analysis of* Doctor Who, Blake's 7, Red Dwarf *and* Torchwood (Jefferson, NC, 2016), p. 230.

81 Lorna Jowett, *Dancing with the Doctor: Dimensions of Gender in the Doctor Who Universe* (London, 2017), p. 146.

82 Ibid., p. 179.

83 Ibid., p. 96.

84 Scott, '#Wheresrey?', p. 139.

85 Huw Fullerton, 'That brilliant new *Doctor Who* series 10 teaser was made by a fan – and there are more to come', *Radio Times* [website] (31 March 2017). Available at http://www.radiotimes.com/news/2017-03-31/that-brilliant-new-doctor-who-series-10-teaser-was-made-by-a-fan--and-there-are-more-to-come (accessed 16 June 2017); Powers, *Gender and the Quest in British Science Fiction Television*, pp. 190–1.

86 Rachel Talalay, quoted in Benjamin Cook, 'The Doctor Falls', *Doctor Who Magazine* 514 (2017), p. 21.

87 Alison Graham, 'The man in the blue box', *Radio Times* (23–29 August 2014), p. 15.

9

THE TRANSCULTURAL FAN

Branding Series 8 of *Doctor Who* in the US

Paul Booth

While *Doctor Who* has always had a global impact and audience, it has arguably never been a more globally recognised brand than it is today. From marketing to paratextual products, from interstitial adverts to worldwide 'events' of magnificent (symbolic) proportions, the name *Doctor Who* reflects 'more than just a television series' and 'can also be seen as part of an ambitious and wide-ranging strategy' of the BBC to brand the programme in a post-2005 global era.[1] This strategy, employed by the commercial wing of the British Broadcasting Corporation, BBC Worldwide, has been one of franchising and marketing across borders and cultures. As Catherine Johnson describes, in fact, the 'history of *Doctor Who* as a text is bound up with the history of television branding' – and such branding has developed across the world and throughout different cultural contexts.[2]

Indeed, as *Doctor Who* series eight neared, promotions in the UK on BBC One and in the US on BBC America ran rampant. This chapter explores this 'hype' of *Who* at the time of the arrival of a new Doctor specifically as it manifested in a US context.[3] First, I analyse the premiere of *Doctor* Who series eight in the light of what Simone Knox describes as the 'transatlantic dimensions' of *Doctor Who*,[4] specifically focusing on promotions like the *Doctor Who* world tour (which travelled to New York City on 14 August 2014) and the simulcast of 'Deep Breath' in cinemas around the world. This analysis examines what Johnson calls the 'programme brand' of *Doctor Who* in the United States, specifically looking at series eight and the Capaldi era (although, as I have previously pointed out, divisions between eras are often exaggerated).[5] I also conduct a semiotic analysis of the BBC One and BBC America trailers and promos for series eight of *Doctor Who*, examining similarities and differences in the way the show was advertised to two different international audiences.[6] I argue in this chapter that BBC America's promotion of Steven Moffat's series eight of *Doctor Who* sought to engage an active fan audience, through a deliberate and focused attempt to create what Bertha Chin and Lori Morimoto call a 'transcultural' appeal to a fan audience,[7] while seeking also to cement a more mainstream viewing public. For Chin and Morimoto, a more nation-centric approach to fandom and fan audiences misses the larger border-crossing realities of the objects of fandom. For instance, they write about East Asian fandom that spans nations and crosses national boundaries and is united by the affective energies of multiple fan audiences, yet the transculturalism they describe is generated by fans working generally outside institutional contexts. For the BBC and BBC Worldwide, the promotion and hype leading up to series eight of *Doctor Who* attempted to concretise these transcultural moments in 'worldwide' events – but also resorted to an aura of 'Britishness' as a way of cementing the unique nature of global *Doctor Who*. I conclude the chapter with a celebrity studies analysis of the then current 'voice' of BBC America, Mark Sheppard, and his intertextual connections and celebrity in relation to a number of popular science fiction television programmes over the past decade, as well as in comparison to the previous 'voice' of BBC America, John Oliver.

Doctor Who: the ongoing branded event

The event of *Doctor Who*'s series eight premiere offers a chance to view shifting notions of promotion and meaning of *Doctor Who* in the

States. Indeed, while Andrew O'Day argues that 'consuming *Doctor Who* has always been an "Event" for fans', different levels of attention at the institutional level can lend more or less *formal* attention to the event-like status of a series.[8] O'Day describes the new series of *Doctor Who* in 2005 as one in which '*Doctor Who* returned [...] in an industrial context where "must-see TV" exists as a category, and is publicized and promoted as such,' and Johnson notes that 'Branding has become particularly important for the BBC in the development of the new series in 2005.'[9] The BBC and BBC Worldwide engaged a highly visible and encompassing promotional package in order to create an event out of the 2005 return of *Doctor Who* – something that attempted to engage a larger and more general audience and reach beyond the stalwart fan audience that would tune in no matter what.

This (para)textual shift became an attempt to transfer the show's appeal from mere niche to more mainstream: Matt Hills argues that this shift 'repositions' *Doctor Who*, and 'although the classic series was merchandised heavily across its existence [...] *Doctor Who* has now been firmly reconceptualised within the contemporary TV industry.'[10] Yet, throughout this branding event, a tension emerges between the nation-specific aspects of the television series and the global audience that BBC Worldwide seemed poised to approach.

Indeed, promotion-branding and event-creating tend to be nationally specific, but also maintain a consistency of message. As Hills claims, *Doctor Who* 'has previously been theorised in relation to [...] national contexts/identities', and understanding *Doctor Who* means trying to parse the nationally specific ways it is viewed and appreciated from the industrial.[11] Indeed, the 'event' of the 2005 premiere of Russell T Davies's *Doctor Who* in the United States tells a very different story from the one in the UK: very little promotion undergirded it, as few (if any) adverts appeared. Indeed, the series' screening was even postponed by a year, after BBC America, in an interesting turn of events, did not premiere the programme in the US. Rather, niche station The Sci-Fi Channel (now known as Syfy) did. Nicholas Cull argues that, initially, Sci-Fi was uninterested in the reboot series as they 'considered the show "too British"'.[12] Reports from the channel reveal that 'some of the executives at the network found the series somewhat lacking and didn't think it would fit into the network's schedule, which already has a number of series, mini-series and films in development.'[13] Whatever the reason, the promotion and branding of 2005 *Doctor Who* in the US highlights this nationally specific context: despite being an 'event' for US fans of the series (many of whom opted to illegally download the show upon its release in the UK[14]), it was nothing like the 'event' of the release in an industrial context in the UK. It was not until Moffat's turn as executive producer and the move to series five that the programme started to become much more heavily promoted in the US by BBC America – with a resulting increase in fan and mainstream attention towards it.[15] These promotions, as outlined by Lynnette Porter, include billboards across major cities in the US, trailers for the series premiering at comic conventions across the country and US news edutainment segments (on the *Today* show) which toured the sets and studios (a huge marketing campaign of posters on the Chicago 'L' public transportation system ramped up my own excitement).[16] As Porter describes, BBC America and BBC Worldwide's promotional strategies in the US had to 'gain the attention of the unconverted masses'.[17]

This differential between the UK and the US promotional context is both expected and also highly surprising, given the oft tumultuous relationship between the US and the UK, in both a *Doctor Who* context and a more general transatlantic one. From its start, *Doctor Who* has always been positioned in relation to US science fiction; it has been the 'other' to the US's 'norm'. Knox argues, in fact, that 'considerations of the Britishness of *Doctor Who* also – inevitably – encounter and take account of the programme's relationship to US television'.[18] For Cull, 'America inevitably provided the cultural model for a British science fiction serial such as *Doctor Who*', and it is the programme's (re) positioning of itself in relation to American science fiction media like *Star Trek* (1966–69) and *Star Wars* (1977) that left 'traces of American science fiction' on the programme.[19] In Tom Baker's era, according to Knox, there was a move to emulate the '"quirky" characteristics' of US science fiction television.[20] During John Nathan-Turner's production era, there was a strong move to internationalise the programme: more international members of the TARDIS crew were added under his tenure (Australian companion Tegan Jovanka, played by Janet Fielding, and American Peri Brown, played by Nicola Bryant), and in 1985 there was also a short-lived move to make each episode 45 minutes long, allowing time for commercial breaks in a nod to US television conventions. The 1996 TV Movie represented another turn to the North American context, as the British series was partially financed by Fox, an American company, and was filmed in Vancouver. The film was not a success, and many blamed the increase in American-ness at the expense of the Britishness.[21]

At the same time, throughout the classic series 'there were elements in American science fiction that the programme's creators took pains to avoid' by drawing specifically on signifiers of unique 'Britishness'.[22] This 'Britishness' is precisely what Dylan Morris argues is the aspect of the programme that is so appealing to US viewers – especially viewers who are members of what he calls 'nerd culture' – who are growing up in a country with little history and cultural mythology of its own.[23] For these American 'nerds' (as a part of an Anglophilic fantasy audience that loves *Lord of the Rings*, *The Chronicles of Narnia*, *Alice in Wonderland* and *Harry Potter*), *Doctor Who* represents a missing part of their cultural history *because* of its Britishness. It is the 'other'-ness that makes it intriguing. For Cull, the Doctor's 'manners and adventures [are] deeply embedded in the stories that British people [tell] themselves about themselves'.[24] Facing the glossy sheen of *Star Trek* and *Star Wars*, *Doctor Who* (under the production thumb of Graham Williams) 'responded to the American challenge by falling back on the time-honoured British response that brains and character could win through'.[25] Despite the fan audience, classic *Doctor Who* never became mainstream in the US. Today, the new series 'brings together [the] heritage and eccentric brand with the cool noticeably differently to the classic series, which [...] experienced problems with US audiences because of how it was managing the brands at different points in time'.[26] That the new 2005 series has also followed a 45-minute episode model and echoes much of the American model of 'quality TV' speaks to the connection between institutional contexts as well. By inscribing that very 'British' heritage as a self-conscious aspect of the *Doctor Who* corpus, *Doctor Who* seemingly becomes both heritage text and promotional material, depending on the institutional and national context in which one views it.

Perhaps nothing reveals this promotional 'hype' of the event more so than the premiere of series eight, which was heavily promoted by both BBC One and BBC America throughout the lead-up to its air date.

Other chapters in this volume have detailed the changes to the series both textually and extra-textually when Peter Capaldi took the reins of the TARDIS from Matt Smith; the shift from the youthful, playful Smith to Capaldi's older and more resolute Doctor also heralded a shift in the style of promotion. One of the most discussed promotional experiences generated by the BBC was a 'world tour' taking place between 7 and 19 August 2014, wherein Capaldi, Moffat and Jenna Coleman (who played companion Clara) visited seven cities across the globe. In the lead-up to the tour, multiple online sources advertised the information, including the main BBC *Doctor Who* website and other sites like *Doctor Who News*. The world tour was advertised as a response to the 2013 50th anniversary special, 'The Day of the Doctor', which was 'broadcast simultaneously in 98 countries and in over 1500 cinemas across the world, setting a new record for event cinema in its first 3 days on general release'.[27] The tour gave select fans at each location the chance to hear from the new Doctor before the premiere of the new series and also to ask questions of the continuing producer and companion. The tour started in Cardiff, then travelled to London. From there, they went to Seoul, Sydney, New York, Mexico City and then Rio de Janeiro.[28]

It is telling to see throughout the tour the negotiation between the Britishness of the programme and the global nature of the promotion and paratextual material. This tension can be witnessed in the tongue-in-cheek image advertising the tour, which was posted in anticipation on the main *Doctor Who* World Tour website. In this image, national monuments and historic buildings from each of the cities visited can be seen, including The Pierhead Building and Millennium Centre at Cardiff Bay (themselves part of the *Doctor Who* text and then near the *Doctor Who Experience*), the skyline of New York City, Big Ben and the Houses of Parliament in London, the statue of Christ the Redeemer at Rio de Janeiro, the Sydney Harbour Bridge, the monument to the Mexican Revolution, and Seoul's Bukchon Village. This emphasis on the cultural and historical background of each city and culture brings a focus on the global aspect of *Doctor Who*. But within each image lies a TARDIS, either flying into the city or hidden among the artefacts (cleverly inside the monument in Mexico City, for example). Obviously created to illustrate the 'arrival' of *Doctor Who* to the city on the tour, the images also create the juxtaposition between that very British symbol (the Police Box) and the national landscapes of the other cities.

Each stop on the tour followed a similar format: developing Matt Hills's discussion in his chapter, there was a screening of the first episode of the new series, 'Deep Breath' and a Q & A with Capaldi, Coleman and Moffat. For some of the tour, there had been plans to live-stream the question-and-answer session; however, after the first session the live stream was halted, with the following reason given:

> We will no longer be live streaming the fan Q & A event from the Doctor Who World Tour in Sydney. We've listened to your feedback and agree that it's much more exciting for fans (both at the events and online) if the Q & A session takes place AFTER screenings of *Deep Breath*. That way, the panel will be able to chat about the Twelfth Doctor and the episode in much more detail. The World Tour is the first time that a current Doctor and companion have officially visited Australia, so we want to make sure that we make the most out of their time with fans.[29]

However, along with concerns about spoilers, more pressing issues might simply have been technical difficulties (delays plagued the Seoul live stream) or fear of negative fan sentiment. Future Q & A sessions, including the one in the US, were recorded, edited into six-minute videos and posted online.

The tension on the tour between the Britishness of *Who* and the global impact of the programme became apparent even from the start. During the Q & A on the Seoul stop on the tour, Peter Capaldi was asked the following question: 'When did you know that *Doctor Who* was so popular around the world?' His answer, perhaps unsurprisingly, echoes many of the sentiments about the national and industrial history of the programme:

> When it came back eight series ago – it exploded in a way. Which was a surprise to all of us, those of us who loved the show from when we were children. I would love to know what it is about it that makes it so popular in South Korea. I'd love to ask the audience why they love it. Because to us it seems a very *British* thing, and yet the world seems to embrace it.[30]

The fan audiences at each of these stops – over 1,000 in Seoul and New York, respectively – demonstrated their passion for this British series;[31] many came in costume, and the Q & As that appeared in the edited videos emphasised a deep knowledge of the series and its production.

By tying together these cities across the globe with a shared focus on and love of *Doctor Who*, the BBC and BBC Worldwide attempted two rather contradictory things at once: to create a coherent global fan community and to market *Doctor Who* as a uniquely British product. This focus appeared to be a major incentive of another BBC Worldwide venture, the simulcast of episodes in the US. For the premiere of Capaldi's first series, BBC Worldwide screened 'Deep Breath' in cinemas across the globe on 23 August 2014 and simulcast a special 3D viewing of the two-part 'Dark Water'/'Death in Heaven' in cinemas in the US only.

The premiere episode of series eight capped the world tour and presented, at least in theory, a unified fan experience. The simulcast drew from the success of 'The Day of the Doctor' 50th anniversary simulcast, which Danny Cohen, controller of BBC One, called an 'event drama'.[32] The 50th anniversary screening brought in $10.2 million at the box office, while the TV premiere (shown at the same time) had almost 13 million viewers in the UK alone.[33] In contrast, the simulcast of 'Deep Breath' was not as popular, with ratings in the US slightly lower than 'The Day of the Doctor' and the episode being shown on fewer screens and with less box office success.[34] A year later, just weeks before the series nine premiere, BBC Worldwide released the series eight finale to cinemas as well, but this seemed to bring in small numbers (on a personal level, the cinema I visited had barely 15 people in attendance). While 'The Day of the Doctor' was an anniversary special, with both textual and paratextual significance for fans and for the BBC, 'Deep Breath' was simply the first episode with a new Doctor – a not-quite unique experience (there have been, of course, many of these so far), leading some to question whether or not there was a valid reason to show 'Deep Breath' in cinemas at all.[35] That the third simulcast of new *Who* occurred *only* in the US is a significant shift in BBC Worldwide's policies. Ostensibly limiting it to a US run 'due to the number of events taking place for Doctor Who this year including the Symphonic Spectacular and the Doctor Who Festival', BBC Worldwide decided not to show the episodes in

UK cinemas.[36] Given the number of *Doctor Who* themed events in the past, however, one wonders if perhaps the limited release stems from the earlier low-rated screening of 'Deep Breath'.

Indeed, the relevance of a simulcast in the internet age – when almost everything is available in almost the same instant as it premieres – speaks to the marketing strategies of BBC Worldwide in terms of *Doctor Who*'s global nature. That the world tour visited those seven cities, and that the simulcast of 'Deep Breath' attempted to unite a global audience at one time, is indicative of the BBC's emphasis on speaking to – and creating – a transcultural audience. As mentioned above, the notion of transculturalism speaks to 'border-crossing fandoms', or the way that fandoms of global texts (like *Doctor Who*) can transcend national or even cultural boundaries as 'cross-border media' are integrated 'into [fans'] own popular cultural contexts'.[37] For Chin and Morimoto, transcultural fandom is rarely the product of an industrial impetus, but rather emerges 'because of affinities of affect between the fan, in his/her various contexts, and the border-crossing object'.[38] In many ways, then, the transcultural fan has agency to move within and around the global (textual) media universes and to create a new mode of fannish engagement with the text.

Therefore, in creating new, branded experiences of *Doctor Who* that specifically target global audiences – a world tour, a simulcast – the BBC and BBC Worldwide are doing more than simply contrasting the Britishness of the series with the global fandom of the audience. They are also attempting to create a transcultural audience that views the programme as more than just a national product. The branding of *Doctor Who* in a United States context reveals this transculturalism. We can see this most overtly for series eight in the way, for example, popular entertainment magazines like *Entertainment Weekly* – a most decidedly *not* niche title – dedicated covers to *Doctor Who* at least three times prior to the Thirteenth Doctor: once for the start of the seventh series (with Matt Smith on the cover and the strapline 'How a British Sci-Fi Series became a Global Geek Obsession'), once for the 50th anniversary (actually two 'collectible' covers) and once for the start of Capaldi's tenure in the TARDIS.

Britishness, in the context of a transcultural *Doctor Who* product, becomes more than a marker of national identity – it becomes a textual attribute that reflects on the both the brand and the experience of *Doctor Who* within a larger global sphere. Johnson argues that 'branding has been used by the BBC to manage both its public service and commercial ambitions for *Doctor Who*', and while that is certainly true, the way this branding co-opts the transculturalism of fandom is rarely discussed.[39] It is not *Britishness* so much as a particular, textually appropriate semiotic appropriation of Britishness that manifests as an aspect of *Doctor Who*, and it is not so much *globalness* that is revealed through the event programming in the promotion of series eight, but a particular view of the global fan audiences as marked as unified by their fandom of *Doctor Who*. As Chin and Morimoto put it, 'fans become fans not (necessarily) because of any cultural or national differences or similarities, but because of a moment of affinity between the fan and transcultural object.'[40] BBC Worldwide seems to want to cultivate this affinity via the worldwide events supporting the start of series eight of *Doctor Who*.

BBC America and ephemera

Series eight of *Doctor Who* saw the emergence of a new Doctor. Promos in the US and the UK focused on Peter Capaldi's seriousness, bringing a sobriety to the role that some fans felt was missing from the Matt Smith years. Indeed, as Knox describes, the turn from Christopher Eccleston to David Tennant and then to Smith demonstrates more a move towards youthfulness that made the show more appealing to a mainstream audience: 'the youthful cast of the reboot is also important in this shift towards the cool.'[41] After seven series of this 'cool', BBC Worldwide faced a challenge in promoting the markedly different take on the character Capaldi brought to the role.

There was a tension, therefore, in the way series eight *Doctor Who* would need to be promoted on both BBC One and BBC America. Although British audiences – especially those fans that grew up with the classic series – might be familiar with an older, angrier Doctor (like Colin Baker's brash portrayal[42]), many new fans would not be. And while *Doctor Who* was much more of a cultural institution in the UK than it was in the US (barring the dedicated attention of hundreds of thousands of fans, of course – but the programme was never mainstream in the US in the way it was in the UK in the 1970s), for the types of transcultural US fans desired by BBC Worldwide and BBC America, as demonstrated by global events like the world tour and the simulcast of 'Deep Breath', promos and adverts needed to augment the already positive feelings about the Time Lord and *Doctor Who* and assuage any resentment/anger/fear that the new Doctor would 'ruin' the programme.

We can see the differing ways that the BBC in the UK (via BBC One) and BBC America promoted the programme in the months approaching the series through a textual analysis of their on-air promotions, or what Paul Grainge calls 'ephemeral media'. For Grainge, ephemeral media are 'short-form texts that populate the audiovisual terrain [...] and throw [...] into relief the durational and circulatory temporalities of media'.[43] Ephemeral media are things like television adverts, interstitial titles, webisodes, mobisodes, user-generated content and other 'paratextual' content.[44]

For John Ellis, television's interstitial content – the breaks within programming that comment on that programming, including broadcaster identifications, adverts, trailers, announcements or anything that 'cannot be classified as a "programme"' – are crucial in the contemporary television environment as they help viewers 'read' TV and how television 'regards itself'.[45] Certainly, interstitials are becoming more and more frequent on television – Ellis estimates as much as 25 per cent of US network television and 15 per cent of UK commercial channels are interstitial. Trailers are a particularly relevant interstitial for *Doctor Who* fans, as they help 'define a number of vectors of significance [...] and excite emotions that often remain unrequited, provoking anger, fear or righteous indignation, and then direct the viewer to the programme for the development and fulfilment of these emotions'.[46] Trailers for series eight of *Doctor Who* had to navigate carefully between not alienating new fans that were unsure about a new Doctor, continue to introduce the programme to audiences that might yet be unfamiliar with it (*Entertainment Weekly*'s proclamation about 'becoming a geek obsession' notwithstanding), and appeal to established fans.

On both BBC One and BBC America, the new series of *Doctor Who* was situated in a number of contexts to create an association between the programme and its viewers. Hills has examined the trailers of series five of *Doctor Who*, specifically in reference to the paratextual material attempting to sustain 'a sense of *Doctor Who*'s ongoing consistency and identity' in the wake of a new producer, Steven Moffat.[47] Hills's discussion also explores the textual differences between the American and the British trailers for series five and six, as the American version of the trailers, he argues, granted Matt Smith a more traditionally masculine role as 'hero' than did the British trailers.

For series eight, however, much of the difference between the two channels' trailers was muted. For instance, both channels ran a 15-second promo called 'Am I a Good Man?'[48] In this trailer, the Doctor stands in shadow in the TARDIS (perhaps indicating the fact that the audience is still unsure about Capaldi's new Doctor) while flames explode around the console. The sound of the TARDIS dematerialising is heard as the Twelfth Doctor intones, 'Clara, be my pal. Tell me, am I a good man?' The camera zooms onto a tight, extreme close-up of the Doctor's eye, in which Clara is reflected; she says, 'I don't think I know who the Doctor is any more.' Finally, the words 'The new Doctor lands' appear on the screen before the image fades to the title of the series and the date of the premiere, topped by the BBC One or the BBC America logo.

In this ad, then, a number of relevant points become visible. First, there is the mystery of the Doctor himself. The running theme throughout the sixth and seventh series of *Doctor Who* had been 'Who is the Doctor?', culminating in the latter's episode 'The Name of the Doctor' (2013). By shrouding the Doctor in shadow and not actually seeing him speak (the words are in voice-over only), the viewer is again asked to question the character's identity and morality. In this case, these questions are made even more evident by the fact that a new actor is playing the Doctor. Capaldi's casting had already been well known: he appeared in the 50th-anniversary episode and was announced to great fanfare in a BBC television special. The trailer here seems to transpose the mystery of the Doctor to the mystery of the actor playing the Doctor: is Capaldi a good Doctor? The answer seems to be that Capaldi will make the role even more nebulous. The trailer also indicates Clara's role in the new series: importantly, she does not directly answer the Doctor, but instead seems to be talking *about* the Doctor to someone else. Her words could be the words of any fan unsure about the direction in which Capaldi might take the series.

With this trailer, both BBC One and BBC America attempt to do precisely what BBC Worldwide was doing with the world tour and the simulcast of 'Deep Breath': create a transcultural fan audience. Instead of reassuring one audience that the new Doctor would be just like Smith's portrayal (which would risk alienating long-term fans who already knew that was not going to be the case, as one Doctor is rarely like another), or placating long-term fans with oblique references to the previous regenerations or changes, the trailer attempts to unify fan audiences around the mystery of the Doctor's moral code. This attempt to generate 'cross-border fandom' engages the 'affinities of affect' that create a 'transnational orientation' towards the media text.[49] In other words, both trailers worked precisely because they focused on a unifying element of the new series – not the new Doctor, but the new tone of the programme.

Other trailers for the two channels' airing of *Doctor Who* do not significantly deviate from each other, but also play up the mystery and unknowability of the Time Lord. In one, the 'official full-length trailer', scenes from the upcoming series are fragmented and edited together to become a choppy, dangerous-looking series of explosions and horror: the eye stalk of a Dalek is juxtaposed with Clara's scared expression; an exploding TARDIS console appears with no explanation. A Dalek intones, 'Life returns', and Clara seemingly responds with 'I don't think I know who the Doctor is any more,' a line familiar from the first trailer. The Dalek then repeats, 'Life prevails'. Then comes a shot of Peter Capaldi as he averts his gaze into the camera and a voice-over explains: 'I'm the Doctor. I've lived for over two thousand years. I've made many mistakes. And it's about time I did something about that.' The images on the screen show unknown aliens and monsters. The trailer then cuts to Capaldi's Doctor in the TARDIS with Clara next to him. 'Where are we going?' she asks. 'Into darkness,' he responds. The rest of the trailer intercuts multiple images of dangerous aliens with dramatic music playing until the strapline familiar from the previously analysed trailer is spoken: 'Am I a good man?' In this trailer, Clara answers him directly: 'I don't know.' The same trailer was shown on both BBC America and BBC One; the only differences between the two were in the opening shot (the BBC One trailer had the words 'Original British Drama' on it, reinforcing the tension between the Britishness and the globalness of the brand) and the end, which had the different logos for the channels inscribed.[50]

Again, as with the previous trailer, there is mystery surrounding not just the character of the Doctor here but also the actor playing him. How will Capaldi handle the new Doctor? The scenes are dark with no humour, which is quite a contrast from the previous few series with Matt Smith at the helm. Smith's youthfulness and his antics are well-established characteristics of his portrayal, and the wittiness and humour of the past series had been a significant element of the programme.[51] The trailers here indicate a massive shift in tone as well as in style from previous seasons. There is nothing comforting about these trailers: there is nothing that says 'Doctor Who is the programme that you've always loved; it will come back and be just as you remember.' Rather, the promos here detail significant shifts in character that unsettle rather than calm.

At the same time, BBC America did try to quell some of that uneasiness with a special marathon of Doctor Who, advertised in an original promo that featured a number of elements from the new series as well as some significant references to the previous ones. For the week leading up to the premiere of 'Deep Breath', BBC America showed every episode of new Doctor Who in order – from 'Rose' (2005) to 'The Time of the Doctor' (2013). To advertise this, BBC America released a promo that featured some of the hallmarks of the previously analysed one – Clara stating, 'I don't think I know who the Doctor is any more' – juxtaposed with images and moments from the past years of the new series.[52] Interestingly, rather than hearing Clara's comment out of context, as one does in the other trailers, in this 'Doctor Who Takeover Week' trailer, her comment is literally answered by the narrator – voice of BBC America, Mark Sheppard – when he replies, 'Refresh your memory with BBC America's Doctor Who Takeover Week!' The scenes then cut between the Eleventh Doctor, the Tenth Doctor, Rose, Daleks and other well-known elements of the series. As Sheppard says, 'From Adipose to Zygons and everything in between – it all leads up to the season premiere of Doctor Who.' In contrast to the other trailers, the music for this trailer is jaunty, a direct pull from the series five 'Onwards!' theme by Murray Gold rather than the dramatic and chilling theme used in the other trailers.

This historical situation of the new series of *Doctor Who* in the context of the previous seven series was important for BBC America, and for the American fan, as it clearly positioned the Doctor not as a menacing figure, not as an unknown, but as one within a trajectory of other Doctors. Emphasising the consistency of the Doctor as a character reduced the tension on Capaldi's appearance by unifying the transcultural fans behind the mystery of his morality: while many new fans may have been apprehensive of the new Doctor, BBC America, by offering a historical view of the new series, may have alleviated some of this concern. At the same time, very few classic *Doctor Who* episodes are even shown on BBC America, apart from the few episodes that appeared on the *Doctors Revisited* DVD sets, released in 2013 and hosted by Steven Moffat.[53] In fact, the BBC America website points interested viewers to streaming services Netflix and Hulu, digital distribution services like iTunes and Google Play, and Video on Demand services via cable companies to find classic episodes, rather than having the ability to host them itself. By 2016, all signs of online streaming for classic *Doctor Who* in the US pointed viewers to the new pay service 'Brit Box', which streamed not just *Doctor Who* but scores of other British television programmes. Thus, the 'marathon' of *Doctor Who* touted by BBC America was in reality a marathon of new *Who*, and ignored much of the previous history of the series.

Fan-made trailers take this historical association one step further. 'Doctor Who: The Twelfth Doctor BBC One TV Trailer' is a fan-made trailer which takes short, key moments from each of the previous Doctors' tenures – Hartnell's Doctor in the Dalek from 'The Space Museum' (1965), Troughton's Second Doctor leaping from an explosion in 1968's 'The Invasion', Pertwee's Third Doctor toasting Jo at the end of 1973's 'The Green Death', etc. These shots are augmented by important lines of dialogue from each of these Doctors: 'There's no point in being grown up if you can't be childish sometimes' (Tom Baker's Fourth Doctor), 'There's always something to look at if you open your eyes' (Peter Davison's Fifth Doctor), for example. Finally, the fan-made trailer ends as the Eleventh Doctor closes the TARDIS door and Peter Capaldi appears on screen: 'My name is Peter Capaldi, and I'm the new Doctor.'[54] Importantly, the clip of Capaldi was ripped from an original BBC promo which was only ten seconds long and was one of the first times Capaldi had appeared as himself-as-the-Doctor.[55]

The official trailers for *Doctor Who* from BBC One and BBC America demonstrated a reliance on the mystery and unknowability of Peter Capaldi as the new Doctor. They brought a sense of drama and seriousness to a series that had become rather self-referential and humorous under the previous Doctor, Matt Smith. And they reflected a maturing of the themes of the series, from a search *for* the Doctor (Smith's eternal question – 'Who is the Doctor?') to a search about the morality *of* the Doctor (Capaldi's, 'Am I a good man?').

Conclusion: bringing gravitas to BBC America

If the promo for *Doctor Who*'s series eight reflected the more serious approach to the series that Capaldi's presence indicated, BBC America's audience may have already been somewhat primed to this shift. As mentioned, in 2011 the 'voice' of BBC America – the narrator who described the programmes and narrated the interstitial promos – changed from comedian and *The Daily Show* contributor John Oliver to the more dramatic actor Mark Sheppard. Sheppard would be familiar to many *Doctor Who* fans, as he played Canton Delaware III in 'The Impossible Astronaut' and 'Day of the Moon' (2011). However, he would also be familiar to genre television fans more generally as he has appeared in scores of classic science fiction and cult television series over the past two decades, including *Star Trek: Voyager* (UPN, 1995–2001), *CSI* (CBS, 2000–15), *Firefly* (Fox, 2002–3), *Monk* (USA, 2002–9), *Battlestar Galactica* (Syfy, 2004–9), *Supernatural* (WB/CW, 2005–), *Chuck* (NBC, 2007–12), *Leverage* (TNT, 2008–12) and *Warehouse 13* (Syfy, 2009–14), among many others. Oliver's work as a comedian on *The Daily Show* and doing stand-up created a more quirky and humorous style of narration, whereas Sheppard's distinctive grave voice and gravitas within genre television brought a more serious and dramatic note to the BBC America promos than his predecessor.

The shift in celebrity 'voice' of BBC America from the humorous Oliver to the sombre Sheppard reflected a similar perceived shift in tone in *Doctor Who* as well. In this way, the US adverts signalled a change in tone that many American audiences were hoping for while tying that change to the hype that surrounded the premiere of the show. Although this took place two years before the change in the

Doctor Who cast, this change of narrator reveals that American audiences had already been primed for a change from the light-hearted to the serious; a move from light to dark.

This shift in tone for series eight matched a renewed reliance on global branding and promotion for *Doctor Who*. As I have argued in this chapter, BBC America's promotion of the series engaged fan and non-fan audiences in a tension between the Britishness of the show and the perceptual global audience of the programme. By creating transcultural links between major global events like the World Tour and the simulcast of 'Deep Breath', BBC Worldwide engaged in a campaign for institutional transculturalism. And just as the transcultural moment transcends national borders and boundaries, BBC Worldwide continued to rely on the national sense of heritage and Britishness within the series as a key textual element. Promos for series eight on both BBC One and BBC America, however, focused on the mystery and horror of the new season and the new Doctor. Rather than shy away from the change in main character, the promos of the new series relished that shift, drawing attention to the more mature Doctor and themes within the show. Instead of asking 'Who is the Doctor?' the new series wanted viewers instead to question the morality of the Doctor, that most British of global characters.

Notes

1   James Chapman, *Inside the TARDIS: The Worlds of Doctor Who* (London, 2013), p. 188.

2   Catherine Johnson, '*Doctor Who* as programme brand', in Matt Hills (ed.), *New Dimensions of Doctor Who: Adventures in Space, Time and Television* (London, 2013), p. 95.

3   Matt Hills, 'Hyping *Who* and marketing the Steven Moffat era: the role of "prior paratexts"', in Andrew O'Day (ed.), *Doctor Who: The Eleventh Hour – A Critical Celebration of the Matt Smith and Steven Moffat Era* (London, 2014), pp. 181–203.

4   Simone Knox, 'The transatlantic dimensions of the Time Lord: *Doctor Who* and the relationships between British and North American television', in O'Day (ed.), *Doctor Who: The Eleventh Hour*, pp. 106–120.

5   For more discussion of *Doctor Who* as a brand, see Johnson, '*Doctor Who* as programme brand'. I discuss the exaggeration of divisions between

eras in Paul Booth, 'Periodising *Doctor Who*', *Science Fiction Film and Television* vii/2 (2014), pp. 195–215.

6   Paul Grainge (ed.), *Ephemeral Media: Transitory Screen Culture from Television to YouTube* (London, 2011).

7   Bertha Chin and Lori Morimoto, 'Towards a theory of transcultural fandom', *Participations: Journal of Audience and Reception Studies* x/1 (2013).

8   Andrew O'Day, 'Event TV: fan consumption of televised *Doctor Who* in Britain', in Gillian I. Leitch (ed.), *Doctor Who in Time and Space: Essays on Themes, Characters, History and Fandom, 1963–2012* (Jefferson, NC, 2013), p. 7.

9   Ibid., p. 16; Johnson, 'Doctor Who as programme brand', p. 95.

10   Matt Hills, *Triumph of a Time Lord: Regenerating Doctor Who in the Twenty-First Century* (London, 2010), p. 66.

11   Idem, *Doctor Who: The Unfolding Event – Marketing, Merchandising and Mediatizing a Brand Anniversary* (Basingstoke, 2015), p. 16.

12   Nicholas Cull, 'TARDIS at the OK Corral: *Doctor Who* and the USA', in John R. Cook and Peter Wright (eds), *British Science Fiction Television: A Hitchhiker's Guide* (London, 2006), p. 67.

13   KJB, 'The *Who* report: did Sci Fi pass on the series?', IGN [website] (1 March 2005). Available at http://www.ign.com/articles/2005/03/02/the-who-report-did-sci-fi-pass-on-the-series (accessed 6 July 2015).

14   Mark Pesce, 'Piracy is good? New models for the distribution of television', Mindjack Magazine [website] (2005). Available at http://hyperreal.org/~mpesce/piracyisgood.pdf (accessed 6 July 2015).

15   Lynnette Porter, *The Doctor Who Franchise: American Influence, Fan Culture and the Spinoffs* (Jefferson, NC, 2012), p. 38.

16   Ibid., pp. 39–40.

17   Ibid., p. 40.

18   Knox, 'The transatlantic dimensions of the Time Lord', p. 106.

19   Cull, 'TARDIS at the OK Corral', pp. 53, 66.

20   Knox, 'The transatlantic dimensions of the Time Lord', p 110.

21   Peter Wright, 'Expatriate! Expatriate! *Doctor Who: The Movie* and commercial negotiation of a multiple text', in Tobias Hochscherf and James Leggott (eds), *British Science Fiction Film and Television: Critical Essays* (Jefferson, NC, 2011).

22   Cull, 'TARDIS at the OK Corral', p. 53; see also Knox, 'The transatlantic dimensions of the Time Lord', p. 112.

23   Morris is here speaking about the European history of the US; the mythology and history of Native Americans is vast, but largely unknown or underappreciated in the US.

24   Cull, 'TARDIS at the OK Corral', p. 55.

25   Ibid., p. 61.

26   Knox, 'The transatlantic dimensions of the Time Lord', p. 114.

27 Christopher Allen, '*Doctor Who*: the world tour takes Capaldi, Coleman and Moffat around the globe', *Doctor Who* [blog] (10 June 2014). Available at http://www.doctorwho.tv/whats-new/article/doctor-who-the-world-tour-takes-capaldi-coleman-and-moffat-around-the-globe (accessed 6 July 2015).

28 Kelly West, '*Doctor Who* world tour featuring Peter Capaldi, Jenna Coleman and Steven Moffat kicks off in August', CinemaBlend [website] (July 2014). Available at http://www.cinemablend.com/television/Doctor-Who-World-Tour-Featuring-Peter-Capaldi-Jenna-Coleman-Steven-Moffat-Kicks-Off-August-64602.html (accessed 6 July 2015).

29 Matt Guenigault, 'Update on the *Doctor Who* world tour live stream from Sydney', *Doctor Who* [blog] (11 August 2014). Available at http://www.doctorwho.tv/whats-new/article/update-on-the-doctor-who-world-tour-live-stream-from-sydney/ (accessed 6 July 2015).

30 Tom Gardiner, '*Doctor Who* world tour – Seoul Q&A highlights are here', TiBS [website] (August 2014). Available at http://www.threeifbyspace.net/2014/08/doctor-who-world-tour-seoul-qa-highlights-are-here/#.U-qeSfldV8E (accessed 6 July 2015).

31 Seoul: Reetu Kabra, 'Globe-trotting with the Doctor', Ariel [website] (22 August 2014). Available at http://www.bbc.co.uk/ariel/28889653 (accessed 6 July 2015); New York: the sold-out Ziegfeld Theatre seats 1,100.

32 Tim Cole, 'BBC1 controller Danny Cohen outlines new commissions and "five key themes" for 2013', *Radio Times* [website] (30 November 2012). Available at http://www.radiotimes.com/news/2012-11-30/bbc1-controller-danny-cohen-outlines-new-commissions-and-five-key-themes-for-2013 (accessed 6 July 2015).

33 Todd Cunningham, '"Doctor Who" anniversary theatrical run scores $10.2M at worldwide box office', Yahoo! Entertainment [website] (27 November 2013). Available at https://www.yahoo.com/movies/s/dr-anniversary-theatrical-run-scores-10-2m-worldwide-185726914.html (accessed 6 July 2015).

34 According to boxofficemojo – which doesn't include data from every country – *Deep Breath* made over $1.7 million in the four countries measured: Australia, New Zealand, Russia and the UK. In contrast, *Day of the Doctor* made, in those same four countries, just over $5 million.

35 For more on the textual and paratextual significance of 'The Day of the Doctor', see Matt Hills, 'The cultural lives of *Doctor Who*: what's special about multiple multi-Doctor specials?', *Antenna* [website] (15 October 2013). Available at http://blog.commarts.wisc.edu/2013/10/15/the-cultural-lives-of-doctor-who-whats-special-about-multiple-multi-doctor-specials/ (accessed 6 July 2015); Idem, *Doctor Who: The Unfolding Event*. One commentator who questioned the validity of showing 'Deep Breath' in cinemas at all was Garrett Castello, in 'Does Deep Breath

really deserve a theatrical release?', *Doctor Who* TV [website] (3 August 2014). Available at http://www.doctorwhotv.co.uk/does-deep-breath-really-deserve-a-theatrical-release-65080.htm (accessed 6 July 2015).

36 PS, 'No 3D *Doctor Who* Death in Heaven cinema showings in UK', Sci-Fi Bulletin [website] (28 July 2015). Available at http://scifibulletin. com/2015/07/28/no-3d-doctor-who-death-in-heaven-cinema-showings-in-uk/ (accessed 28 July 2015).

37 Chin and Morimoto, 'Towards a theory of transcultural fandom', pp. 92–3.

38 Ibid., p. 93.

39 The BBC's use of branding: Johnson, 'Doctor Who as programme brand'. Lack of discussion around branding as co-opting the transculturalism of fandom: Paul Booth, *Playing Fans: Negotiating Fandom and Media in the Digital Age* (Iowa City, IA, 2015).

40 Chin and Morimoto, 'Towards a theory of transcultural fandom', p. 105.

41 Knox, 'The transatlantic dimensions of the Time Lord', p. 108.

42 See 'Colin Baker: it wounds me when my Doctor is lowest rated', *Doctor Who* TV [website] (22 July 2015). Available at http://www. doctorwhotv.co.uk/colin-baker-it-wounds-me-when-my-doctor-is-lowest-rated-74952.htm (accessed 27 July 2015).

43 Paul Grainge, 'Introduction: ephemeral media', in idem (ed.), *Ephemeral Media*, pp. 3–4.

44 Jonathan Gray, *Show Sold Separately* (New York, 2010). See also Hills, 'Hyping *Who* and marketing the Steven Moffat era'.

45 John Ellis, 'Interstitials: how the "bits in between" define the programmes', in Grainge (ed.), *Ephemeral Media*, p. 60.

46 Ibid., p. 66.

47 Hills, 'Hyping *Who* and marketing the Steven Moffat era', p. 185.

48 British trailer: 'Am I a good man? – Doctor Who series 8 2014: teaser trailer – BBC One' [video], YouTube (uploaded 27 June 2014), https:// www.youtube.com/watch?v=CIzg0B8pXuc (accessed 6 July 2015); BBC America trailer: http://www.bbcamerica.com/doctor-who/videos/am-i-a-good-man/ (accessed 6 July 2015).

49 Chin and Morimoto, 'Towards a theory of transcultural fandom', p. 93.

50 'The official full length TV launch trailer – Doctor Who series 8 2014 – BBC One' [video], YouTube (uploaded 13 July 2014), https://www. youtube.com/watch?v=TivqZTq5u6Y (accessed 6 July 2015); http://www. bbcamerica.com/doctor-who/videos/official-season-8-full-length-trailer/ (accessed 6 July 2015). Link no longer working.

51 Richard Hewett, 'Who is Matt Smith? Performing the Doctor', in O'Day (ed.), *Doctor Who: The Eleventh Hour*.

52 'Doctor Who Takeover Week on BBC America – nonstop Who starts Mon Aug 18' [video], YouTube (uploaded 14 August 2014), https://www. youtube.com/watch?v=emzc77f0VEo (accessed 6 July 2015).

53 In late 2015, BBC America did start showing a few classic Tom Baker serials – 'Genesis of the Daleks', 'The Hand of Fear', etc. – but there remains no regular showing of classic episodes on the channel.

54 Doctor Who Hub, 'Doctor Who: the Twelfth Doctor BBC One TV trailer' [video], YouTube (uploaded 4 August 2013), https://www.youtube.com/watch?v=aPC9LepU9rs (accessed 6 July 2015).

55 BBC, '*SPOILERS* Peter Capaldi is the new Doctor! – Doctor Who (2013) – BBC' [video], YouTube (uploaded 4 August 2014), https://www.youtube.com/watch?v=VDGzzGRKukE, (accessed 6 July 2015).

PART FOUR

FANDOM

10

'DOCTOR WHO BELONGS TO ALL OF US'

Fan Texts and Fans' Imaginings of the Future Twelfth Doctor

Brigid Cherry

'Tonight we reveal the identity of Doctor number twelve.' With this voice-over the BBC opened a live programme organised around its announcement of the next actor to play the lead role in *Doctor Who*. Such announcements have long been the subject of considerable media coverage, and when the replacement for Matt Smith was cast, the BBC surrounded the announcement with an example of live global event television. The half-hour-long *Doctor Who Live: The Next Doctor* was broadcast on BBC One on 4 August 2013 and also screened simultaneously around the world (in the US, Canada and Australia). This media event – which was celebrity-studded (Liza Tarbuck, Rufus Hound, Stephen Hawking) and included interviews with *Doctor Who* cast members past and present – built to a climax with the reveal of Peter Capaldi as the new Doctor in the final few minutes.

With any casting announcement for *Doctor Who* there is a range of attendant media and fan interest, frequently enthusiastic, but not always positive. In previous research into responses to a new Doctor, I analysed the discursive responses online, particularly in respect of fans' emotional reactions to the actor.[1] But fans do not (always) simply discuss, debate and argue about the casting while waiting for the new series to begin. They also incorporate their responses into transformative works. In fact, even as Peter Capaldi was being announced as the actor to play the next regeneration of the Doctor, *Doctor Who* fans were already writing him into their own fan texts. Twelfth Doctor fan fiction started to appear the same day, and fan art – including Photoshopped images and videos – began circulating on the evening of the announcement, making tangible Capaldi's statement to Zoe Ball on *Doctor Who Live* that '*Doctor Who* belongs to all of us. Everyone made *Doctor Who.*'

Capaldi was referring to the dedicated audiences who have viewed the series over the years as one of the main reasons for its longevity, but the idea that *Doctor Who* belongs to everyone also underlies the transformative work that takes place within fan culture. It is already well established that fans make their own contributions – both material and textual – to popular culture texts. They remediate narratives by writing fan fiction, making fan films and music videos, and painting, drawing or digitally manipulating images in fan art, as well as making props and costumes for cosplay. Accounts of fan cultures have already established the importance of understanding producerly activities undertaken by fans.[2] Fans, of course, have long been recognised as prosumers, producers and consumers of their own contributions to the archontic narrative, the archive of all texts including fan fiction as well as canonical texts.[3] In these kinds of transformative works, anyone can indeed make *Doctor Who.*

The key interest I have here relates to the kinds of transformations that fans undertake and how these relate to affective responses not only to the text (which has been widely recognised already), but to extra-textual factors – the casting announcement being a case in point. The build-up to a new actor in the role of the Doctor, or indeed any changes to the main cast and production/writing team, presents fans with unknowns. They may well have emotional responses to an actor – as indeed I explored with the casting of Matt Smith – but they are also (temporarily, at least) in a period of uncertainty as to the characterisation, personality, mannerisms, performance and even costume of the new Doctor. Of course, fans can speculate in the discursive spaces of fan forums and social networking communities, but they can also produce transformative works that incorporate not only their responses to the casting announcement, but how they see, or would like to see, the new Doctor.

In order to explore this further, this chapter analyses a range of fan texts and how they incorporate the fans' own versions of Capaldi's Doctor well in advance of any revelations as to his character or hint of the storylines in which he will appear. This research therefore sets out to analyse the fan art and fan fiction that circulated within *Doctor Who* fandom in the ten-day period after *Doctor Who Live*. This timescale was selected so as to capture the most immediate responses, but in-depth interviews were also subsequently undertaken with fan artists and writers in the months between the announcement and Capaldi's first appearance after the regeneration in 'The Time of the Doctor'. Drawing on key examples, selected from fan fiction on Archive of Our Own, fanfiction.net and A Teaspoon and An Open Mind,[4] fan-Photoshopped images of Capaldi as the Doctor on Tumblr and DeviantArt, and fan-made title sequences and other fanvids on YouTube (many of which fall outside the ten-day period), I explore what these fan texts reveal about fandom's predictions and desires for what the new era of *Doctor Who* would bring. I analyse key examples of fan productivity, comparing the ways in which they incorporate the responses and cultural capital of the fans.

The data

On each of fanfiction.net, A Teaspoon and An Open Mind and An Archive of Our Own the first Twelfth Doctor fan fiction started to appear by the next day (the same evening, if the time in the US is taken into account). Eight fics were published over the following ten days on fanfiction.net, with five on Teaspoon and 17 on An Archive of Our Own. While this is a relatively small sample, it represents a cross-section of responses to the casting of Capaldi (and of course fics continued to be published after this initial period and up to the first story with the Twelfth Doctor, at which point fics settle around the on-screen characterisation).

Similarly, fan art had appeared in the immediate post-announcement period (though this is much harder to quantify). The majority of the early art had consisted of montages compiled from pre-existing screenshots and publicity material, frequently captioned in some way. It is difficult to estimate the quantities of fan art produced and circulated, since it was spread across a broad range of social media and microblogging sites, including Tumblr, Deviant Art, Twitter and Facebook, and then often reblogged and circulated on other sites including the *Doctor Who* forums and news sites. This also means that it is sometimes difficult, unlike with fan fiction and other forms of fan art (especially hand- or digitally drawn original art as opposed to manipulated pre-existing images), to establish its origin or the individual artist responsible. Nonetheless, it provides a useful case study in how fan art can incorporate affective responses to extra-textual events – in this case the casting announcement.

Responding to the new Doctor

Before going on to analyse these examples of fan art and fiction and the interviews with the writers and artists, it is useful to firstly contextualise the writing of the Twelfth Doctor into fan art and fan fiction by setting out the broad strokes of the fans' reception of the announcement programme and reactions to the casting of Peter Capaldi. For the most part the announcement was welcomed, enthusiastically so, with Capaldi being exceptionally popular among the established fan communities such as Gallifrey Base. By 7 August 2013, 2,637 members of Gallifrey Base had voted in a poll to record their verdict on the casting. Of those who responded, 90 per cent clicked 'Thumbs up' and less than 2 per cent gave a 'Thumbs down' (the other 8 per cent reserved judgement by clicking 'Don't know yet'). Just prior to the casting he was also the subject of much anticipation in terms of rumour and speculation and by the fact that many in this group were already aware of his status as 'one of the fans'.

However, it is important to also note that some concerns were raised, especially among other fan demographics. There were some reports of fans complaining about Capaldi's age, although many fans in different communities – including newer and younger fans – felt these were exaggerated, had not witnessed such complaints in their own communities, felt the exact opposite themselves and were not happy that assumptions were being made about younger fans not having knowledge of the original series when older actors frequently played the role. Fan fiction writer sein Henker says:

> Interestingly, there was a lot of moral outrage from certain parts of the fandom about teenage girls and young women being upset that Capaldi isn't young or attractive, but late-teen-to-early-twenties women is my demographic and the group of people I discussed Capaldi's casting with the most, and I never once saw this sentiment from anyone around my age group, on the internet or at my university [...] I was actually hoping for an older Doctor when I found out that Matt Smith's Doctor would be dying. The accusations and the insults started almost immediately after the announcement, and a lot of women were left wondering where it was coming from. Older male fans seemed to want to dismiss the feelings of younger female fans before we even had a chance to *have* feelings.

The notion of age being problematical is thus disputed by some fans as a constructed objection that was not widely experienced. On the other hand, there were a number of unfulfilled hopes or expectations that were also discussed. Among groups of female fan writers and artists in particular there were many who were disappointed that the new Doctor was not to be played by a female actor, but other fans were also hoping for a black or other non-white British actor to be cast. Sein Henker went on to describe this reaction as

> there being some well-deserved backlash due to the fact that no one but a white man was even considered for the role, but no one being particularly surprised, and most of us were careful not to blame Capaldi for this.

These fans are, then, careful to separate out their wishes for wider non-hegemonic representation in the role from their responses to Capaldi's casting.

The immediacy of responses in fan art and fiction

In the analysis of fan art and fiction that follows, I discuss how fans worked through their responses. One important factor in the analysis is that the art and fiction encapsulates the immediacy of responses, as sein Henker indicates:

> I wrote [a] fic in a few hours on a whim, mostly to get something on paper and to help me sort out my thoughts and set a tone for longer and more serious fics that I will almost certainly write after the season begins airing.

A useful approach to researching the way fans incorporate their affective responses into their art and fiction is Amber Davisson and Paul Booth's model of projected interactivity.[5] The combination of analysis of fan fiction (they are specifically interested in fan fiction, though it is also possible to apply their approach to other categories of fan production) and interviews with fan fiction writers permits exploration of the complicated identity play occurring in fan communities. Such analysis is designed to explore what the fan production reveals about the fan identities that are present in the community. Fan fiction gives the writer control over these identities through their play with the character's traits, actions and environment in their own writing. Analysis of fan discourse alongside fan production, in this case via interviews with fan artists and writers, facilitates understanding of these fans' affective responses to extra-textual material as well as the textual. What is interesting here is that the art and fiction published in the ten days after the announcement dealt with the first thoughts or connections that fans had around Peter Capaldi as an actor and how he might play the role. The art and fiction thus frequently dealt with how these responses might be played out in the storyworld, making links between pre-existing elements of the post-2005 text that fans privilege and the fan discourses emerging around expectations of Capaldi's star persona and his possible future Doctor.

In addition to the observations outlined above, one of the interesting points made by one of the fans interviewed in depth for this study was to link Capaldi to his background as an art student (many of the fans linked him to his career in film and television). Heather explicitly links the importance of fan art to the Capaldi era because Capaldi himself trained as an artist:

> As I found out more about Peter, though, I discovered that he's an artist and that he's really quite good. Went to art school and all. That was so exciting, and I felt a lot of very old sparks start to flicker in me: inspiration.

This linking of the actor's life history to one specific form of fan production led her to ponder whether the Capaldi era will be the time when fan art becomes significant in the same way that fan fiction has been to post-2000s *Doctor Who* fandom during David Tennant's and Matt Smith's roles in the series. Aside from the fact that fan production is an important area for study in its own right, and fan art has been somewhat neglected alongside fan fiction, it therefore seems appropriate to make a specific study of fan art. However, there are also many connections between various forms of fan art and fan fiction that demand to be explored further. One such connection is the fact that visual imagery is increasingly dominating online communication and discourse (with memes, emojis and so forth), which is linked to the popularity of gif fics and the inclusion of fan art and craft in fan fiction archives. Whether Heather's assumption that fan art will be of primary importance in the Capaldi era is true or not – and certainly the move to a more visual approach to social networking, especially via Tumblr and the exponential growth in internet memes as a means of computer-mediated discourse points this way regardless of Capaldi's background – it indicates that key forms of fan production, including art and fiction, are important in researching the ways in which extra-textual factors are incorporated into fans' work (in Heather's case Capaldi's biography). In the analysis that follows, I therefore analyse the fan art and fan fiction alongside each other, exploring the ways that various responses play out in the various forms of fan production.

Cult stardom

One of the reasons many fans welcomed Capaldi being cast as the Doctor was related to his star persona, and that, in addition to being recognised as a fan himself, he was also well known for his previous roles in film and television, some of them having cult appeal. Capaldi is a well-liked actor among fans of *Doctor Who* and British telefantasy and other cult series, having appeared in *Lair of the White Worm* (1988), *Neverwhere* (BBC, 1996), *Skins* (Channel 4, 2007–13), *The Crow Road* (BBC, 1996) and the cult comedy *The Thick of It* (BBC, 2005–12). One of the categories of the fan art and fiction (but especially the fan art) that circulated immediately after the announcement envisaged Capaldi as the Doctor through the filter of his previous acting roles. In the discourses in the fan groups after the announcement this included amusement about the fact that he was credited as 'W.H.O. doctor' (as in World Health Organisation) in *World War Z* (2013) and how playing the Doctor might fit alongside his role as Cardinal Richelieu in the (then upcoming) *The Musketeers* (BBC, 2014–16), as well as also referencing past performances. Stills or clips from *Lair of the White Worm* and the *Crown Court* episode 'Big Deal' (Granada, 1984) were used to illustrate his sex appeal and for amusement respectively. The former was circulated as a rare example of Capaldi wearing a kilt (bekilted Scots actors are perennially popular among female fans, as their enjoyment of photos of David Tennant and John Barrowman in kilts affirms) and the latter for his performance as a rockabilly (which also linked to his history in the punk band Dreamboys, with Craig Ferguson). Predominantly, however, the role of most interest to the fans was Malcolm Tucker in *The Thick of It*. Cult star persona is an important factor in this respect, and in the entanglement of star and character that Roberta Pearson points out with respect to cult TV stardom,[6] focused in this instance around the cult appeal of the Tucker performance.

One anonymous fan felt this was partly due to the fact that Capaldi's casting was the first time in the history of *Doctor Who* that such a cult star had been cast. While recognising that other actors were well known as character actors, and that Jon Pertwee and Peter Davison had previously had star status prior to playing the Doctor, it was Capaldi's cult appeal, as well as his own fan profile, that made this significant among fans who acknowledged it in their fan art. Many examples of fan art centred around the incorporation of Malcolm Tucker's personality into the Doctor. Many pieces of photomontage consisted of a 'mash-up' of Malcolm Tucker and the Doctor to create a foul-mouthed, misanthropic version of the Doctor. This emphasised the disconnection between the 'not safe for work' Tucker and the family drama of *Doctor Who*, and the fact that Tucker has become a cult character that many fans (and also cultural workers, since the media continued the trend) recognised. Several examples inserted an image of Capaldi as Tucker into a background from the *Doctor Who* storyworld, such as Tucker leaning against a corner of the TARDIS, or looking out of the TARDIS door.[7] Both these images were captioned with the most quotable Tucker line, 'Come the fuck in or fuck the fuck off.' This line of dialogue in particular has cult status – it was titled 'Malcolm Tucker's Best Line Ever' on YouTube, heads the top ten favourite Tucker quotes in the *Guardian*, could at the time of writing be purchased as a doormat from the website malcolmtuckershop.com and is the main title of the fuckitybye tumblr.[8] The 'Come the fuck in or fuck the fuck off' line proved so popular with these artists that it was used with images that did not otherwise reference Malcolm Tucker. Jonny Eveson, a fan artist who produces and sells posters of his art for many fandoms including but not restricted to *Doctor Who*, posted his piece of art celebrating Capaldi's casting within hours of the announcement.[9] This depicted Capaldi's face with Matt Smith's tweed-jacket-and-bowtie costume, the left-hand side of the image flaring with bright white light from the sonic screwdriver and the right-hand side the black depths of space surrounding a small spinning TARDIS. The text Eveson chose to add is Tucker's invitation, suggesting that Capaldi's role as Tucker is a significant component of his star persona for these fans and *The Thick of It* a cult comedy whose appeal dominates Capaldi's star persona.

The 'fuckity bye' line also appears in examples of fan art. One comprises a sequence of identifiable Doctor costumes captioned with the relevant Doctor's war cry/catchphrase – 'fantastic' over the Ninth Doctor's leather jacket, 'allons-y' across the Tenth's brown pinstripe, 'geronimo' beneath Eleven's red bow tie, and then Malcolm Tucker's grey suit with 'fuckity bye'. Other 'Tuckerisms' were also employed to similarly suggest the next Doctor incorporating Tucker's persona. Another widely circulated piece of fan art Photoshops a Dalek (replacing *The Thick of It*'s Ollie), slightly askew so it appears as if it leans to the right, cowering against a wall while Tucker looms over it saying 'I'm gonna lock you in a fucking flotation tank and pump it full of sewage until you fucking drown' – a Tucker line from *In the Loop* (the film spin-off of *The Thick of It*). Another artist, didnotts, circulated a digital sketch via Twitter captioned 'More Malcolm Tucker as Doctor Who', depicting the character wearing a bow tie (an iconic element of the Matt Smith costume) and wielding the sonic screwdriver while a speech bubble quotes another favourite Malcolm Tucker line: 'About as much use as a marzipan dildo'.[10] In the 'Malcolm Tucker IS Dr Who' vid, Pete Nottage edits together clips from *The Thick of It* and recent episodes of *Doctor Who* to create a dialogue between Tucker and various characters from *Who*. It opens with Clara asking, 'What happened to me?' and the Tucker-Doctor replying, 'We fucking time travelled, yes!' followed by edits which suggest he is telling River off with 'E-fucking-nough, you need to learn to shut your fucking cave.' Later in the vid, Clara tells the Tucker-Doctor to 'Run, you clever boy,' but he responds with 'Oh, fuck off!'[11] Tucker-Doctor also promises the fan a new approach, with the clip of Tucker saying, 'Life is interesting at last, I've been so fucking bored for the last two years' evoking the fans' excitement about the casting announcement and its cult cachet but also ironically seeming to write off or play down the Matt Smith era.

All of these mash-ups between *Doctor Who* and *The Thick of It* are playful, designed for amusement and also celebrate the cult status of the character and the star. But they are also a way of getting the connection with the star persona of the cult character of Malcolm Tucker out of the way quickly. The characters of Malcolm Tucker and the Doctor are very different, though this is not a poor fit between the character and the actor's star persona as much as between the two characters; it recognises in a knowing and even ironic way Capaldi's range as an actor. Moreover, in the immediate aftermath of the announcement these playful recognitions of difference were quickly produced, widely circulated and prolific. For Eveson, his poster design was an instinctive choice. He threw the piece together very quickly, adding, 'I had to commemorate Peter Capaldi with another bit of a cop out guff piece of Photoshopping today to mark the 12th Doctor's announcement. Had to be done.'[12] It was irresistible for many of the artists to instantly produce such pieces for their own entertainment and that of other fans (the speed at which this was produced was what led Eveson to describe his piece as 'guff'). Digital editing packages and image-manipulation software allow fan artists to produce such images very quickly, but fan writers were not slow to run with the cult appeal of Capaldi's role as Malcolm Tucker either. ladygrey99 uploaded her fic 'Fob Watches and VHS' the same day as the announcement, saying, 'Well someone had to do it and the baby was asleep for a whole half hour this morning,' echoing the same immediate connections as the fan artists but also emphasising the inevitability of the connection.[13]

In her fic, which takes place after the final episode of *The Thick of It* (after Tucker has been arrested), Ollie hesitates outside Malcolm's front door, holding a pocket watch:

> The watch was heavy in Ollie's hand as he braced himself to knock on Malcolm's door. He'd stopped thinking of Malcolm as The Doctor the first time Malcolm had shoved him against the wall of the tea room and called him a cunt. That had been years ago. The Doctor was going to be pissed. It was only supposed to be a few weeks. A couple of months, tops. But every few months River would pop in to tell them the threat was not yet gone. In truth things had cleared up a few months earlier but it was in the middle of the whole Mr. Tickle nightmare and Nicola stepping down, plus Ollie was in hospital for that week.

ladygrey99 thus makes reference to the storyworlds of both series – the events in the *Doctor Who* episodes 'Human Nature' and 'The Family of Blood' (2007) (which establish the use of the Chameleon Arch and the storing of Time Lord essence in a fob watch) as well as a reference to River Song on the one hand and the main plot thread from the final series of *The Thick of It* about the suicide of a housing campaigner and Ollie's appendicitis. The fic thus represents a particular example of retcon, the term for narrative elements that retrospectively fit later storyworld events into the continuity of the text. In this instance, though, the fact that the casting of Capaldi makes many fans immediately think of his cult character from *The Thick of It* leads ladygrey99 to retcon Malcolm Tucker into the *Doctor Who* storyworld. This is distinct from crossover fics which take characters from one storyworld and insert them wholesale into another. Malcolm's misanthropic demeanour is explained by something going wrong with the Chameleon Arch process, and Ollie – in fact, the companion – is worried that the Doctor will be stuck this way: 'The words gob shite should never come from the

Doctor's face. Not his Doctor who had given him a kindly smirk while he lay in rubble, took his hand, and told him to run.' This deals with the disjunction between roles, and ladygrey99 restores equilibrium. Once Malcolm has opened the watch, Ollie can again '[look] up into the face of the Doctor'. Her comment about her fic that 'someone had to do it' suggests a light-hearted imperative. But it also allows fans who might be thinking that Capaldi's most famous role at that point is counterproductive to him playing the role of the Doctor to integrate the two roles using canonical instances (and widely enjoyed ones) from the storyworld up to that point. It reassures her and other fans that Capaldi-as-Tucker need not get in the way of the characterisation, and that typecasting is not a concern.

A familiar face

It is, however, not Capaldi's cult star profile that exercises the fans most, but the fact that he has been in *Doctor Who* before. Capaldi's prior roles in the series (as Caecilius in 2008's 'The Fires of Pompeii') and in *Torchwood* (as Frobisher in 'Children of Earth', BBC, 2009) worried some fans of post-2005 *Who*. Those who had been fans from earlier, as well as those who had acquired fan knowledge of the classic era, were not so anxious, pointing out that it was not unusual for actors to make reappearances and that they were in any case performing different roles. However, discourse in online fan forums and across social media now means that concerns such as these are debated at length,[14] leading to fans remediating the text to reflect their concerns.

Several key examples of the fan fiction written by *Torchwood* fans immediately after the announcement reflect anxieties about Capaldi now reappearing as the Doctor. The characters of Captain Jack Harkness and Ianto Jones, and the relationship between them, was extremely important to this fan cohort. For them, Capaldi was most memorable as Frobisher, the antagonist (though ultimately a tragic figure) of 'Children of Earth' who had ordered the assassination of anyone previously involved with the 456, resulting in Jack (John Barrowman) and the Torchwood hub being blown up and ultimately leading to the death of Ianto (Gareth David-Lloyd). Sein Henker explains:

Capaldi's casting announcement was all that I remember anyone on (my corners of) the internet talking about for two or three days [...] I'm heavily involved in what's left of the *Torchwood* fandom, so the primary question on all of our minds was 'How are they going to reconcile Capaldi's new role as the Doctor with the role he's already played in "Children of Earth"?' There were a lot of theories bouncing around, and I threw out a couple of my own. This discussion was the primary inspiration behind my fic, since it's a Jack/Twelve fic that focuses on Jack's response to the regeneration.

Pir8grl was another one of these *Torchwood* fans, and she felt some anxiety despite her fan knowledge of the classic era:

I was a bit startled by the idea of Peter Capaldi, only because his role in 'Children of Earth' was so conspicuous. There's a precedent for actors (even playing the Doctor) having appeared in previous episodes, but I don't think any of those roles have been as prominent as John Frobisher.

It is thus not simply the recasting of an actor in the central role that concerns them, but the specific part that the actor played previously. These writers reconcile the Twelfth Doctor's appearance with their own responses to 'Children of Earth'. Moreover, these fans also position the problems of the Doctor's appearance in the context of a slashed relationship between Jack and the Doctor. Trobadora's 'Under the Skin' deals with the new Doctor's similarity to Frobisher by having Jack keep the Doctor awake and sexually active. It is only when asleep that Jack sees Frobisher in the Doctor's face:

A wicked edge slides into the light in the Doctor's eyes, and the corners of his mouth go up, and up. That grin is like nothing that ever crossed John Frobisher's face. Those eyes, the weight and the lightness of them, bear no similarity to John Frobisher's.

It's the Doctor, every bit of him, and Jack is all right.

Just so long as the Doctor doesn't fall asleep.[15]

Trobadora quickly establishes in this fic that there is a clear difference between the very different characters despite a surface similarity. On the other hand, in sein Henker's fic 'Doctor', a Doctor/Jack slash from the point of view of Jack after the regeneration, Jack finds it harder to see past Frobisher's face. His thoughts can be read as resembling those of a fan adapting to a 'new' Doctor, especially where the past Doctor was 'their' Doctor (fans often feel possessive of one or more Doctors, and in the case of many David Tennant fans this is the Tenth Doctor, who is often the focus of the Doctor/Jack fic):

> 'Doctor,' Jack said, because maybe if he just kept saying it, he would start to believe it. Doctor. He could almost do it, from the back. Almost forget. Almost not see it. Doctor. He closed his eyes and kissed his old Doctor's new shoulder, but as he did so he caught himself picturing the last and different Doctor he'd kissed. No. The same Doctor. His Doctor. His Doctor, who would always be his Doctor, no matter how he looked.[16]

These reactions are of course amplified for the *Torchwood* fans, as sein Henker's are. In 'Doctor', Jack flinches when he tries to kiss the Doctor, and his passion is extinguished:

> Jack had been doing well, too. He'd lost lovers before. He knew how the grief process worked. He had finally started to move on from Ianto's death [...] He hadn't been ready for his Doctor to regenerate into a constant reminder of the 456 incident. The universe had thrown some shit at Jack before, but it had really outdone itself with this one.[17]

This suggests that *Torchwood* fans in particular, and fans of other regular characters in the wider *Doctor Who* universe, have very strong affective investments in those characters and character relationships. Capaldi's casting raised some problems for members of this fan audience because for them Capaldi's most memorable role is as a villain. This is not to say that these fans cannot adapt to the casting and even accept it; sein Henker's fic ends on a note of hope when the Doctor, recognising Jack's reticence in making love to the person who looks like the man responsible for his lover Ianto's death, brings Jack a banana milkshake: 'Jack grinned. "Doctor ..." he repeated. It didn't make things better, but it helped a lot. His Doctor liked bananas. They'd be okay.'

The significance of bananas here takes Jack, and the Jack fans, back to their Doctor – the Tenth. And it is of course the David Tennant Doctor specifically who attracted many of the new female fans who came to the series in the early years of the post-2005 series, fans who were also attracted to Jack Harkness and later during *Torchwood* to Ianto. The feelings written into the fic thus become an account of the fans themselves.

This is further illustrated by Eloriekam's 'Mistaken Identity'. This fic opens with a chance encounter between Jack and someone he takes to be Frobisher but who is in fact the newly regenerated Twelfth Doctor:

> He's out for a rather aimless walk when he sees them. There's a short young woman, with dark hair and a knee-length dress, examining something with a tall, slim man with mostly gray hair. The man says something, and Jack puts together the voice and the nose and the hair, even though the clothes are not what he expected that person to be wearing, and runs forward.[18]

As with the previous examples, the fic is written as an immediate response to the casting announcement. Eloriekam says that 'I had three thoughts after learning of the casting for Twelve: this is the third. I don't usually do this sort of thing, but I couldn't resist.' Her indication that this is irresistible suggests an intense emotional response, and this links to the fact that her fic focuses on Jack's instinctual act of revenge: he shoots the Doctor, believing him to be Frobisher. Just as Eloriekam cannot resist, neither can Jack, who 'is done thinking, and draws his gun and aims it square at the other man's heart, at Frobisher's heart, knowing that even with this it will never make up for bomb, concrete, Ianto'. The fan and Jack share a distaste for Frobisher, 'glaring harder, wishing for the satisfaction of his gaze turning Frobisher to ash, breaking his body'. Told from Jack's point of view, the character is frequently referred to as Frobisher, not the Doctor. The repetition emphasises the conflation of characters – 'Frobisher says', 'Frobisher's expression darkens', 'to support Frobisher as he staggers', 'the muzzle of his gun under Frobisher's chin'. Although the writer and the reader know that this is the Doctor, the characters are one and the same (to Jack and thus to the reader through narrative point of view) in this section. Here too, fan knowledge of Capaldi's past role is paralleled by Jack's experiences: 'all the memories of what Frobisher did snap in Jack, and the crack echoes around them.'

The Doctor does not die when Jack shoots him, and though injured manages, in a lengthy middle section of the fic, to convince the sceptical Jack that he is indeed the Doctor. This section spends a lot of time depicting Jack being talked around, needing to be convinced that this is indeed the Doctor, and this suggests the fan herself coming to an acceptance of this man who looks like Frobisher as the Doctor. Having got the Doctor back to the TARDIS to heal, Jack's reasoning in reassuring himself – and thus the fan – is that:

> 'We're diverse, but at the end of the day there really are a finite number of faces.'
>
> 'I suppose,' Clara answers thoughtfully.
>
> 'Tell me more about how you're the impossible girl?' Jack asks her, thinking about the newest impossible face on the friend who calls him impossible.[19]

This is not just acceptance of the new Doctor, but of the 'impossible' narrative possibilities of *Doctor Who*.

Affective investments

For female fans such as these, character relationships are of paramount importance; furthermore, this has been a significant factor in the appeal of post-2005 *Doctor Who* for female fans and the growth of the female cohort in both the audience for the programme and its fandom. Accordingly, a large amount of fan fiction, particularly that in the genres of slash and shipper fic, has developed the relationships – established, perceived and desired – between characters. This is closely related to the appeal of the actors, with the Tenth Doctor and Rose 'ship' and the Doctor/Captain Jack slashed relationship being extremely productive, but the Eleventh Doctor and River Song or Doctor/Clara relationships have also been the subject of transformative works. The casting of Capaldi re-establishes the fact (after Tennant and Smith giving the Doctor a 'younger' face) that older actors have frequently played the role, and fans work through the changes to the character that this brings into play through their preferred ships.

Sein Henker gives particular consideration to the age difference between actors playing the Doctor and the companion. She says:

> My one initial caveat was that I didn't want to see any sort of romantic relationship between the Twelfth Doctor and Clara Oswald when there was such a large age difference between the actors. Twenty years is roughly the largest gap I'm willing to allow for between actors, especially when Jenna Coleman is so young-looking. I'm less picky about character ages!

She thus opens up the contradictions in writing shipper fics in the *Doctor Who* storyworld and the difference in age between Capaldi and Coleman. Consequently, romantic relationships between Clara and the Doctor when he looks older (being played by an actor in his fifties) are problematised. Pir8grl notes this is '[a]n obvious starting point, and one that other writers have touched on in various ways'. In her own writing, she negotiates this problematic with a series of short fics. (Drabbles and other forms of short fic are very popular in a wide range of fandoms, and are very often written in response to a challenge or topic thrown out by other fans. In one sense, the casting announcement created a similar challenge for the *Doctor Who* fan fiction writers.) Pir8grl's fics explore how she sees the relationship progressing: 'Clara and Eleven had a very close relationship with definite romantic overtones. How would that hold up through his regeneration, especially into someone who looks so different?' Her fic 'A Journey Begins' reflects on the Doctor feeling self-conscious about the visible difference in his and Clara's ages.[20] In 'Be My Mirror' she deals with the appearance issue through humour, using this to deflect concerns.[21] Her 'Christmas Serenade' assumes the same relationship as Clara had with Eleven, but again she counterpoints this by dwelling on the Doctor's lousy driving skills and the ability to find hope in the worst situations, thus drawing on canonical aspects of the character to contextualise the relationship in an established continuity for the character.[22] In 'Time to Begin', on the other hand, Pir8grl presents a series of short scenes that alternate between Eleven interacting with Clara and Twelve now being uncertain about their relationship.[23]

Pir8grl's fics illustrate the ways in which this early, pre-emptive Twelfth Doctor fan fiction is speculative. She says:

It's just fun to imagine what might happen, and see how close it ends up to the 'real thing'. I've done it before – I wrote a block of Clara fics before 'The Bells of Saint John' aired, and also a few speculating on the 50th anniversary show.

I think that's the appeal of writing a story when we haven't really seen the character yet – there are so many 'what ifs' to explore.

The crucial 'what if', as Pir8grl's short fics indicate, explores the effect the apparent age difference has on the relationships fan writers have already remediated in their fiction. In 'New Body – Same Hearts', Pir8grl envisages the regeneration scene with Clara and the Doctor. Immediately after the change, Clara has to process the 'new man lying on the deck in front of her'. She is afraid of what his new personality might bring more than his changed appearance. He looks 'a bit older' but 'rather distinguished' and there is 'something about his face that hinted of easy smiles and laughter', but Clara also fears that he might not be in 'his right mind'. In this fic, Pir8grl assumes that Clara remembers all her encounters with past Doctors in 'The Name of the Doctor' (the fic was of course written before Clara's memory is established as hazy in 'The Day of the Doctor'). And she remembers the Sixth Doctor's prickly personality: 'She shuddered slightly – his sixth incarnation had been ... unique ... in so many ways. She rather hoped it would remain that way.' In this way, with Clara watching the unconscious Doctor, the fic is reflexive of Clara's emotions rather than her love and passion for the Doctor. Pir8grl classifies it as romance, and the fic concludes with the sense that the romantic feeling Clara and the Doctor share will continue:

Clara stared into eyes that were filled with wisdom, and mischief, and heartache, and insatiable curiosity. She *knew* those eyes, even if they happened to look a bit different now.

The Doctor reached out and tucked a lock of hair behind her ear. 'You've been with me from the very beginning. Did you think I could ever – *ever* – forget all that? Of course you're still my Clara. That is ... unless ... if you ...?'

Clara couldn't bear the look of anguished uncertainty that crossed his face, and she offered the first response that came to mind, sliding her arms around his waist and laying her head against his chest. After a moment, his arms settled around her, holding her close. She felt the Doctor's familiar double heartbeat against her cheek and smiled.[24]

This serves also to express the reassurances the fan seeks that *Doctor Who* will continue unchanged through the turmoil of regeneration and cast change, but also promises that the fans will stay loyal to the series. The emphasis on romance deflects any remaining concerns the fans might have about the age difference and that might emerge more explicitly in the sexual relationships of Doctor/Clara shipper fics. This is not an immediate impediment in many of the fics in this category that focus on the Doctor's relationship with River, however, with the age difference between actors conforming more to socially acceptable norms.

Fans considered River's relationship with the older Capaldi to reflect societal views around the age of partners in sexual relationships, even though in storyworld terms the Doctor has always been much older than she. Many fan artists use River's 'Hello, sweetie' catchphrase in various expressive fonts to welcome Capaldi's Doctor. River's personality as established in the storyworld is maintained, but this is matched with a Doctor who appears more mature and connotes a more mature relationship. For example, in areyoumarriedriver's montage, River, dressed in the blue suit from 'Day of the Moon' (2011), is turned to the left and slightly overlapping a publicity still of Capaldi in *The Ladykillers*, making it appear as though they are posing together as a couple. This unity is enhanced by the fact that both figures look out from the image, engaging with the viewer. They do not gaze into each other's eyes lovingly, nor does one look dreamily upon the other, but they both own the gaze, suggesting strength and an equal partnership. The 'hello' is a sans serif font and the 'sweetie' an angular 'felt pen' style, evocative of River's spontaneity, and the background of a blueprint of the TARDIS offers a *tabula rasa* for adventures together.[25] Another art piece by tribeoftyrones has a softer focus as she chooses to construct her montage by Photoshopping images that evoke sensuality. Her composition superimposes a headshot of

Capaldi onto a glamorous publicity still of Alex Kingston, taken by the Hollywood photographer Sheryl Nields. In this still, Kingston is facing the camera in a sexualised pose: wearing a one-shouldered black gown, she stands with her hands behind her head, looking down slightly, eyes closed or semi-closed so that only the lids are visible, lips slightly parted. Although Kingston is standing in the original shot, the white background of the photo together with the pose and expression suggest that she is lying seductively on a bed. Covering most of Kingston's torso, the chosen image of Capaldi – looking to the left, his eyes at the level of her breasts, Kingston appearing to look down at him – suggests desire and a longing for each other. In fact, tribeoftyrones refers to it as 'creepy'. However, the image has been liked by other fans on Tumblr and widely reblogged and reproduced, as well as being featured on BuzzFeed.[26] This merely illustrates that fans are often self-deprecating, even about their own work, but also shows that key examples of fan production often bring status, and even a form of celebrity, within fandom. Regardless of this, such images bring characters together to fulfil the wishes and desires of the fan community (in this case to continue the preferred sexual relationship).

With the Doctor/River shipper fic, the appearance of age was a major factor. AmaranteReikaChan addresses this directly in 'Always My Sweetie'. River appraises the Doctor when she sees him for the first time in his new body, concluding: 'Can't say I'm not pleased you look older this time. It'll be nice to be able to take you in public without people judging me.'[27] Amarante acknowledges this is a common thought that the Doctor/River shippers have: 'I know this is probably going to be a very overused idea. But I couldn't help it. It was the first thing I thought of as soon as I saw who the new actor was.'[28] To further illustrate this, 'Aging God' by PrincessPinky is an inward-looking reflection by the Doctor himself on his new body and much is made of the fact that his appearance is older. The Doctor contemplates his wrinkles and grey hair: 'He'd redecorated and he didn't like it [...] So much *older*.'[29] This is not only a reference to some of the reported objection to Capaldi's casting, however. His angst is not only at seeming to be old, but at the very fact of regeneration. The new body signifies the loss of the family, Amy and Rory, that he had established as the Eleventh Doctor:

Holding onto that body had been like holding onto a piece of them somehow. Now even that had fallen into the blackness; the void of the time vortex. His new face reflected the passage of their time; his laugh lines – though he'd never laughed in this body – and more, the wrinkles, were their memories, their endings.[30]

The Doctor's older appearance is thus connected to his grief over his lost companions, his life experiences, and thus does not reflect an objection to an older-looking Doctor. Furthermore, it facilitates the seduction that is expressed when this Doctor meets River in his new body: 'River stroked his cheek and leaned on her tip toes to kiss one of his silver brows. "So ... *mature*."' In the passionate foreplay that follows, River is perfectly accepting of his maturity, and thus so too is the fan. Interestingly, Clara is not present in this fic, being redundant to the relationship between the Doctor and River and not a part of the Pond family that is privileged in this story, reflecting both the fan's affective investment in a particular era of *Doctor Who* and in the Doctor/River ship. Fan fictions such as these thus serve to smooth over the changes in the series that come with major cast changes and act as proof that sexy is not equated with young for these fans.[31]

Costume and title sequence

Many of the examples of fan art and fiction explored thus far are connected with affective investments in the series, the star and the fan community to which the artists and writers belong. But fan producers also engage with many aspects of art design, especially of extra-textual material and extra-diegetic elements of the programme such as trailers and titles. There is of course overlap and feedback between the fans' interest in official design and publicity material of the series and their responses to the text. For example, how the fan artists and writers dress the Twelfth Doctor in their work immediately after the announcement (and well before the official costume publicity shots) relates to Capaldi's star persona and prior performances, though this varies between individual examples of fan work. Unlike fan artists, many of the slash and shipper fic writers discussed above ignore or avoid the question of what the Doctor's costume would be. They leave the Doctor in Eleven's clothing, make no reference to what he is wearing (or in some instances, as with some examples of the slash and shipper fic, have him wearing no clothes at all). Eloriekam is unusual in describing a costume – she dresses her Twelve in 'a patchwork jacket and light shirt' – but, more typically for this kind of fiction, Amarante 'didn't want to speculate on anything clothing related'. PrincessPinky sets her story immediately post-regeneration and her Twelve still wears the tweed jacket and bow tie of Matt Smith's Doctor, before River tears off this clothing, preferring the Doctor in his 'birthday suit'.[32]

On the other hand, many of the fan artists explore costume possibilities. They often link closely to Capaldi's costumes in other roles, and among the photomontages they have produced the Capaldi Doctor has been depicted wearing the black-framed spectacles from *The Hour* and the goatee from *Musketeers*. For many of the image manipulation artists, working with costume was a matter of finding suitable prior roles from Capaldi's CV, but some artists looked further afield, adding Capaldi's face and head to shots of other actors in what they envisaged as suitable costumes from other programmes or films. Many of these were costumes from historical dramas that tapped into the notion of the history of the Doctor's costumes as having an Edwardian feel. Most prominent in this category of post-announcement fan art, however, was Capaldi in costume as Professor Marcus from Graham Linehan's stage version of *The Ladykillers*. The *Ladykillers* costume was selected because the artists felt it to be in keeping with the character of the Doctor; Kasterborous, who posts art on DeviantArt, commented that 'There's something very Doctorly about it, but then he was playing an absent-minded professor, or at least playing someone playing an absent-minded professor ... not a bad look really!' Significantly, this costume included a striped and fringed long scarf looped loosely twice around the neck, which while not looking like the iconic Tom Baker scarf in terms of colour or width of stripes, nevertheless recalled it for the fan artists.

This shot was used by areyoumarriedriver in her Doctor/River art discussed above. MrPacinoHead uses the *Ladykillers* costume shot in a montage with existing *Doctor Who* publicity photos of Clara, Vastra and Jenny on a background of Gallifreyan ideograms, space and stormy sky effects with embossed metallicised teal and copper lettering for the words 'Doctor Who'.[33] This is designed to resemble existing BBC publicity material for upcoming seasons. This image was also used in art designed to resemble official costume reveals, being Photoshopped onto backgrounds that anchored it in the *Doctor Who* storyworld, most often the interior of the TARDIS or the police box exterior itself. The most widely recirculated image (in fact, it can be said to have gone viral as it was shared by fans across the *Doctor Who* forums, Facebook and the fan groups on the crafting site Ravelry) also Photoshopped in the sonic screwdriver in one hand and changed the background to an image of the TARDIS in a garden.[34]

So widely circulated was this piece of fan art that some fans mistook the shot for an official costume. In fact, one fan crafter, who wished to remain anonymous, created a yarn colourway based on this image (a mix of blues and silver-greys in cool tones) to sell in her Etsy shop. When images go viral, they are often circulated beyond the confines of the intensely fannish groups and are shared across a much wider range of communities. In the age of social media, where 'we are all fans now', the fan art is shared with groups of viewers on different 'trajectories of fannish behaviour'.[35] Some of these fans might be more accurately described as being at the casual end of the spectrum; although their affective investments may be quite high, their fan capital may be low, meaning that they are not involved in or aware of the more focused fan groups. A case in point is the fibre artist I referred to above who dyed yarn in response to what she thought was the official costume release. She initially referred to this as a 'publicity photo' and called her yarn colourway The Twelfth Doctor 'based on this'. She edited her post to read 'FAKE publicity photo' after it was pointed out this was fan art, and later on in the discussion referred to it again as a fake. This can be read as suggesting irritation at being taken in by the art, but this is not an overall rejection of, or antagonism towards, fan art in general, fan handicrafters often being as inspired by fan fiction and art as they are by features of the official text. In this instance, the general response was that the colourway is 'awesome' and the dyer herself says, 'I love that photo' and thinks her yarn fits well with her other *Doctor Who* colours (which include a TARDIS blue, a bow-tie red and a Mad Man with a Box colourway for the Eleventh Doctor).

Confusion as to the origins of an image, and most especially the mistaken assumption that an image is an official BBC release, is exacerbated by the fact that fan art often incorporates BBC and

Doctor Who trademarks and brand logos. Jonny Eveson's early piece of fan art, for example, incorporates the official *Doctor Who* logo from the Matt Smith era (the blue-and-white lettering using the specially designed Eleventh Doctor font for the title *Doctor Who*, with the DW in the shape of the TARDIS between the words).[36] This does have the potential to add to the confusion of those fans who have little way to distinguish the fan art from official BBC publicity. While this raises questions around the legality of copyright, trademark use and intellectual property rights, it is – in the context of this discussion – more significant in terms of some fan artists working in the territory of official design. Rather than their work reflecting their affective responses to the text, or even their own tastes and preferences, these are sometimes more academic exercises in transforming the look or style associated with *Doctor Who*. In this category are examples of fan-made trailers and title sequences. Key examples of these fell outside the period of the original research, partly because of the longer time it can take to construct often complex videos, but also because some artists matched the official release dates of trailers and other publicity. For example, fan-made trailers became much more prolific once the official costume shots and trailers started to appear in January and May 2014 respectively, suggesting that fan video makers were more inspired to incorporate their visions of the Capaldi Doctor into extra-textual vids at this stage rather than at the point of the announcement. While this suggests that these videos do not reflect the fan producers' initial affective responses in the way that the post-announcement fan art and fiction does, it is nevertheless worth considering further, particularly in light of the fact that fan title sequences in particular went viral towards the end of 2013.

This is not to say that viral fan title sequences should be of more weight in terms of research into fan production, but distinctions between fans do open up, particularly in terms of the perceived quality of their fan work. Take for example CHMagIII's titles. This vid was made relatively quickly and uploaded to YouTube on 19 September. It does not incorporate Capaldi's face, just his name along with Jenna Coleman's, and it is a variation on the coloured streamer time vortex from the Tennant era and an asteroid field reminiscent of the McCoy titles, as well as the TARDIS hanging over a planet. CHMagIII admits that it is 'not very good' and that some of his other sequences, given more time and consideration, were of much higher quality.[37] By comparison, NeonVisual's title sequence, uploaded to YouTube in early September – a fast-paced and highly detailed sequence showing the TARDIS navigating an asteroid field and flying around a Gallifreyan city – was picked up on by fan news and comment sites such as The Mary Sue and Kasterborous, as well as by BBC News.[38] What is an important consideration in this respect is that, talent aside and despite easy access to editing software, those fans with access to professional equipment and with training or professional experience may have an advantage in this field of fan art. NeonVisual, for example, is a small, independent company producing digital content in both online and offline media specifically for fan and non-profit groups. Also falling into this category is the most celebrated of the fan-made title sequences produced after the announcement, the fob watch title sequence by motion graphics professional Billy Hanshaw, uploaded to YouTube in mid-September.[39] Enjoyed by many fans (including Moffat, who described it as 'absolutely stunning'[40]) for the very different visualisation of the time vortex as cogs and a spiralling clock face (and also for its borrowing of a popular steampunk aesthetic), this eventually formed the basis of the series titles used in season eight when Moffat commissioned Hanshaw to work with the BBC on the new title sequence for the Capaldi era.[41]

The fan excitement surrounding Hanshaw's titles was significant in relation to how the fan community saw it, that is as a transformative work produced by a member of the community. Comments on the Ravelry group included 'the credits were based on a fan's idea for the intro' and they 'were actually created by a fan [...] that makes a difference for me; I like to think of it all being part of the huge fan base'. In her interview, Heather talked about the 'gorgeous fanmade title sequence that came out earlier this year' and felt that it was 'very awesome' of Moffat to contact the fan to use his titles for the programme. But this belief that the video was an example of fan work was something of a misnomer, led to an extent by the media, including the *Mirror*, MTV, technology publications and the BBC itself, who all reiterated the discourse that the sequence was made by a fan. Considering that Hanshaw made the video as a professional advertising his services, the idea that he is 'just' a fan is rather misleading. This is not to imply that a professional working in the media cannot also be a fan, but Hanshaw himself admits to watching *Doctor Who* only sporadically and takes care to distance himself from being an 'uber-fan'.[42] On the one hand, this does illustrate the difficulties of defining fan status when fannish behaviours are so widespread and encouraged by the culture industries, but on the other it also gives rise to questions about the relationship between fans (as prosumers, producing and consuming their own fan works) and workers in the culture industry – including Moffat and Hanshaw (as producers, making programmes for consumers). Many fans made the assumption that the fan video adapted for the series titles was the work of a fan amateur, fitting the discourse of the 'star' fan who is eventually recognised by the producers for their inspirational work (before they knew the details, some fans also entered into a discussion around the assumption that this was an instance of the culture industries ripping off the work of the fan artists, though this reproduces an altogether different discourse).

Of course, *Doctor Who* fandom has an interesting history of fans moving into professional roles in the culture industries. In fact, a number of the production team who have worked on the post-2005 series are self-confessed fans, including Russell T Davies, Steven Moffat, Mark Gatiss and Paul Cornell, as well as actors David Tennant and Peter Capaldi. The possession of fan credentials (not just being a fan, but being a *participatory fan*) is an important point in relation to the continuation of *Doctor Who* in novels and audio plays after the cancellation in 1989. However, as Matt Hills points out, these fans represent an elite (borrowing the term used by the editor of *Doctor Who Magazine*, he refers to them as a 'mafia') in which a gender bias is evident.[43] What is perhaps most telling in the media coverage is the fact that the professional fans' title sequences were highlighted, often in a celebratory way, whereas the fan art and fiction (vast amounts of it produced by female fans) was overlooked. This is not to say that male fans who enter the production teams of *Doctor Who* are deliberately excluding female fans from their ranks, but it does perpetuate the patriarchal structures of the media industries and the demographic of classic *Who* fandom. As Busse discusses, negative outsider notions of what constitutes a 'good' and a 'bad' fan are often perpetuated within fandom.[44] Bad fandom often involves the emotional responses that are at the heart of female fans' transformative works. Busse argues that 'accusations of being too attached, too obsessed, and too invested get thrown around readily, and all too often such affect is criticized for being too girly or like a teen'.[45] Perhaps tellingly, this underlines the dichotomy between the fan art and fic produced in response to the casting announcement, which through projected interactivity encodes the affective responses of the largely female fans, and the technical exercises undertaken by male fans producing the title sequences that get them noticed by the wider media and the members of the fan 'mafia' now producing *Doctor Who*.

Conclusion: processing regeneration through fan work

As the field of fan studies has already well established, fans produce transformative works in response to the official narrative. However, the examples of fan work discussed in this chapter also illustrate the way fans incorporate their responses to extra-textual material into their art and fiction. These transformative works incorporate the fans' own reflections, hopes and ideas for directions which they would like the character to take, regardless of whether there is much – or indeed any – primary material to transform. Most importantly, fan fiction also encodes the concerns and expectations of the fan writers. The kinds of transformative work the fans undertake represent affective investments in the Capaldi Doctor by fitting him into a preferred ship or slashed pairing, imagining how other characters in the storyworld might deal with the Doctor's new appearance and speculating on his new look and personality (even where these are playful or recognised as out of character). The work can thus deal with different responses to the narrative, but in one sense it is also regarded as ephemeral. It exists in the gap between Doctors, and is a way for fans to both play with and work through their responses as they approach a major transition point in the series (and character) they love.

Further, in describing her early Twelfth Doctor fics, Pir8grl describes imagining future narratives with the new Doctor and seeing how close she comes to the eventual episodes as 'fun'. Even though female fandom might have few opportunities to achieve input into the production process, writing speculative fan fiction can be an amusing and entertaining pastime. Fanfic writers may never expect to see their scenarios come to fruition on screen (for fanfic is, in any case, an attempt to transform the canonical text in order to address perceived narrative gaps or unfulfilled *relationships* in the on-screen series); nevertheless, writers such as Pir8grl might well take pleasure in seeing some of their expectations and desires met (at least in part). Although the series was extremely unlikely to address the concerns of the *Torchwood* fan writers regarding the Doctor's resemblance to Frobisher, the Doctor did address his similar appearance to Caecilius in 'The Fires of Pompeii' (noted in the introduction to this collection), which does acknowledge the new face as something fans were concerned with. Similarly, while desires around a slashed relationship with Jack or a ship involving Clara are unlikely to be the subject of TV episodes, again they are acknowledged to some extent: in 'Deep Breath', the Doctor tells Clara he cannot be her boyfriend. This does echo the concerns of some fans about the age gap, but it also serves to re-establish an asexual/paternal Doctor, drawing a line under the possibility of Doctor–companion romantic or sexual relationships as there had been with the Tenth Doctor. One exception, of course, is the already established relationship with River Song. This fits the now more socially age-appropriate pairing (as least in terms of the actors' ages). Moreover, the Doctor/River shippers do get to see their desires for River and the Twelfth Doctor come to fruition in 'The Husbands of River Song' when River and the Doctor 'live happily ever after' (as the on-screen caption reads) on Darillium for a night lasting 24 years. So while fan fiction remains a segment of the archontic text that stands apart from the canonical narrative in the main (not least because female fans continue to have less access to official production channels and therefore use fan fiction to remediate and transform the narrative), echoes of their desires for narrative events and relationships that do appear on screen can contribute to the pleasures of writing speculative fan fiction.

However, these additional viewing pleasures strongly contrast with a minority of fan work, specifically that which is used by professionals or fans aspiring to careers in the media and arts as a showcase for their skills, talents and imagination. This is not to argue that all the other fan artists and writers do not also produce work to achieve such recognition (there are plenty of fanfic artists and writers who achieve fan celebrity status or whose work goes viral), but they continue not to be recognised by the very media industries in which the 'poachers-turned-gamekeepers' of *Doctor Who* fandom operate.

To frame this in the context of projected interactivity, two fan identities are revealed that suggest male and female fandom remains oppositional to some extent. While these may not always be mutually exclusive, the different outcomes lead us to question whether the idea that '*Doctor Who* belongs to all of us' is not without its tensions after all.

Notes

Unless otherwise indicated, all quotes from fans in this chapter are taken from direct interviews with the author.

1 Brigid Cherry, '"Oh, no, that won't do at all ... it's ridiculous!": observations on the *Doctor Who* audience', in Andrew O'Day (ed.), *Doctor Who: The Eleventh Hour – A Critical Celebration of the Matt Smith and Steven Moffat Era* (London, 2014), pp. 204–27.

2 See Karen Hellekson and Kristina Busse (eds), *Fan Fiction and Fan Communities in the Age of the Internet* (Jefferson, NC, 2006) and *The Fan Fiction Studies Reader* (Iowa City, 2014), for example.

3 Abigail Derecho, 'Archontic literature: a definition, a history, and several theories of fan fiction', in Hellekson and Busse (eds), *Fan Fiction and Fan Communities*, pp. 61–78.

4 Archive of Our Own, available at https://archiveofourown.org/; Fanfiction.net, available at https://www.fanfiction.net/; A Teaspoon and an Open Mind, available at http://www.whofic.com/ (all accessed 5 August 2013).

5 Amber Davisson and Paul Booth, 'Reconceptualizing communication and agency in fan activity: a proposal for a projected interactivity model for fan studies', *Texas Speech Communication Journal* xxiii/1 (2007), pp. 33–43.

6 Roberta Pearson, '"Bright particular star": Patrick Stewart, Jean-Luc Picard, and cult television', in Sara Gwenllian-Jones and Roberta Pearson (eds), *Cult Television* (Minneapolis, MN, 2004), pp. 61–80.

7 Leaning against a corner of the TARDIS: Space Dad, Available at http://FuckYesPeterCapaldi.tumblr.com (accessed 18 August 2013). Looking out of the TARDIS door: 'Peter Capaldi is finally in a "Doctor Who" and "The Thick of It" f#%kety mashup', Uproxx [website] (8 May 2013). Available at http://uproxx.com/tv/2013/08/peter-capaldi-doctor-who-the-thick-of-it-mashup/ (accessed 19 August 2013).

8   YouTube accolade: mjam555666, 'Malcolm Tucker's best line ever!' [video], YouTube, https://m.youtube.com/watch?v=D6Qrt43PYtE (accessed 7 August 2013). Link no longer working. Top ten favourite Tucker quotes: Johnny Dee, '*The Thick of It*: top ten Malcolm Tucker moments', *Guardian* (15 October 2009). Available at https://www.theguardian.com/tv-and-radio/tvandradioblog/2009/oct/15/thick-of-it-malcolm-tucker (accessed 15 March 2015). Fuckitybye Tumblr: 'Come the fuck in or fuck the fuck off' [blog]. Available at http://fuckitybye.tumblr.com/ (accessed 7 August 2013).

9   Jonny Eveson Posters. Available at http://jonnyevesonposters.tumblr.com/ (accessed 9 August 2013). Link no longer working.

10   D.I.D, 'More Malcolm Tucker as Doctor Who!' [Twitter post], 10.14 a.m., 5 August 2013, https://twitter.com/didnotts/status/364434168433750018 (accessed 15 August 2013).

11   Pete Nottage, 'Malcolm Tucker IS Dr Who!' [video], YouTube (uploaded 4 August 2013), https://youtube.com/watch?v=5Blf073f2Lc (accessed 12 August 2013).

12   Jonny Eveson Posters.

13   ladygrey99, 'Fob watches and VHS', Archive of Our Own [website] (4 August 2013). Available at http://archiveofourown.org/works/912456 (accessed 6 August 2013).

14   Steven Moffat has also addressed the issue both in the narrative and in interviews.

15   Trobadora, 'Under the skin', Archive of Our Own [website] (7 August 2013). Available at http://archiveofourown.org/works/916278 (accessed 9 August 2013).

16   sein Henker, 'Doctor', FanFiction [website] (6 August 2013). Available at https://www.fanfiction.net/s/9569067/1/Doctor (accessed 14 August 2013).

17   Ibid.

18   Eloriekam, 'Mistaken identity', A Teaspoon and an Open Mind [website] (n.d.). Available at http://www.whofic.com/viewstory.php?sid=51548 (accessed 17 August 2013).

19   Ibid.

20   Pir8grl, 'A journey begins', FanFiction [website] (22 September 2013). Available at https://www.fanfiction.net/s/9705232/1/A-Journey-Begins (accessed 22 June 2018).

21   Idem, 'Be my mirror', FanFiction [website] (22 October 2013). Available at https://www.fanfiction.net/s/9784756/1/Be-My-Mirror (accessed 22 June 2018).

22   Idem, 'Christmas serenade', FanFiction [website] (19 February 2014). Available at https://www.fanfiction.net/s/10125277/1/Christmas-Serenade (accessed 22 June 2018).

23   Idem, 'Time to begin', FanFiction [website] (13 February 2014). Available

at https://www.fanfiction.net/s/9978714/1/Time-to-Begin (accessed 22 June 2018).

24 Idem, 'New body – same hearts', FanFiction [website] (7 August 2013). Available at https://www.fanfiction.net/s/9572321/1/New-Body-Same-Hearts (accessed 16 August 2013).

25 The image can be found, numbered 22 in a list, in Ailbhe Malone, '23 reasons to love Peter Capaldi', Buzzfeed [website] (5 August 2013). Available at http://www.buzzfeed.com/ailbhemalone/reasons-to-love-peter-capaldi (accessed 19 June 2015).

26 This image is numbered 21 in a list in Malone, '23 reasons'.

27 AmaranteReikaChan, 'Always my sweetie', Archive of Our Own [website] (6 August 2013). Available at http://archiveofourown.org/works/914171 (accessed 29 August 2013).

28 Ibid.

29 Princess Pinky, 'Aging god', FanFiction [website] (5 August 2013). Available at https://www.fanfiction.net/s/9566744/1/Aging-God (accessed 25 August 2013).

30 Ibid.

31 And in the female fan groups, the discussion of Capaldi in terms of his sex appeal and the sharing of images which can be lusted over, while not as prolific, is as intense as it is for Tennant.

32 Princess Pinky, 'Aging god'.

33 MrPacinoHead, 'Doctor Who series 8 wallpaper'. Available at http://mrpacinohead.deviantart.com/art/Doctor-Who-Series-8-Wallpaper-391510282 (accessed 13 August 2013).

34 When it comes to fan memes that are reposted, retweeted and reblogged continually it is sometimes hard to establish where they originated. For example, the image of Peter Capaldi in costume from *The Ladykillers* with a sonic screwdriver added is also taken from its Photoshopped background and added to other backgrounds. The work of one fan artist is thus co-opted by another.

35 Kristina Busse, 'Fandom-is-a-way-of-life versus watercooler discussion; or, the geek hierarchy as fannish identity politics', Flow [website] (17 November 2006). Available at http://www.flowjournal.org/2006/11/taste-and-fandom/ (accessed 10 October 2009).

36 Jonny Eveson Posters.

37 CHMagIII, '12th Doctor opening title sequence' [video], YouTube (uploaded 19 September 2013), https://www.youtube.com/watch?v=jrNZoz1WnI8 (accessed 24 September 2013).

38 The title sequence itself: NeonVisual, 'Peter Capaldi *Doctor Who* series 8 opening sequence – finalized – 2014 NeonVisual fan intro' [video], YouTube (uploaded 18 January 2014), https://www.youtube.com/watch?v=LzNuZuRcUxM (accessed 27 January 2014). Article on The Mary Sue: Sam Maggs, 'Can this fan-made *Doctor Who* opening credit

sequence for Peter Capaldi be real please?', The Mary Sue [website] (9 February 2014). Available at http://www.themarysue.com/doctor-who-opening-credits/ (accessed 6 July 2014). Article on Kasterborous: 'Delicious fan-made Peter Capaldi *Doctor Who* titles', Kasterborous [website] (1 September 2013). Available at http://www.kasterborous. com/2013/09/delicious-fan-made-peter-capaldi-doctor-who-titles-video/ (accessed 6 July 2014). BBC News feature: Neil Bowdler, 'Fan unveils "new" *Doctor Who* titles', BBC News [website] (7 November 2013). Available at http://www.bbc.co.uk/news/technology-24812380 (accessed 9 July 2014).

39 billydakiduk, 'Doctor Who original concept Peter Capaldi intro' [video], YouTube (uploaded 16 September 2013), https://www.youtube.com/watch?v=oXOBHnWiinY.

40 Karen Hyland, '*Doctor Who*: fan's sequence has become new titles sequence', *Mirror* [website] (15 August 2014). Available at http://www.mirror.co.uk/tv/tv-news/doctor-who-fans-sequence-become-4056067 (accessed 28 September 2015).

41 Ian Youngs, 'The *Doctor Who* fan who created the show's new titles', BBC News [website] (23 August 2014). Available at http://www.bbc.co.uk/news/entertainment-arts-28871058 (accessed 5 October 2014).

42 Henry Mance, 'For the fans, by the fans – lessons from the new *Doctor Who*', *Financial Times* (21 August 2014). Available to subscribers at https://www.ft.com/content/a4f6e280-27bc-11e4-b7a9-00144feabdc0 (accessed 27 September 2015).

43 Matt Hills, *Triumph of a Time Lord: Regenerating Doctor Who in the Twenty-First Century* (London, 2010), p. 54.

44 Kristina Busse, 'Geek hierarchies, boundary policing, and the gendering of the good fan', *Participations: Journal of Audience and Reception Studies* x/1 (2013), pp. 73–91.

45 Ibid., p. 73.

11

HIT OR MISS?

Fan Responses to the *Regenderation* of the Master

Dene October

Sora 2311: Missy is the best thing to happen to Doctor Who since the idea of regeneration.

Matt_Wilson: You are kidding right? Missy will sink Doctor Who.[1]

As *Doctor Who* series eight drew to an end, its mysterious recurring character, Missy (Michelle Gomez), finally introduced herself as the Doctor's arch-enemy, the Master. The BBC had treated the dramatic reveal as top secret, using ADR (Automated Dialogue Replacement) so onlookers could not spoil the surprise, and posting press preview screeners with the scene removed. As fans spread the reveal across *Doctor Who* forums, surprise turned to consternation, anger, grief and glee, as what posters dubbed *regenderation* stirred up old debates.

Studying forum responses to the build-up and reveal of Missy as the Master necessarily involves issues of internal canonical as well as external cultural significance, and highlights the language and motivations of fans. The relationship between online fan practices and television viewing (social television) has attracted rising scholarly attention over the last decade, applying the ethnographer's tools to the online space, which Matt Hills reminds us is 'a form of public space' where a widely distributed membership come to 'talk' through mundane computer-mediated interactions.[2] Fans are arguably the most visible of television audiences, although not the only ones worth studying. While producers of media have preferred to research the widest possible audience, partly due to the negative image of the fan, the field of fan studies leaves other viewing positions undertheorised. Since fans are not the only ones who experience *Doctor Who* as a meaningful cultural product, this chapter also considers the responses of students from the Doctor Who by Design class I teach,[3] whose interest in the programme is framed by the historical and theoretical contexts of their study, and a random test sample (whose relationship to the programme was unknown prior to interview). Although this additional research represents a minor part of this chapter, the recognition of a wider public reception for Missy helps contextualise the forum responses.

Studying fans and 'fan talk'

Fans are increasingly part of everyday cultural life, and this visibility encourages the media to mine 'fan talk' for news even while presenting the fan as a figure of ridicule. The academic focus has shifted from fan as media dupe or resistant textual poacher,[4] to cultivated brand advocate and social media influencer. Fans are, according to Paul Booth, in a 'liminal state between resistant and complicit'; thus, for Cornel Sandvoss, 'fan places are places of consumption', while for Mark Duffett, 'fans often like things for free, and [...] they are always *more than* consumers.'[5] The latter sentiment highlights the emotional attachments formed with fan objects beyond their official use. Fans exploit a range of analytical, interpretative and technical skills that put them on a par with producers, academics and artists but share skills, expertise and opinions.[6]

Sandvoss defines fandom as the 'emotionally involved consumption of a given popular narrative or text', while John Fiske argues that texts are chosen by fans who 'discriminate fiercely' in a self-interested and functional act.[7] However, it does not follow that emotional involvement leads to active fandom or fannish behaviour to fannish identity. The label 'fan' disguises varying levels of investment and engagement,[8] which are expressed through a range of activities including cosplay (costume play) and fans' talk in physical or online communities.

The domestication of the computer and internet, which has afforded media companies the ability to disseminate products and promotions widely, has also afforded fans tools to create Web pages, gain access to information and archives, have a visible presence, interact with others and engage in sometimes self-conscious public performance. Online interaction turns the fan community 'from a network of local cultures or periodic rituals into a non-stop process of social effervescence',[9] enabling swift and untimely interactions such as posting 'spoilers' (material leaked ahead of scheduled broadcast), changing television from a 'lean-back experience' to a lean-forward interactive one. The paradigm shift has been from an age of scarcity in broadcasting to one of plenty, one where 'technological digitization and convergence are starting to reach maturity', evidenced by the spread of broadband, interactive sets, mobile, smart and wireless technologies, and interactive user practices.[10] The media-savvy fan is a familiar cultural figure, acknowledged on programmes and networks and deployed as an *organic invitation* for audience engagement,[11] as in the *Doctor Who* series nine episode 'Before the Flood', where the Doctor invites viewers to google 'bootstrap paradox'.

The community and social bond aspects of fan participation have picked up from Donald Horton and R. Richard Wohl's psychology of PSI (parasocial interaction), an influence in media communications studies in describing the *illusory* connection fans make with fictional characters and celebrities.[12] Such interactions also broaden the fan's 'scope of interpersonal relations [...] rather than compensate for a lack of relationships',[13] thus undermining the negative assumptions of online fans as friendless. Henry Jenkins suggests that fans use fandoms as an 'alternative social community' through which they communicate and share.[14] Communication is *the* 'primal instinct' of fans, according to Susan Clerc, while for Kirsten Pullen it is about finding like-minded others.[15] For Arthur Lizie, sharing interpretations of the fan object is but one of the opportunities opened up by 'fan talk'; fans can also negotiate private issues and engage in commerce and relationship building.[16] In order to study 'fan talk' it is important, as Hills remarks, to do more than set up a 'discursive justification' of fandom and fans and instead engage with the construction of fan language – *how* fans engage each other through computer-mediated discourse.[17] Studies of online fan communities have documented how spaces evolve a sense of place through etiquette, behavioural norms and unique forms of expression, how and whether they abide over time or adapt to new technologies, and whether 'fan talk' or personal chat dominates interactions.[18] Precedents to such work include Brigid Cherry, who looks at 'the language and discourses that are employed in talking' about fan experiences and how fans react to regeneration, Paul Booth and Peter Kelly, who study how fans talk about each other, and Douglas McNaughton's study of online 'Whospeak'.[19]

The forums studied for the current chapter are DSF (Digital Spy Forums) and DWF (Doctor Who Forum).[20] DSF is part of Hearst Entertainment, the UK's largest entertainment forum and digital publisher, with an online audience of 16 million users per month.[21] The forum provides over one million posts and 26,000 different threads on *Doctor Who*.[22] DWF is much smaller, with around 3,700 active members who have made almost 55,000 posts, and carries the strapline 'Theories even more insane than what's actually happening'.[23] These forums are organised into threads, some by episode titles and others as started by individual posters, and into posts running from earliest to latest, pages which can be reorganised or filtered by search terms accessible to both fan contributor and academic researcher.

These forums are ungated public spaces where members make comments in full view. Although only registered members can post and comment upon each other's posts, anyone may see the posts – unlike the popular Gallifrey Base, for example, where threads are blocked from search engine results.[24] In the lead-up to the 'Missy reveal', these public threads were harvested by online news sites and British tabloids, such as the *Daily Mirror*, in a way that sometimes inflated how representative and significant certain dramatic forum voices were. Sometimes the discussions became heated, and despite forum rules that prohibit 'racism, homophobia and sexism' (DSF), it quickly became evident there were variations in tolerance and respect. While other private forums offer safe gathering spaces, promoting feminist and LGBTQ voices, these forums often relied on moderation: there were instances where moderators deleted offensive posts and even barred members, but there were also instances where members moderated each other, attacking misogynistic, sexist and transphobic posts. All of this was publicly visible – acting as a protean textual production that dramatised the heterogeneity of fans as players on a public stage where the range of views about the 'Missy reveal' spoke to a wider scope of gender attitudes than private forums would have revealed – and is hence important to this survey.

There is clearly a case for reporting the gender of participants when foregrounding discourses in computer-mediated communications, particularly where the population and practices of fan communities may be changing. Making demographics visible has benefits such as exploring fan migrations across texts perceived as dominated by male or female audiences, for example.[25] *Doctor Who* fandom has been a masculine preserve in the past and 'carried a whiff of the Old Boys' Club', and is coded through the programme's 'masculinised genre', so its fanzines and conventions may provide a gendered template for online communications.[26] Several commentators have remarked on how women use media to build relationships or to illuminate character relationships, whereas men focus on demonstrating knowledge and solving 'narrative problems'.[27] Susan Herring, Deborah Johnson and Tamra DiBenedetto have argued that men's success in 'defining computers and computer networks as male domains' means many women feel more comfortable in women-centred online discussion groups where they can 'set the terms of the discourse'.[28] Several commentators have pointed out how the interests and engagements of female fans are easily dismissed, their responses derided, their textual readings denigrated, their emotions feared and their attachments mocked.[29]

On the other hand, posters may choose to present an 'unmarked' self in forums which offer gender anonymity. This may be to maintain a discreet online identity or to leave offline prejudices behind.[30] While online anonymity is more often the resort of parties wishing to attack others, it also offers the opportunity to 'express thoughts and emotions without fear of being identified and socially evaluated'.[31] Ann-Marie Cook and Deirdre Hynes's study of female posters on European football forums reveals that the tactics used to combat online chauvinism include appropriation of 'male language styles, concealment of femininity [...] the protection of one's forum persona by simply avoiding situations that could lead to being "outed" as a woman' as well as 'brandishing their mastery of facts and figures'.[32]

On the forums studied, specific details about individual posters, such as their gender, are difficult to establish, since neither DSF nor DWF requests such data upon registration or provides the means for members to profile it beyond a customisable username and avatar. DSF, as part of 'netiquette', even warns posters not to divulge personal details. Naturally, personal details do emerge, particularly in sustained member interactions, and the popularity of the thread 'Age, Sex, Location of Posters ... just curious' indicates both curiosity and willingness to match online with offline identity (for more on the congruence of off- and online identities, see Nancy Baym and Sarah Bird[33]).[34]

Some posters used gendered handles or avatars. Some volunteered personal details; for others, these 'leaked' during the course of posting. Some used the same social identity across other platforms, leaving gendered internet footprints. From this information the following demographic profile of the threads was ascertained. On DSF's Missy threads, only 11 per cent of posters could be identified as women, compared with 53 per cent who were identifiable as men; this leaves 36 per cent whose profile and posts did not reveal gender information. On DWF's Missy threads, 22 per cent of posters could be identified as women, compared to 40 per cent who were men and 38 per cent whose gender could not be ascertained. Some users used gay iconography or references in their profiles, while others openly declared their heterosexuality – there were many more who did so on threads like 'Doctor Who's male fanbase – all gay?' (DSF, 2008). Some users changed their handles during the period of study to variations of 'Missy'. While extreme caution should be used in interpreting this data, what is noteworthy – particularly given the early remarks about online and offline congruence – is the percentage of gender-neutral profiles.

More specific identification of these posters raises ethical concerns. The 'doxing' (research and broadcast of private information in order to expose individuals), trolling and online harassment of gamer and fan women, particularly over issues of cultural diversification, has been much reported since 2014, the year of Missy's debut. The issue of ethics in digital ethnography is a live and practical one, not least due to fans' fears of misrepresentation.[35] While posters in ungated communities should perhaps have a 'reasonable expectation' of being observed, they may in fact assume their audience is sympathetic; consequently for the academic writer who is editing and placing posts into a new critical context, decisions about uncovering identities cannot be taken lightly.[36]

Given all the above, it would be an error to assume that posters here are male 'until proven otherwise'.[37] When G. G. uses the phrase 'raving cross-dresser', while this implies a position in relation to conservative ideas about gender, the issue of G. G.'s gender is less the point than how certitudes work across gender. This may in some cases lead women to accept masculine sensibilities and regulate their posts to gain peer acceptance. On the other hand, many posters whose gender markers indicate they are male were early adopters of 'regendering'.

In addition, it is possible to discern with some posters' profiles more than others whether the attachment to fandom is long-lived (stretching back to the 'classic' series) or based exclusively on the post-2005 'new' series (although many of those who were clearly new fans also made reference to the classic series). Again, there is no clear correlation between length of fandom and attitudes towards the 'Missy reveal' that could not be accounted for by more general cultural attitudes about gender. While there were many negative and reactionary voices, the forum responses to the 'Missy reveal' were mixed, if not generally positive.

A miss is as good as a mile: fan responses to messing with the Master

The 'Missy reveal' in 'Dark Water' generated media headlines, viewer comment and a spike in fan posts typical of the denouement to most *Doctor Who* season arcs. 'Missy is River Song ... the Rani ... Clara Oswald ...' speculated a breathless C. B. (DSF) even amid the thrill of Peter Capaldi's first outing as the Twelfth Doctor in 'Deep Breath'. 'Nah, shes [sic] the Master,' opined C. J. Others, like T. S., were dubious how 'a female Master would go down' with the fans. 'Without sounding sexist,' began C. W., 'I seriously hope the master isn't a woman [...] This IMO would be the death of doctor who.' Just a couple of months later, the conjecture gave way to cries of delight and shrieks of disapproval:

I think a re-GENDER-ation is a great idea. (J. J., DSF)

It's inspired casting. I'm sure, in his own afterlife, he's [Roger Delgado] laughing his head off himself [...] Also – it gives me a wonderful opportunity for cross-dressing in the future. (P. S. 1., DWF)

In welcoming Missy to the programme, such posts can be seen as attempts to position their authors in opposition to the anticipated furore and demonstrate knowledge, attachment and loyalty as 'true fans'. But not all posters expressed their attachment through supportive comments and many threads, such as 'The Master is NOT a Woman' (DSF), coordinated the campaign against *regenderation*:

Am I supposed to forget EVERYTHING I have ever seen and now accept that the Master is a raving cross-dresser (G. G., DSF)

This is fucking bullshit, the Master is the Master not the Mistress! (E. P., DWF)

Expressions of anxiety and uncertainty about the programme direction were common – perhaps since, as Paul Booth points out, 'Fandom is an inherently nostalgic practice.'[38] Many posters pitched their complaints as a desire for stability, or at least for slowing down the programme changes. For some the need to stop and take stock was an imperative: 'If it's not necessary to change, it's necessary not to change' (I. B., DSF).

But others defended change as one of the show's traditions, expressing a wanderlust for fresh takes on old ideas. Disputes about the show's *strange and familiar* mix are common, as indicated by forum archives, particularly given the accelerated pace and broadcast context of storytelling since the 2005 return of the show:[39]

A show that doesn't create discussion (or controversy) once in a while risks falling into realms of irrelevancy [...] it just so happens that the rules in Doctor Who are flexible enough to allow gender change to be an element up for change within that formula. (A. M., DSF)

I am sick of the phrase 'Dw is about change'. Hartnell regenerated because otherwise the show would end after he left [...] sometimes change is necessary evil, but this time it is not necessary (A. B., DSF)

Many posters were anxious that the events in 'Dark Water'/'Death in Heaven' would not be fully explained, their mysteries either deferred until series nine or left for fans to fight over. The porous boundaries between fans and the media industry were highlighted by those who felt that showrunner Steven Moffat was likely to troll fans with misdirection and stories that nudged in the direction of their 'bonkers theorising' (the light-hearted fan term on DWF for imaginative speculation) and *fanwank* (where continuity references appeal to fans but make little sense to the plot).[40] As Cherry points out, fans make it their business to have and share concerns about continuity, and this is particularly so where the responsibilities for writing out textual inconsistencies (retconning) do not have clear ownership.[41] This concern with canon (an officially sanctioned body of work) is particularly precarious given the complexity of the paracanonical universe of *Doctor Who* and the 'official' narrative unfolding in a transmedia setting (across various media) and alongside parallel competing stories. Such concerns are often alleviated when explanations are stitched into future programmes. There is some relief, for example, when Missy begins to conform to character in series nine. Discussing the season opener, 'The Magician's Apprentice', P. M. (DWF) admits to being happily confused by Missy's intentions in helping the Doctor against the Daleks, adding, 'but I've been watching the show since the 70's and can't help but trust the Mixmaster as far as I can throw her, it's instinct by now, lol'.

Much of the concern with canon was focused on the established character of the Master and the lore of regeneration. The Master's early regenerations – unlike the Doctor's – are surprisingly consistent, his goatee beard, high hairline and love of dark outfits defining him, but the female Missy character writes out this physical familiarity. Indeed, criticism of Missy is part of the wider context for not enjoying any iteration of the Master since Roger Delgado, a point made by a few posters, for example, 'I did not like Simms nutcase version at all' (D. M., DSF). Others pointed out that the Master's physical appearance had taken many odd turns; it wasn't *regendering* that was the problem, but the textual gap that left *regeneration* as a possibility:

If you can except [*sic*] him [...] merging with Tremas in The Keeper of Traken [and] turning into a cat in Survival [...] turning into a woman really is nothing. The only thing is I hope it is not a regeneration because I don't think the history of the programme supports that. I hope he's 'stolen' the body again. (J. R., DSF)

If it's not a straight regeneration, as with The Doctor, then the problem about the biology of gender is irrelevant [...] The Master obtaining a female body is perfectly playing by the rules that the show had already set up a long time ago. (A. M., DSF)

Character consistency worried others. In 'Dark Water', Missy refers to the Doctor as her boyfriend and proceeds to kiss him, an event that proved to be a sticking point. It 'is something I don't think I will ever get over', stated K. M. (DWF), rationalising this upset as 'not because The Doctor kissed somebody who used to be a man' but because 'it just doesn't seem like something any of the other incarnations of The Master would ever do'. While some characterised Missy's behaviour as more appropriate to slash, an extreme version of fanfic where two characters of the same gender are linked in romantic or sexual liaison (and which is no stranger to Doctor/Master pairings[42]), others disputed the kiss as problematic, recalling the longstanding ambiguity in the Doctor/Master relationship: 'It's the history between Missy/the Master and the Doctor that gives extra meaning to those exchanges' (G. K., DSF). Others felt the kiss emphasised the new gender dynamic between the Doctor and Missy. As such, the debate tested the emotional sense of ownership for the character since fans may feel 'they have a better understanding of [...] characters than the producers', a conviction often taken up through fan fiction, which offers the opportunity for fans to remediate texts 'involving themselves in the creative process', and foster a sense of being in control.[43] As Jenkins reminds us, passive audiences lack control over the text, and leave it to producers to 'protect the integrity of their favorite character',[44] while active audiences exert control through 'fan talk' and fiction.[45]

One of the ways that fans are able to exert control and marshal their fan knowledge is through displays of creative speculation and forensic detective work. These skills, alongside posting frequently and eloquently, tend to be rewarded by the admiration of peers and act to classify the poster as both erudite and tasteful. The tradition of 'bonkers theorising' also means boasting elaborate plot ideas in comparison with, and criticism of, the showrunner. One poster remarked:

'I was just sure that Moffat wouldn't do anything so obvious as have Missy be the Master!' (A. B., DWF).

The scale of some posters' dedication and detective work was evident in the attention paid to particular scenes: 'I think there's more than one time line,' theorised P. F. (DWF), having listed the probable order of scenes based on the changing lengths and styles of the Doctor's hair, a clue in unravelling the complications of the narrative. The contents of Clara's kitchen were also combed through as fans demonstrated non-linear ways of viewing, such as slowing and pausing the episode, tactics which received plaudits from other posters. As S. B. (DWF) said, directly addressing B. B., 'Bless you for the foray into Clara's kitchen [...] Seriously – the rest of us just aren't worthy!!'

Displays of cultural capital extend beyond the television stories. D. F. (DWF) enlightened posters about the Big Finish 'Timelord Unbound' audio adventures, pointing out that, in this alternative canon, 'Time Lords regenerate into the opposit [sic] sex when they commit suicide.' In researching his theory, D. F. rewatched old episodes and found correspondences with how the Master sacrifices himself to stop Rassilon ('The End of Time', 2010): 'Self-sacrifice is a form of suicide, right? Which means that [the] Master had no choice – he had to become the Mistress.' Such forensic attention to the text (despite not being correct), as well as the emphasis on peer acknowledgement, invites a comparison between academics and fans.[46] On the other hand, posters differed from academics in not setting debate into wider cultural and political contexts.

Responses to Missy(ing) the Master: transgender studies

My Doctor Who by Design class – split 60/40 female/male – enjoyed Missy, but they feared for her cultural potential. She lacked a backstory that examined gender dysphoria or required the audience to identify with her as transgender. The same students recalled the Doctor's speech in 'A Town Called Mercy' (2012), where the horse called Susan 'wants [one] to respect his life choices' as glibly reducing gender struggle and identity politics to a matter of lifestyle. The storylines were well-intentioned, according to the students, but ones that merely borrowed the trope of the trans woman without contesting popular assumptions, thus trans character Cassandra O'Brien (Zoe Wanamaker) in 'The End of the World' (2005) and 'New Earth' (2006) is represented as vain and surgery-obsessed. Worse still, the BBC did not take up the opportunity to discuss such issues, leaving negative voices to complain about 'ghastly rumours' that the Doctor will regenerate as female and fears that discussing transgenderism might 'introduce genitalia into family viewing'[47] – voices that reduced transgender to sex change.

Missy (and Bethany Black, who became the programme's first transgender actress, starring as 474 in the series nine episode 'Sleep No More') appears in a context where commissioners were attempting to plug the biggest 'single absence in broadcasting' despite lacking confidence in understanding the issues involved.[48] Thus, while the twenty-first century has seen an acceleration in representations, these tend to be negative ones, with 40 per cent cast as victims, 21 per cent as killers and 20 per cent as sex workers.[49] At the same time, academia has seen a rise in university courses for Transgender Studies as well as several themed journals, edited books and conferences, making transgenderism one of the most written-about subjects and offering 'new opportunities to broaden the horizons' of others.[50]

Academic fans are often well versed in the language of identity politics which contextualises their fan reception, although Richard Wallace complains that little work has been done to address the issue of gender politics in *Doctor Who*.[51] This helps make sense of why 'representations often failed' despite the good intentions of the programme's makers. Subject positions are mediated by access to privileged discourses, or the moderation of discourses, for example in the policing of 'fan talk' on forums.

This differentiation in reader positions caused tensions between articulate posters and those for whom language skills and powerful discourses lay out of reach. Many posts worried about being labelled transgenderist and misogynistic while simultaneously mocking those they characterised as politically correct. When M. W. stated that 'Missy is an alien and a monster,' D. M.'s response lampooned the language being used in the debate: 'Now, that's just being alienist and monstrophobic' (DSF).

Humour was one form of defence. T. I. (DWF) referenced UK comedy show *Little Britain* (BBC, 2003–7), which features the running joke of a man making a poor attempt to pass off as a woman, by saying, 'The Master is a lady, he does ladies' things.' Others were indignant: 'There seems to be a concerted feminist campaign to bring feminist issues into all of the media we interact with [...] I just want to watch tv and play games to escape all this nonsense, it's getting ridiculous' (M. M., DSF). Some compensated for the programme's reticence by suggesting that answers could be found within its textual openness: 'Gender is fluid on Gallifrey. It's not a big deal within the show, but unfortunately it seems to be so here' (B. S., DSF). Others were happy, both with Missy as a character and the lack of potentially controversial discussion:

> We have a lead character who can change his face and flies around the universe in a blue box, and people get caught up on a gender change. The only thing that [the programme makers] could have done wrong would have been to fixate upon the change and make a huge deal out of it – they didn't and I like that a lot. (A. N., DSF)

Fan communities engender a sense of belonging and the expectations of 'shared experience'.[52] Fans are therefore invested in the 'active communality with kindred spirits',[53] and in protecting the online 'family' even while comparing it with the 'not-we' family watching in front of the television at home. Communities operate according to what Jenkins calls 'moral economy', leveraging consensus to promote values and positions, something which irritated W. W. (DSF): 'This is the one thing that really annoys me. People who have some kind of inner loathing of the show and pin unfounded labels on it because they want to see changes to a well established format.'

Here fan identity is constructed in comparison with the 'other', those less intensive viewers, lurkers (who observe without participation), trolls, non-fans and press critics as likely to focus on programme flaws as qualities:

> Can't all these issues [...] be addressed by the writing, the actors and the production (J. T., DSF)

Stop judging and just enjoy. It's fiction for crying out loud, and I'm sick of the people thinking it's ok to judge a person's acting on their gender (T. B., DSF)

These appeals present loyalty to the fan object as more important than individual tastes, *bonkerising* and *ARSE*, which S. B. defines on DWF as the 'Righteous Sense of Entitlement' on display when a 'fan thinks they [know] better than the current showrunner what the showrunner wants to say'. Canon is framed finally as a matter for 'the writers/directors/producers' to 'tell the story they want to tell' (ibid.) rather than the 'headcanon' through which fans make sense of stories in ways not supported by official events:

> I've been watching the show since 1963, and have gone thro [*sic*] various degrees of ARSE along the way. I was upset when Susan left FFS! [...] My point is that the show encourages us to embrace changes. They may not always be to our personal liking. (S. B., DWF)

> No amount of headcanon is going to undo this. But I look forward to seeing viewers try for years to come and these debates being utterly one-sided, with no regard for what is on screen or actually possible within the confines of the show. (C. D., DSF)

Fan-critics were reminded that the weight of opinion was against them. A poll on DSF carried out by the poster S. R. showed that 58.56 per cent of posters favoured Missy. Meanwhile, when A. O. (DSF) asserted that 'many' agreed with him that 'the Master should have remained a male character', T.F. was able to come back with, 'You say "many", but that doesn't appear to be true of the general public. This episode was ranked the joint highest of the series with an AI [Audience Appreciation Index] of 85.'

Many conceded they had been too quick with emotional responses. Initial postings, made hastily during and immediately following broadcast of 'Dark Water', included threats to never watch the show again. After consideration, some of the posters cooled down, while others even back-pedalled. B. B. (DWF) was not alone in revisiting first thoughts, justifying their change of heart with the comment 'Michelle

Gomez is just too brilliant!' The forums thus afford time and space for reflection and jolts to consciousness.

As Missy conversions became an observable feature of posts, S. D. (DWF) parodied 'the five stages of grief' as exhibited by posters, these being denial, anger, bargaining, depression and acceptance. But for those who dug in, the message from one poster was stark:

> My 10y/o was very cross that the master, who he loves, had changed into a woman! However, about 15 mins later he was loving it!' (T. M., DWF)

> Your ten-year-old is wise. Object, absorb, accept, move on. I have done the same! (A. B., DWF)

By series ten, the programme signalled it was ready to move on again, an advance trailer teasing the return of John Simm. 'The forum hasn't been this busy in AGES', remarked S. F. as posters on DSF debated the potential implications. Some worried the clock was being reset on the gender debate sparked by Missy: 'If this turns out to be a *degeneration* then I'm going to be even more annoyed' (P. T.). For others, the precedent for 'multiple Doctors' stories meant the two Masters might interact, and even 'flirt with one another' (A. B.). As the series got under way, many of the threads lamented the programme's reliance on spoilers and speculated that Simm's return was only to satisfy departing showrunner Steven Moffat's 'completionist desire' for a Master/Missy regeneration. Many gender disputes resurfaced; thus, discussions about the Razor character really being the Master in disguise ('World Enough and Time') were met with frustration: 'I thought Missy was the Master' (K. T.). John Simm proponents were '[s]o glad his Master is back, he has the right balance of being scary/ sinister and humourous [*sic*]' (A. T.): 'the Simm master unmasking was a nice nod to the Delgado years' (B. C.) and gave the actor 'a second chance to come back and do himself and the character some justice' (D. B.). Some indulged the possibility that his return meant Missy 'might not be The master?' (S. S.). Meanwhile, Missy advocates insisted the Gomez version was 'the better Master!' (H. S.) and, after the final episode 'The Doctor Falls', were '[d]evastated that this is the end of Michelle Gomez as Missy' (J. M.).

Audiences and contexts

The disagreement over what constitutes a true fan was reflected in attempts to steer the *regendering* debate into a consensus of forum support for the show, reminding us that fans are not homogenous and indeed differentiate themselves from one another (for example, this study notes how forum users identified their differences from slash fans). Fans can become anti-fans crusading against an aspect of the show they find reprehensible, corralling other fans and organising discursive resistance. We are also reminded that fans are not the only viewers for whom *Doctor Who* has cultural significance. Kristina Busse points out that a tight definition of what constitutes a 'fan' means excluding 'the emotional and intellectual engagement of large numbers of viewers for whom a given show may have immense impact on their lives'.[54]

Jonathan Gray cautions us not to ignore non-fans – those who occasionally watch, but without intense engagement – and anti-fans – who have an intolerance for the text but form judgements about it and may view it 'as closely as fans do'.[55] The sample studied as part of this research comprised largely casual viewers or non-viewers, yet most respondents held opinions about Missy and were mainly supportive of the notion of greater visibility for transgender characters on television. These views seemed to run across gender profiles:

> I support transgender, but I think this was just done for shock. (casual viewer)

> People shouldn't rip their dicks off about trans issues. Support, love and solidarity. Let's all be ALLIES!! (non-fan)

It was also clear that these non-fans and anti-fans had, through the adoption of social media, spread the Missy reveal through tweets, texts, blogs and Facebook entries, and the wider viewer is likely to be an important area for digital ethnography in the future. By and large, students in my Doctor Who by Design class defined their fandom in terms of their viewing and discreet blogging rather than highly visible fan practices. While non-academic fans exhibit academic-type skills in textual analysis, academic fans are positioned in ways that afford a peculiar focus to their enjoyment of the text; it is this communicative distance between text and reader that enables 'the reader to construct a specific meaning reflective of his or her interpretative frameworks'.[56]

Blasting the canon: a female Doctor

The negative reception of Missy fits into the wider casting choices taking place recently, and subsequent debates in both the mainstream and social media in response to the *regendering* of Marvel's legacy hero Thor and creation of alternative-world hero Spider-Gwen, both attempts to appeal to new readers.[57] However, falling sales have been linked to disputes about the popularity of these characters. J. A. Micheline notes that Marvel's talk about diversity and inclusiveness is set for failure 'when it continues to push white men as its "real audience" and makes them the metric for success'.[58] One example of the extent to which an audience might go in protecting its inherited privileges was when actor Leslie Jones was subjected to sexist and racist abuse on social media after appearing in the all-female *Ghostbusters* remake (2015). As with these instances, the *Doctor Who* forums demonstrated that disputes can stem from a sense of entitlement: a loyal audience may become hostile and misogynistic, with complaints ranging from issues of character ownership and canon, to anxiety about change and the extraneous discourses directing it. In the latter camp, there was disquiet about 'political correctness' (A. B., DSF) and perceived attempts to put the interests of the 'do-gooder equal opportunities brigade' (C. W., DSF) ahead of the fans. Some posters, meanwhile, felt that the gender swap was about generating headlines in the short term. I. B. (DSF), for example, compared it with 3D television, labelling it 'a gimmick', while others, before the announcement that the Thirteenth Doctor would be played by a woman, feared there would be long-term implications: 'I don't like the Master being a woman as that means that the doctor will be a woman at some point in the future and I DO NOT want that to happen' (B. R., DWF). Some posters who identified themselves as viewers since the classic series insisted they would 'struggle' (N. O., DSF) with seeing 'how a woman could be the best person for the role' (G. S., DSF) and that such a change was 'stunt casting' (R. N., DSF). While some forecasted the end of the programme and wished 'this whole "female doctor" thing would go away' (S. P., DSF), or opined that fangirls would only continue to watch if 'the Doctor was an extremely sexy bloke' (G. M., DSF), others seemed resigned to change, hoping for a 'cute female Doctor' (I. N., DSF). Some felt that only quality writing would support a female Doctor (A. J. B., DSF), others that 'it just depends on who it will be really' (L. L., DSF), while for a few a broader change would include more female writers and producers (for example S. T., DSF).

Many who suggested change was inevitable offered the programme's own history as support. During his tenure as producer (1980–9), John Nathan-Turner teased that the Doctor could become a woman. Joanna Lumley plays a non-canonical female Doctor in 'The Curse of Fatal Death' (a BBC production for Red Nose Day, 1999), and Matt Smith's Doctor hints at the possibility during his opening lines: 'Chin, blimey. Hair. I'm a girl! No. No. I'm not a girl.' In *The Sarah Jane Adventures* (BBC, 2007–11) episode, 'Death of the Doctor' (2010), he insists he can regenerate as 'anything' while in 'The Doctor's Wife' (2011) he claims that a Time Lord called the Corsair regenerated as a woman. In 'The Night of the Doctor' (2013), the Sisterhood of Karn offer the regenerating Eighth Doctor a choice of gender. In series nine's 'Hell Bent', the Time Lord general, having been shot by the Doctor, regenerates from a white man into a black woman. But it is the casting of Missy which made the discussion of a female Doctor a mainstream topic, both in the press and on the forums.

When pressed on the subject, Steven Moffat, showrunner between 2010 and 2017, claims both to have made a female Doctor possible and that his tenure had been simply the wrong time for it. Certainly, many posters put the blame at his door. M. M. (DSF), for example, commented rhetorically: 'Moffat's got a boner for Timelord sex changes.' Some hinted at factionalism between classic and new series fans, suggesting that Hartnell, Troughton and Pertwee (the first three doctors) would be 'spinning furiously in their graves' (DSF), while others felt under personal attack: 'What is wrong with adults having a warm, safe, familiar feeling about our old friend the Doctor? Safe in the knowledge that when he regenerates he will regenerate into another dear old male Doctor' (W. W., DSF). When D. B. asked on DWF, 'If the Doctor regenerated into a woman, would he change his name to The Nurse?' there were a number of jokey responses, such as

'She'll have to call herself Nurse Who and fancy the Brigadier if she is anything like Missy' (M. W.), while others attacked the unknowing sexism of the poster, J. F. included, who answered, 'No. Because a woman doctor is called "a doctor".'

Returning to the point that the programme itself failed to discuss transgender issues, discussions on the forums were necessarily limited in scope, and many pitched their arguments within 'common sense' accounts of identity, one poster stating: 'I think the whole gender think [sic] is farcical. The Dr was perceived from the outset as a cantankerous grandfather not a grandma!!' (J. W., DSF). Others relied on unproblematised assumptions based on gender binaries (e.g. rational /emotional): 'The Doctor is generally far more rational [than the Master] and therefore it is less credible to think of him turning into a woman' (W. W., DSF).

Conclusion: new dawn

Public forums afford opportunities for engagement in 'fan talk', which in turn affords further viewing, dispute and reinterpretation.[59] Fan forums mediate and shape content, and online fan forums are technologies of convergence affording communal, rather than individual, modes of reception.[60] They become what Stanley Fish calls 'interpretative communities', where posts are shared and reviewed by peers as part of a public process of meaning-production.[61] Fan communities can act as 'moral communities' and even 'echo chambers', where fans are guided by articulate appeals to fandom loyalty.[62] However, 'fan talk' also affords the opportunity for disagreement about interpretation of fan texts and what constitutes fan behaviour, as well as challenges to the community hierarchies. *Doctor Who* fans in particular frequently find themselves in a new paradigm for making sense of the programme, given its propensity to reinvention, regeneration and *regendering*. Big changes, such as the Missy reveal, become opportunities for studying fans and forums at times of discursive crisis and how, through fan talk, fans negotiate change within a community context. The announcement that the Thirteenth Doctor would be played by a woman provides a further opportunity to mine fans' reactions to the Time Lord's *regenderation* which, as noted above, many posters feared.

Notes

1 The full thread from which this interaction is taken can be read at Matt_Wilson, 'What do you think of Missy' (2014), Digital Spy Forum. Available at https://forums.digitalspy.com/discussion/2032173/what-do-you-think-of-missy (accessed 22 June 2018).

2 Rising scholarly attention over the last decade: see Francisco Segado, María-del-Mar Grandio and Erika Fernández-Gómez, 'Social media and television: a bibliographic review on the Web of Science', *El profesional de la información* xxiv/3 (2015), pp. 227–34. 'A form of public space': Matt Hills, *Fan Cultures* (London, 2002), p. 172. Mundane computer-mediated interactions: Adrienne Evans and Mafalda Stasi, 'Desperately seeking methodology: new directions in fan studies research', *Participations: Journal of Audience and Reception Studies* xi/2 (2014), p. 16.

3 This class is offered as an option to Graphics and Media Design students at the University of the Arts London.

4 Henry Jenkins, *Textual Poachers: Television Fans and Participatory Culture* (New York, 1992).

5 Paul Booth, *Playing Fans: Negotiating Fandom and Media in the Digital Age* (Iowa City, 2015), p. 4; Cornel Sandvoss, *Fans: The Mirror of Consumption* (Cambridge, 2005), p. 53; Mark Duffett, *Understanding Fandom: An Introduction to the Study of Media Fan Culture* (New York and London, 2013), p. 21.

6 On a par with producers: Nicholas Abercrombie and Brian Longhurst, *Audiences: A Sociological Theory of Performance and Imagination* (London, 1998), p. 144. Sharing skills, expertise and opinions: Tisha Turk and Joshua Johnson. 'Toward an ecology of vidding', *Transformative Works and Cultures* 9 [special issue: Francesca Coppa and Julie Levin Russo (eds), *Fan/Remix Video*] (2012).

7 Sandvoss, *Fans*, p. 8; John Fiske, 'The cultural economy of fandom', in Lisa A. Lewis (ed.), *The Adoring Audience: Fan Culture and Popular Media* (London, 1992), pp. 34–5.

8 Jonathan Gray 'New audiences, new textualities: anti-fans and non-fans', *International Journal of Cultural Studies* vi/1 (2003), pp. 64–81.

9 Hills, *Fan Cultures*, p. 181.

10 Jo Pierson and Joke Bauwens, *Digital Broadcasting: An Introduction to New Media* (London and New York, 2015), pp. 23–7.

11 Sharon Marie Ross, *Beyond the Box: TV and the Internet* (New York, 2008).

12 Donald Horton and R. Richard Wohl, 'Mass communication and para-social interaction', *Psychiatry* xix/3 (1956), pp. 215–29.

13 Paul W. Ballantine and Brett A. S. Martin, 'Forming parasocial

relationships in online communities', *Advances in Consumer Research* xxxii/1 (2005), pp. 197–201.

14 Jenkins, *Textual Poachers*, p. 280.

15 Susan J. Clerc, 'Estrogen brigades and "big tits" threads: media fandom online and off', in Lynn Cherny and Elizabeth Reba Weise (eds), *Wired Women: Gender and New Realities in Cyberspace* (Seattle, WA, 1996), p. 74; Kirsten Pullen, 'I love Xena.com: creating online fan communities', in David Gauntlett (ed.), *Web.Studies: Rewiring Media Studies for the Digital Age* (London, 2000), p. 53.

16 For a discussion of opportunities opened up by 'fan talk', see Arthur E. Lizie, *Dreaming the World: U2 Fans, Online Community and Intercultural Communication* (Cresskill, NJ, 2009), p. 80; the expression 'fan talk', and its meaning, can be found in John Fiske, 'The cultural economy of fandom', in Lisa A. Lewis (ed.), *The Adoring Audience: Fan Culture and Popular Media* (London, 1992).

17 Hills, *Fan Cultures*, p. 66.

18 Ruth, A. Deller, 'A decade in the life of online fan communities', in Linda Duits, Koos Zwaan and Stijn Reijnders (eds), *The Ashgate Research Companion to Fan Cultures* (Farnham, 2014), pp. 237–48.

19 Brigid Cherry, 'Squee, retcon, fanwank and the not-we: computer-mediated discourse and the online audience for NuWho', in Christopher J. Hansen (ed.), *Ruminations, Peregrinations, and Regenerations: A Critical Approach to Doctor Who* (Newcastle upon Tyne, 2010), pp. 209–10; '"Oh, no, that won't do at all... it's ridiculous!": observations on the *Doctor Who* audience', in Andrew O'Day (ed.), *Doctor Who: The Eleventh Hour – A Critical Celebration of the Matt Smith and Steven Moffat Era* (London, 2014), pp. 204–27; Paul Booth and Peter Kelly, 'The changing faces of *Doctor Who* fandom: new fans, new technologies, old practices', *Participations: Journal of Audience and Reception Studies* x/1 (2013); Douglas McNaughton, 'Regeneration of a brand: the fan audience and the 2005 *Doctor Who* revival', in Hansen (ed.), *Ruminations, Peregrinations, and Regenerations*, pp.192–208.

20 DSF can be found online at https://forums.digitalspy.com; DWF is at https://www.thedoctorwhoforum.com.

21 'About us', Hearst UK (undated). Available at http://www.hearst.co.uk/about-us. The figure of 16 million appeared on the Hearst website at the time of writing; by July 2018, this had risen to 17 million.

22 'Doctor Who', Digital Spy Forums. Available at https://forums.digitalspy.com. The figures quoted in this chapter appeared on the DSF forums at the time of writing; by July 2018, these stood at 1.1 million posts and 26,900 different threads.

23 'Members directory' and 'Forums', DWF. Available, respectively, at https://www.thedoctorwhoforum.com/members/ and https://www.thedoctorwhoforum.com/forums/. The figures quoted in ths chapter

appeared on DWF at the time of writing; by July 2018, there were 3,716 active members listed on the site, and 54,676 posts.

24 Gallifrey Base is available to registered users at http://gallifreybase.com.

25 Jenkins, *Textual Poachers*; Brigid Cherry, 'Screaming for release: femininity and horror film fandom in Britain', in Steve Chibnall and Julian Petley (eds), *British Horror Cinema* (London, 2002), pp. 42–57.

26 'Old Boys' Club': Deborah Stanish, 'My fandom regenerates', in Lynne M. Thomas and Tara O'Shea (eds), *Chicks Dig Time Lords: A Celebration of Doctor Who by the Women Who Love It* (Des Moines, IA, 2010), p. 35. 'Masculinised genre': Rebecca Williams, 'Desiring the Doctor: identity, gender and genre in online science-fiction fandom', in Tobias Hochscherf and James Leggott (eds), *British Science Fiction Film and Television: Critical Essays* (Jefferson, NC, 2011). Gendered template for online communications: Henry Jenkins and John Tulloch, *Science Fiction Audiences: Watching* Doctor Who *and* Star Trek (London, 1995).

27 Ganz-Blättler's 1999 study of the *Little Voices* fanzine (for US crime drama *Magnum, P. I.*, 1980–8) is one example of the usage of media by women to build relationships: Ursula Ganz-Blättler, 'Shareware or prestigious privilege? Television fans as knowledge brokers' [paper presented at the Media in Transition Conference at MIT on 8 October 1999]. Available at http://web.mit.edu/m-i-t/articles/ganz.html (accessed 1 July 2017). Media to illuminate character relationships: see for example Susan Clerc's 1996 study of The X-Files, 'DDEB, GATB, MPPB, and Ratboy: *The X-Files*' media fandom, online and off', in David Lavery, Angela Hague and Maria Cartwright (eds), *Deny All Knowledge: Reading the X-Files* (London, 1996), pp. 36–51. Discussion of men's usage of media: ibid., p. 41.

28 Susan C. Herring, Deborah Johnson and Tamra DiBenedetto, '"This discussion is going too far!" Male resistance to female participation on the internet', in Kira Hall and Mary Bucholtz (eds), *Gender Articulated: Language and the Socially Constructed Self* (New York, 1995), pp. 67–96.

29 Dismissal of female fans' interests and engagements: Kristina Busse, 'Geek hierarchies, boundary policing, and the gendering of the good fan', *Participations: Journal of Audience and Reception Studies* x/1 (2013). Derision of female fans' responses: Matt Hills, 'Michael Jackson fans on trial? "Documenting" emotivism and fandom in *Wacko about Jacko*', *Social Semiotics* xvii/4 (2007), pp. 459–77. The denigration of female fans' textual readings and fear of their emotions are are discussed in Rebecca Williams, 'Wandering off into soapland: fandom, genre and "shipping" *The West Wing*', in *Participations: Journal of Audience and Reception Studies* viii/1 (2011). For more on fear of female fans' emotions and mockery of their attachments, see for example Melissa Click's paper on the 'gendered mockery' of *Twilight*

fans, '"Rabid", "obsessed", and "frenzied": understanding *Twilight* fangirls and the gendered politics of fandom', Flow TV [website] (18 December 2009). Available at https://www.flowjournal.org/2009/12/rabid-obsessed-and-frenzied-understanding-twilight-fangirls-and-the-gendered-politics-of-fandom-melissa-click-university-of-missouri/ (accessed 1 July 2017).

30 Maintaining a discreet online identity: Louisa Ellen Stein, 'Subject: "Off topic: oh my God, US terrorism!": *Roswell* fans respond to 11 September', *European Journal of Cultural Studies* v/4 (2002), pp. 471–91. Leaving online prejudices behind: Debra Ferreday, *Online Belongings: Fantasy, Virtuality, Community* (Oxford, 2009).

31 Online anonymity as used to attack others: Michael J. Moore et al., 'Anonymity and roles associated with aggressive posts in an online forum', *Computers in Human Behavior* xxviii/3 (2012), p. 2. Expression of 'thoughts and emotions': Kimberly M. Christopherson, 'The positive and negative implications of anonymity in internet social interactions: "on the internet, nobody knows you're a dog"', *Computers in Human Behavior* xxiii/6 (2007), p. 3041.

32 Ann-Marie Cook and Deirdre Hynes, 'From the terraces to the television screen: gender, sexuality and the challenges of online fandom', Inter-Disciplinary Net [website] (2012). Available at http://www.inter-disciplinary.net/research/wp-content/uploads/2013/03/Cook-Hynes-Fandom.pdf (accessed 1 July 2017). Link no longer available.

33 Nancy Baym, *Tune In, Log On: Soaps, Fandom, and Online Communities* (London, 2000); Sarah Elizabeth Bird, *The Audience in Everyday Life: Living in a Media World* (London, 2003).

34 The thread was started back in July 2004 and still attracts posts.

35 The question of informed consent (ethics in digital ethnography) is discussed by Busse and Hellekson, while Freund and Feilding raise concerns about academic presence affecting results: see Kristina Busse and Karen Hellekson, 'Identity, ethics, and fan privacy', in Katherine Larsen and Lynn Zubernis (eds), *Fan Culture: Theory/Practice* (Newcastle upon Tyne, 2012), pp. 38–56; Katharina Freund and Dianna Fielding, 'Research ethics in fan studies', *Participations: Journal of Audience and Reception Studies* x/1 (2013). For discussion of fans' fears of misrepresentation, see Evans and Stasi, 'Desperately seeking methodology', p. 11.

36 'Reasonable expectation' of being observed: Freund and Fielding, 'Research ethics in fan studies', p. 332. Assumption of sympathetic audience: Emma Hutchinson, 'Researching forums in online ethnography: practice and ethics', in Martin Hand and Sam Hillyard (ed.), *Big Data? Qualitative Approaches to Digital Research* (Bingley, 2014), pp. 91–112. Available at http://www.emeraldinsight.com/doi/abs/10.1108/S1042-31922014000013007 (accessed 1 July 2017).

37 Cook and Hynes, 'From the terraces to the television screen', p. 21.
38 Booth, *Playing Fans*, p. 6.
39 Andrew O'Day, 'On speed: the ordering of time and pace of action in *Doctor Who*', in Matt Hills (ed.), *New Dimensions of Doctor Who: Adventures in Space, Time and Television* (London, 2013), pp. 113–33.
40 Matt Hills, *Triumph of a Time Lord: Regenerating Doctor Who in the Twenty-First Century* (London, 2010), pp. 58–61.
41 Cherry, 'Squee, retcon, fanwank and the not-we', pp. 224–5.
42 See sites like *Best_Enemies*, where the emphasis is on the classic Doctor/ Master pairing, and *slash_lords*, focused on the new *Who* iteration. Both are hosted at livejournal.com (accessed July 2015). Online fanfic can be found at A Teaspoon and an Open Mind, at whofic.com (accessed July 2015).
43 'Better understanding of characters': McNaughton, 'Regeneration of a brand', pp. 192–3. Involvement in the creative process: Amber Davisson and Paul Booth, 'Reconceptualizing communication and agency in fan activity: a proposal for a projected interactivity model for fan studies', *Texas Speech Communication Journal* xxiii/1 (2007), pp. 33–43.
44 Jenkins, *Textual Poachers*, p. 27.
45 Davisson and Booth, 'Reconceptualizing communication', p. 34.
46 Kristina Busse and Karen Hellekson, 'Introduction: work in progress', in Karen Hellekson and Kristina Busse (eds), *Fan Fiction and Fan Communities in the Age of the Internet* (Jefferson, NC, 2006) and *The Fan Fiction Studies Reader* (Iowa City, 2014), p. 6; Matt Hills, 'Foreword: the eleven fandoms', in Paul Booth (ed.), *Fan Phenomena: Doctor Who* (Bristol, 2013), pp. vi–vii.
47 'Ghastly rumours' that the Doctor will regenerate as female: Terrance Dicks interviewed by Simon Guerrier, 'Cruel intentions', *Essential Doctor Who 4: The Master* (March 2015), pp. 9–11. 'Introduce genitalia into family viewing': Russell T Davies, quoted in Ben Dowell, 'Amy Winehouse would be a great Doctor', *Guardian* (7 July 2008). Available at http:// www.theguardian.com/media/2008/jul/07/television.bbc (accessed 1 June 2015).
48 Matthew Hemley, 'Transgender roles and storylines "missing" from UK programmes, admit C4 and BBC', *Stage* (7 October 2010). Available at https://www.thestage.co.uk/news/2010/transgender-roles-and-storylines-missing-from-uk-programmes-admit-c4-and-bbc/ (accessed 26 June 2018).
49 Natalie Jarvey. 'Transgender TV takes the spotlight', *Hollywood Reporter* cdxx/34 (2014).
50 Stephen Whittle, 'Foreword', in Susan Stryker and Stephen Whittle (eds), *The Transgender Studies Reader* (London, 2006), p. xi.
51 Richard Wallace, '"But Doctor?" A feminist perspective of *Doctor Who*', in Christopher J. Hansen (ed.), *Ruminations, Peregrinations, and*

Regenerations: A Critical Approach to Doctor Who (Newcastle upon Tyne, 2010), pp. 102–3.

52 Fan communities as engendering a sense of belonging: Jenkins, *Textual Poachers*, p. 23. Shared experience: Daniel Cavicchi, *Tramps Like Us: Music and Meaning among Springsteen Fans* (Oxford, 1998), p. 161.

53 Henry Jenkins, *Fans, Bloggers, and Gamers: Exploring Participatory Culture* (New York, 2006), pp. 41–55.

54 Hellekson and Busse (eds), *Fan Fiction and Fan Communities*.

55 Bethan Jones, 'Antifan activism as a response to MTV's *The Valleys*', in *Transformative Works and Cultures* 19 [special issue: Anne Kustritz (ed.), *European Fans and European Fan Objects: Localization and Translation*] (2015).

56 Sandvoss, *Fans*, pp. 138–9.

57 Axel Alonso, Marvel editor-in-chief, quoted in Noelene Clark, 'Marvel Comics shaking up its superhero roster to attract new readers', *Los Angeles Times* (4 June 2015). Available at http://www.latimes.com/entertainment/herocomplex/la-et-hc-marvel-comics-axel-alonso-all-new-all-different-lineup-20150603-story.html (accessed 2 April 2017).

58 J. A. Micheline, 'Marvel superheroes aren't just for white men – true diversity could boost sales', *Guardian* (4 April 2017). Available at https://www.theguardian.com/commentisfree/2017/apr/04/marvel-comics-blaming-diversity-bad-sales (accessed 2 April 2018).

59 Jenkins, *Textual Poachers*, p. 58.

60 Duffett, *Understanding Fandom*, p. 239.

61 Stanley Fish, *Is There a Text in This Class? The Authority of Interpretive Communities* (Cambridge, MA, 1980).

62 Andrew Leonard, quoted in Duffett, *Understanding Fandom*, p. 242.

APPENDIX

AUDIENCE DATA

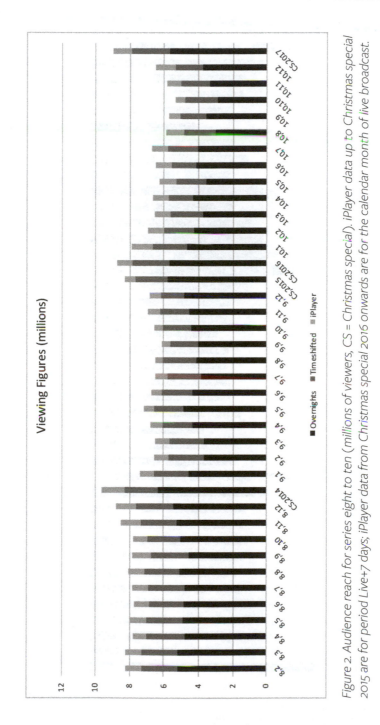

Figure 2. Audience reach for series eight to ten (millions of viewers, CS = Christmas special). iPlayer data up to Christmas special 2015 are for period Live+7 days; iPlayer data from Christmas special 2016 onwards are for the calendar month of live broadcast.

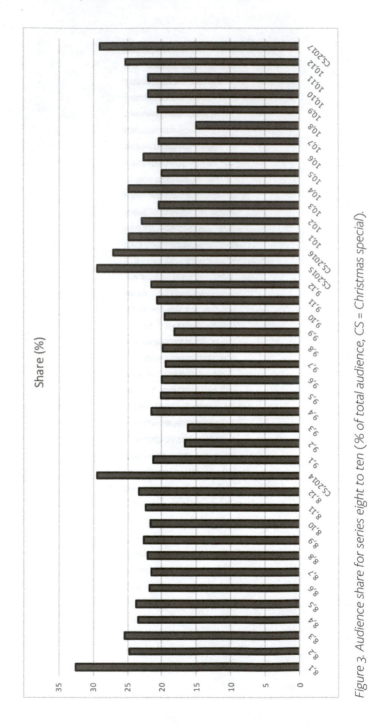

Figure 3. Audience share for series eight to ten (% of total audience, CS = Christmas special).

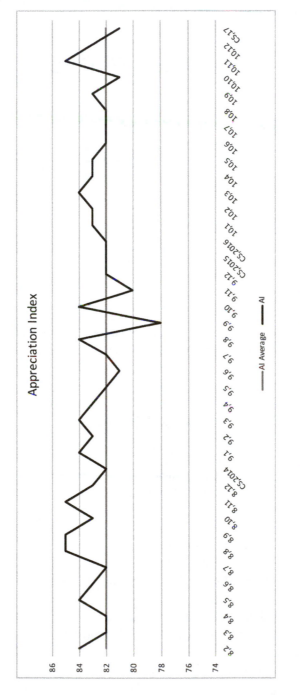

Figure 4. Audience Appreciation Index (AI) for series eight to ten (CS = Christmas special).

LIST OF EPISODES

THE STEVEN MOFFAT/ PETER CAPALDI ERA

CS = Christmas special

Note: Peter Capaldi's face was evident in the 50th-anniversary episode 'The Day of the Doctor' (2013), and he made a brief appearance at the close of 'The Time of the Doctor' (2013).

Series eight (2014)

8.01 'Deep Breath'
8.02 'Into the Dalek'
8.03 'Robot of Sherwood'
8.04 'Listen'
8.05 'Time Heist'
8.06 'The Caretaker'
8.07 'Kill the Moon'
8.08 'Mummy on the Orient Express'
8.09 'Flatline'
8.10 'In the Forest of the Night'
8.11/8.12 'Dark Water'/'Death in Heaven'

CS 'Last Christmas' (2014)

Series nine (2015)

9.01/9.02 'The Magician's Apprentice'/'The Witch's Familiar'
9.03/9.04 'Under the Lake'/'Before the Flood'
9.05/9.06 'The Girl Who Died'/'The Woman Who Lived'
9.07/9.08 'The Zygon Invasion'/'The Zygon Inversion'
9.09 'Sleep No More'
9.10/9.11/9.12 'Face the Raven'/'Heaven Sent'/'Hell Bent'

CS 'The Husbands of River Song' (2015)

Sidestep *Class* (2016): 'For Tonight We Might Die'

CS 'The Return of Doctor Mysterio' (2016)

Series ten (2017)

10.01 'The Pilot'
10.02 'Smile'
10.03 'Thin Ice'
10.04 'Knock Knock'
10.05 'Oxygen'
10.06/10.07/10.08 'Extremis'/'The Pyramid at the End of the World'/'The Lie of the Land'
10.09 'Empress of Mars'
10.10 'The Eaters of Light'
10.11/10.12 'World Enough and Time'/'The Doctor Falls'

CS 'Twice upon a Time' (2017)

... and introducing Chris Chibnall as the new showrunner...
... and Jodie Whittaker as Doctor Thirteen!

INDEX

References to notes are indicated by n. Character names are filed by their first names.

WHO WATCHING

EXPLORING AND CELEBRATING
THE WORLDS OF DOCTOR WHO